MW00339010

LOVE IN THE TIME OF
SELF-PUBLISHING

Love in the Time of Self-Publishing

HOW ROMANCE WRITERS CHANGED THE RULES OF WRITING AND SUCCESS

CHRISTINE LARSON

PRINCETON UNIVERSITY PRESS

PRINCETON & OXFORD

Copyright © 2024 by Princeton University Press

Princeton University Press is committed to the protection of copyright and the intellectual property our authors entrust to us. Copyright promotes the progress and integrity of knowledge. Thank you for supporting free speech and the global exchange of ideas by purchasing an authorized edition of this book. If you wish to reproduce or distribute any part of it in any form, please obtain permission.

Requests for permission to reproduce material from this work should be sent to permissions@press.princeton.edu

Published by Princeton University Press
41 William Street, Princeton, New Jersey 08540
99 Banbury Road, Oxford OX2 6JX

press.princeton.edu

All Rights Reserved

ISBN 9780691217406
ISBN (e-book) 9780691217390

British Library Cataloging-in-Publication Data is available

Editorial: Meagan Levinson and Erik Beranek
Production Editorial: Mark Bellis
Jacket Design: Jessica Massabrook
Production: Erin Suydam
Publicity: Alyssa Sanford and Kathryn Stevens
Copyeditor: Lachlan Brooks

Jacket illustration by Cha Pornea

This book has been composed in Arno

Printed on acid-free paper. ∞

Printed in the United States of America

10 9 8 7 6 5 4 3 2 1

To the men I love most:

Alex and Zach Rojo

Erik Urdang

Scott and Evan Larson

In the short run, actors make relations. In the long run, relations make actors.

—JOHN PADGETT AND WALTER POWELL,
THE EMERGENCE OF ORGANIZATIONS AND MARKETS

It is not often that someone comes along who is a true friend and a good writer.

—E. B WHITE, *CHARLOTTE'S WEB*

CONTENTS

LOVE IN THE TIME OF
SELF-PUBLISHING

Introduction

I'M A SUCKER FOR a happy ending. Especially when my own prospects have felt a bit precarious. As a teen, when my parents divorced, I escaped to the orderly world of Jane Austen. Later, when I worked in New York as a young magazine editor, Jennifer Weiner's *Good in Bed* taught me you don't have to be a size two to find love. After a heartbreak in my twenties, Terry McMillan's romance-adjacent *Waiting to Exhale* reminded me that lovers come and go, but girlfriends are forever.

Then came a time when I couldn't read romance at all. In graduate school, with my twin boys in second grade, my marriage suddenly, unexpectedly evaporated. A newly single mom, the *last* thing I wanted to read was romance: I was too busy sobbing in the produce aisle. I regrouped, moved onto campus with my boys, and settled them in a new school.

On the sunny morning when I finally sat down to resume my research, I couldn't write. I stared at my blank screen, anxious, overwhelmed, and terrified by uncertainty.

This time, it was romance writers themselves, rather than their books, who gave me hope.

After a decade as a freelance journalist, I'd entered graduate school to study how digital technologies changed life for journalists and other media workers. In the early 2000s, I'd noticed friends outside media starting to work like freelancers, moving to the project-based self-employment glorified by books like Daniel Pink's *Free Agent Nation* and Richard Florida's *Rise of the Creative Class*. Magazine editor Tina Brown dubbed this ostensibly liberating New Economy workstyle "the gig economy." The term conjured images of carefree musicians sleeping by day and partying by night.

But I knew better. My own freelance career had its glamorous moments— like writing for the *New York Times* and the *Wall Street Journal*—but to fund those high points, I had to write corporate reports and press releases and teach as an adjunct. I constantly hustled for work and hounded clients for payment. Most years, I earned more than my then-spouse, but it was his steady paycheck and benefits that made my career possible. Now, with no marriage and no steady job, even with all the privilege that comes with being white, well educated, healthy, and middle-class, I felt more than ever the high anxiety of working in the gig economy.

Although my research had focused on journalists, other media workers were also feeling insecure as new technologies disrupted old patterns. A writer friend had mentioned in passing that, of all the authors he knew, *only* the romance writers were thriving in the digital economy. Idly, I'd wondered why that was. Maybe an interesting side project? Then I'd forgotten about it.

But that morning in California in 2014, feeling lost and terrified, I remembered the romance writers. Unable to focus on the "real" research in front of me, I emailed some authors. To my surprise, several responded almost immediately. I set up interviews. I asked them how publishing was changing. What were they earning? How was technology affecting their work?

After each call, I felt miraculously better. Recharged, hopeful, focused. The rise of e-books and digital publishing, just a few years old at the time, offered these writers new ways to make money and set their own terms in an industry where they'd had little power before. Many, especially authors of color and writers of LGBTQ+ love stories, had started self-publishing, reaching audiences long slighted by major publishing houses. Meanwhile, traditionally published authors were finding new ways to connect with readers.

My early interviews were all with women (defined in this book as anyone who self-identifies as a woman), who make up more than 90 percent of romance novelists. Every one of them deeply understood precarity, both personal and professional. They'd faced every flavor of personal hardship—divorce, infidelity, sick children, natural disasters, racism, sexism, homophobia. They handled all this while pursuing a notoriously unstable and solitary career. Most started out writing at night or early in the morning, held multiple jobs and did most of the family caregiving. Their sales were unpredictable, their incomes rose and fell, and contracts were hard to come by, especially for marginalized authors. And yet not a single romance author said they felt isolated or unsupported in their work.

Without exception, every author I spoke with talked about how the romance community of writers, readers, and other fans—which many affectionately dubbed "Romancelandia"—offered the emotional and professional support needed to thrive in an uncertain, digitally disrupted cultural industry. At the same time, this was no hearts-and-rainbows story. The network never served all authors equally or fairly. For far too long, authors of color, LGBTQ+ authors, and other marginalized writers reaped less advantage from the network than white, heterosexual authors—I would come to call this persistent pattern *inclusive access/unequal benefits*. Tensions would come to a head in the near implosion of Romance Writers of America in 2019, offering valuable lessons in network repair and social justice. This inclusive access/unequal benefits tension seemed to reflect other networks I'd seen, in journalism and academia. As one Black author told me, in this way, Romancelandia "is a microcosm of America."

All this would unfurl as I continued to research the community. The more people I spoke with, the more I came to see that this much-mocked, largely dismissed group of creators was grappling with some of the most compelling issues of our time: How can isolated workers create community and solidarity? How can racism, homophobia and forms of discrimination be redressed? How do digital platforms change power dynamics? In pursuit of answers, my explorations of Romancelandia expanded to include eighty in-depth interviews with writers, editors, agents, and industry observers along with a survey of 4,270 romance authors and a network analysis of their advice patterns. Over the years, I also engaged in countless informal interviews with readers, writers, and other Romancelandians at conferences and online. Here's what I found:

- For forty years, American romance writers have developed an unusual type of professional network, based on practices historically associated with women, where they shared critical business information about contracts, payments, publishers, and the craft. This gave them a massive advantage when e-books came along.
- Romance authors pioneered electronic publishing, nearly a decade before the Kindle launched. Marginalized authors in particular were first to experiment with e-books and new forms of self-promotion.
- After the e-book boom, between 2009 and 2014, romance writers' median income rose 73 percent, while the median income of all other authors dropped 42 percent. Among romance writers, authors of color saw more income growth than white authors, with their median income rising 150 percent compared to 63 percent for white authors.
- Through their solidarity, romance writers improved their power vis-à-vis publishers and even—sometimes—held their ground against Amazon, as the company came to monopolize digital publishing.

For romance writers, none of this happened overnight. Rather, over four decades, romance writers created a powerful model of female solidarity, which, while flawed, drastically improved their working conditions.

All this matters because work today feels unstable, uncertain, and isolating for a huge number of people—not just writers. More than half of Americans today, and more women than men, do not work a "traditional job" with a steady wage, predictable earnings, and a regular schedule.[1] In 2022, 36 percent of respondents in a nationally representative survey identified themselves as independent contractors, up from 27 percent in 2016.[2] Another survey in 2018 found that a third of Americans freelanced either full time or as a side hustle.[3] It's no wonder that some 60 percent of Americans feel increasingly insecure and isolated in their jobs.[4] Meanwhile, the most coveted careers of the future like video streaming, gaming, and social media influencing involve highly individualized working conditions, calling for new kinds of organization.

All this characterizes what sociologist Ulrich Beck dubbed "the risk regime . . . a political economy of insecurity, uncertainty and loss of boundaries."[5] Many scholars link this risk regime to "precarity," defined as work with unpredictable pay, little access to health benefits, individualized working conditions, and no guarantee of continued employment.[6] These risks and insecurities are not equally distributed: people of color and other marginalized groups suffer more.

More and more workers are responding to increasing insecurity. In the summer of 2023, screenwriters and actors went on strike together for the first time in sixty years, protesting the impact of streaming and, potentially, artificial intelligence on their incomes. A few months later, twenty-five thousand members of the Auto Workers Union walked off the job in three states, demanding wage increases, better retirement benefits, and shorter hours.[7] Meanwhile, employees at Starbucks and Amazon warehouses have been forming unions. Public support for unions is higher than it has been in five decades.

Labor arrangements and networks don't have to be the way they are. As a thought experiment, for instance, media scholar Angela McRobbie asks how creative work might be organized differently had production structures not originally been designed by and for men. "What would it mean to bring a feminist perspective to bear on social and cultural entrepreneurship?" she asks. What might "new forms of community and cultural economy" look like?[8]

I believe it might look a lot like Romancelandia.

This is a book about how informal labor networks, self-organization, and mutual aid can improve the nature of work. It's about forging communities where no community existed before, based on a philosophy, however imperfectly realized, of attending to the needs of every member. The story of Romancelandia shows that alternative forms of organization, based on historically feminized practices, can improve "platformized," isolated, and precarious working conditions. At the same time, this is a cautionary tale, warning how informal networks can, however unwittingly, absorb and reproduce broader social patterns of exclusion and marginalization—which, in turn, can spur new forms of self-organizing. In the end, it holds a two-part lesson for independent workers, especially platform creators, seeking more equitable treatment from corporations: If you want to be treated fairly, you need a united community. And if you want a united community, you have to treat everyone fairly.

This book adds to expanding conversations around platformized cultural labor, where old careers like writing, music, filmmaking, and journalism, and new ones like social media influencing and streaming, all depend on digital platforms dominated by vast, impenetrable corporations. Media and communication scholars including Brooke Duffy, Nicole Cohen, Stuart Cunningham, David Craig, David Hesmondhalgh, Emily Hund, Nancy Baym, and many, many others are examining how social media and the digital economy change the way we think about work and community. This book adds to these conversations by analyzing how emerging forms of self-organization, communication, and technology affect the flow of cultural power and inequality.

More broadly, though, this book offers a few ideas, and a little hope, for people pursuing insecure work that they love, and for the communities that support them. Anyone who works alone or who feels isolated and unprotected in their job can learn from Romancelandia. So can organizations looking to redress exclusions and create unity in an age of increasing division and declining trust. Right now, creators—who symbolize the way more and more people work—are turning their attention to long-neglected conversations around labor conditions, both in grassroots efforts like Instagram influencers working together to game algorithms, and in broader professional organizations, from the brand new American Influencer Council to the Future of Music Coalition to the plethora of digital journalism unions.[9] Many of these groups are just starting to form their own version of Romancelandia: I hope the history and trajectory of this community will inform their conversations.

My own story ended up happily, at least for now, which is plenty good enough for me. My boys and I resettled in Colorado; I love my job as a professor; and yes, I found a life-changing new romance. I hope this book can be part of a much larger positive change, by helping isolated and precarious workers build communities in ways that advance fairer, more satisfying, humane, and dignified work.

That would be a very happy ending indeed.

PART I

Why Romancelandia Matters

1

Brenna's Choice

ROMANCE WRITERS IN THE DIGITAL ECONOMY

IN THE FALL OF 2013, Brenna Aubrey, a high school French teacher in Southern California, got the call of a lifetime. Her literary agent was on the line. A major publisher had just made a six-figure offer for Aubrey's first book, *At Any Price*.

Aubrey, then forty-six, had imagined this moment for nearly a decade. So, no one was more surprised than Aubrey herself when she turned it down.

"I did the unthinkable," she told me.

A self-described geek with chunky glasses and honey-colored, shoulder-length hair, Aubrey had spent years writing a fantasy novella. Her husband and friends encouraged her to publish it, but like most first-time authors, she had no clue where to start. "In the 1990s and 2000s, you'd go out and buy a *Writer's Market* directory, find a list of agents and send query letters," she said. She searched online for advice but couldn't find it. Major writing associations like the Science Fiction and Fantasy Writers of America (SFWA) and Mystery Writers of America (MWA) seemed the best source for guidance, but they only accepted published authors as members.

But there was one exception. An acquaintance recommended Romance Writers of America (RWA), which both published and unpublished authors could join. It didn't matter that Aubrey wrote fantasy, her friend said. RWA was a great place for anyone to learn story craft, especially women authors.[1]

So, Aubrey ventured out to a Southern California chapter meeting, tentatively taking a seat at a table with several other writers. One, it turned out, was a *New York Times* bestselling author. Another had published seventy-five books.

"I thought, 'This is impressive,'" she said. "I'd read romance in my 20s, before I started fantasy and sci-fi, but the genre had changed a lot in that time. It had become smarter, and the women characters had more agency. I made the shift to romance."

Three years later, Aubrey finished *At Any Price*, a digital-era romance featuring a whip-smart, video-gaming, aspiring med student who's broke and, inconveniently, a virgin. The plot, in which her heroine sets out to solve both problems at once, proved irresistible to agents and editors. The manuscript sold at auction, with four publishers vying for rights. While first-time romance authors at the time could expect an advance of $3,000–$5,000 USD, Aubrey was offered $120,000 for three books to be published over eighteen months. It was every debut novelist's dream come true.

But while her agent had been shopping her manuscript, Aubrey had been watching other writers. Things were changing in publishing. Since 2007, when the Kindle had come out, authors had started to self-publish their works, sometimes with remarkable results. In 2010, twenty-six-year-old Amanda Hocking went almost literally from rags to riches when she self-published a series of paranormal romance novels she'd written while working a low-wage job. H. M. Ward had started self-publishing in 2011 and sold more than two million books. E. L. James's blockbuster *Fifty Shades of Grey* had started out as online fan fiction based on *Twilight*. Self-published books, which had almost never hit best-seller lists before 2010,[2] represented 8.6 percent of *USA Today's* bestseller list by 2013. On romance-only bestseller lists, up to 50 percent of books were self-published.[3]

Aubrey began to wonder if she, too, might do better as an indie author. So, when her dream offer came in, she paused. She cold called several self-published RWA members, including H. M. Ward and Courtney Milan. Though they'd never met, she recalls, both writers happily shared their experiences.

Ward told her that "if you have a good book, and it sounds like you do, you can make the same money" as the publisher was offering.

Both authors shared detailed advice, the kind considered sensitive and proprietary in many other industries. Ward, for instance, talked about her earnings, her book pricing strategy, her promotional techniques, and more. She also promised to promote Aubrey's novel to her own readers.

Aubrey agonized over the decision. The money was only part of it: She wanted freedom over her writing schedule and control of her cover design, book release dates, and marketing. None of those were available through traditional publishing.

In the end, she made her unthinkable choice.

She declined the bid, cut ties with her agent, and published her books through Kindle Direct Publishing (KDP), Amazon's online platform. A year later, she'd already earned more than her New York publisher would have paid over three years. By 2016, she had quit her teaching job to write full time, and was earning enough to support both herself and her husband, who now worked as her publishing assistant.

"Do I regret turning down the deal?" she wrote on her blog a year later. "Nope. Not one bit."

From Unthinkable to Unstoppable

As I mentioned in the introduction, this book is about women's informal labor networks and how alternative forms of self-organizing can improve insecure working conditions, especially in the digital era. On one level, it explains how Aubrey's decision—not only unthinkable, but essentially *impossible* for most of nineteenth- and twentieth-century publishing history—came to make sense by 2013. On another level, it resolves two puzzles. First, why did romance writers, arguably the most mocked, maligned, and mistreated group of authors in history, become the most successful and innovative writers in the e-book revolution? Second, why did a key pillar of Romancelandia—Romance Writers of America—collapse at the very height of that digital success?

Solving these puzzles takes us through a forty-year history of women, work, and power, in which Romancelandia reflected major social, communication, and labor trends in the United States.

Aubrey's choice, and her success, came to pass in part because book publishing underwent a digital disruption in 2007 with the introduction of the Kindle. This shift, in turn, sparked a revolution in the way books are published, distributed, marketed, written, and read.

But even more importantly, Aubrey's choice was possible because she wrote romance—and romance authors, over four decades, had developed a vast informal network to share information and improve their conditions. Without realizing it, romance writers organized themselves into a rare network structure called an "open-elite" network, which promotes bonds between elite members and newcomers. Such networks have been associated with innovation and disruption in settings as diverse as Renaissance Italy and Silicon Valley. Underpinned by an ethic of care that strove to meet the needs of all community members (though it often failed), the network improved authors' contracts, trained new talent, and ultimately fostered jaw-dropping success in the world of e-books. Meanwhile, marginalized authors used similar social tactics and new communication technologies to address inequity in the network and the industry.

As I mentioned in the intro, I found that romance authors nearly *doubled* their median income in the five years after the rise of e-books, while authors overall saw a whopping 42 percent decline.[4] The income gap between Black and white authors closed. *The Guardian* credited romance writers with driving the adoption of e-readers and tablets.[5] The *New York Times* called romance writers "publishing's most innovative participants."[6] By 2022, the romance renaissance was still flourishing: *Publisher's Weekly* reported a staggering 52 percent increase in romance sales over the previous year.[7]

But, as I noted in the intro, these gains were not shared evenly. The network, though initially inclusive, was dominated by white heterosexual women and its ethic of care was largely "color-blind," a form of discrimination analyzed by sociologist Eduard Bonilla-Silva and others, which fails to acknowledge individual needs rising from racial and other identity-based exclusions.[8] While "not seeing color" or other difference sounds like a good intention from well-meaning people, in this case, it meant that Romancelandia, and RWA in particular, assumed that marginalized authors had the same needs as the white, middle-class, heterosexual women who dominate romance writing. Lacking "identity-aware care"—a term coined by media scholar Sue Robinson, which recognizes the differing needs of all community members—the network failed to help marginalized authors as much as white, heterosexual writers. In the context of a larger cultural reckoning in the late 2010s, the long-standing reality of inclusive access/unequal benefits ultimately led to a high-profile, social-media-driven implosion of RWA in late 2019. But even as that key community pillar collapsed, others have risen to take its place, leading to new opportunities for diverse authors and new efforts to diversify the lily-white, heterosexually oriented publishing industry.

Why Romancelandia Matters

When I tell people I've spent the last eight years researching romance writers, I get two reactions. The first is delight—mostly from romance readers, and mostly from women. That's not surprising, given that romance as a genre has historically been *about* women, *by* women, and *for* women, although that's changing even as I write this. Romance is one of the most popular themes of all storytelling, enduring across time and geography, weaving through myths and fairy tales and Netflix series. In 2022, booksellers sold more than 58 million print or digital copies of romance novels, *not even counting* self-published books.[9] If those novels populated a country, it would be the twenty-fifth largest nation in the world. Bigger than Canada. Bigger than Australia, South Africa, or Argentina. Cultural analysts tell us romances are foundational cultural stories, along with myths and fairy tales, reflecting "primal structures" in our social relations.[10] In the 1980s, media scholar Janice Radway argued that romance novels aren't just great stories, but a "form of individual resistance" for women, a way to claim time for themselves in a life dedicated to caring for others (although she also warned that romance sometimes supports an unequal status quo).[11] More recently, gender and cultural studies professor Catherine Roach noted that despite its problematic aspects, romance offers women a chance to imagine happiness in a patriarchal world, providing a "play space to roll around in the fields of fantasy with sister readers."[12]

The second reaction I get to my research, usually from anyone who doesn't read romance, is a subtle blend of confusion, disdain, and disinterest. This is also not surprising. At least since 1855, when Nathaniel Hawthorne enviously dismissed the "damned mob of scribbling women" who monopolized book sales "with their trash,"[13] women's writing has been undervalued, especially when women are writing about love, emotion, family, and relationships— devalued concepts historically designated to women in Western society. Romances, we're told, are trashy. They're bodice-rippers. They're poorly written. Worse, some say, they're retrograde and anti-feminist, "Valium for the mind," as one critic told newscaster Ted Koppel on national TV.[14] In 2017, in a flippant, condescending New York Times article, publishing luminary Robert Gottlieb dismissed romance novels as "harmless, I would imagine," although often "preposterous" and "flatly written."[15] As late as 2020, the New York Times could still write that "other forms of genre fiction, like the detective novel or the space opera, have achieved mainstream respect, but the reputation of the romance novel and its writers languishes."[16]

Why Should We Care?
Romance as a Site of Women's Labor

Many literary scholars and cultural critics argue that romance novels, whether playful or preposterous, matter because they convey messages about women and their role in society. An entire generation of women scholars in the 1980s and 1990s, including Janice Radway, Tania Modleski, Ann Barr Snitow, and others risked their careers by taking romance seriously as an academic topic. A new generation of romance scholars, including Julie Moody-Freeman,

Jayashree Kamblé, Catherine Roach, Eric Murphy Selinger, and many, many more are probing romance themes and texts in new ways. I agree that the romance genre matters for all the messages, positive and negative, that it conveys about gender roles.

But that's not what this book is about. I take romance seriously as a genre because it's a *unique site of feminized labor*—where "feminized" refers to skills, responsibilities, or roles historically associated with women even when executed by men or nonbinary people.[17] Feminized expectations and practices are less valued compared to those of men, even though what "feminine" means differs by race, sexual orientation, and other aspects of identity. In Romancelandia's woman-dominated enclave of cultural work, we see what self-organization might look like if women's experiences shaped the cultural and commercial economy.

This matters because the nature of work is changing—not only for creative workers like writers, musicians, and journalists, but also for a much broader set of workers outside the cultural industries (which are fields that center on the "making and circulation of texts," according to David Hesmondhalgh).[18] Fully a third of Americans performed some gig work in 2022, and Black, Hispanic, Asian, and immigrant groups were even more likely than white Americans to work this way.[19] The characteristics of cultural labor—independence, self-enterprise, uncertainty, risk, lack of protection—now apply to a vast and growing number of independent workers and contractors: Uber drivers, adjunct professors, software developers, accountants, food servers, telemarketers, marketing specialists, lawyers, traveling nurses, and consultants—advisors and specialists of every flavor. More and more, employment security is not a given (and never really was for many Americans). As media scholar Mark Banks put it, "the future of all work is now widely assumed to be adopting a cultural industry model."[20]

The Women's Economy

While many call this insecure work regime the "gig economy,"[21] it might more accurately be dubbed the "women's economy." Women in the United States, especially women of color and immigrants, have *always* worked part-time, taken piecework or freelance work, and labored in insecure jobs. In fact, I suspect, along with media scholar Nancy Baym, that the term "gig economy" caught on because it sounds not only more glamorous, but more masculine, evoking images of footloose rock stars.[22] But the term also cloaks the potential for exploitative conditions, including vast inequalities, underpay, and over-work, particularly for underrepresented groups. Some economists go so far as to argue that "women's work has become the paradigmatic model of labor and working in contemporary capitalism," as economists Lisa Adkins and Eeva Jokinen put it (while noting it's not quite that simple).[23]

Within the cultural industries, workers old and new are grouping into new informal networks and communities. Baym argues that musicians today need to forge ongoing, personal, digital relationships with fans, whether they like it or not.[24] They're also banding together to protect their digital rights through groups like the Future of Music Coalition. Freelance and full-time journalists have launched dozens of new unions in recent years, according to communication professors Nicole Cohen and Greig de Peuter.[25] Instagram influencers are creating "engagement pods" to resist platform invisibility, as media studies scholar Vicky O'Meara writes.[26] So far, these and other informal efforts at solidarity and mutual aid are still small in scope, with little real impact on the vast power differences between producers and platforms.[27] Still, these emerging networks may lay the groundwork needed for broader protections against precarity.[28] For these emerging industries, Romancelandia offers a mature and long-established model of how informal networks and self-organization can improve working lives—as well as a warning about how self-organized networks can exclude marginalized creators.

Beyond cultural industries, workers are looking for new ways to connect and organize. Traditional labor unions don't appeal to most Americans today. Although support for labor is at a fifty-year high, only 10 percent of US workers actually belonged to a union in 2022 (in part, this is because independent contractors can't unionize, according to current US labor law). Efforts by Amazon warehouse employees and Starbucks baristas to unionize evince a growing desire for solidarity in the face of corporate power but haven't yet created substantial change.[29] In a time of declining trust in institutions and increased suspicion of digital platforms, alternative models of self-organization could offer a missing sense of community and solidarity for the 60 percent of Americans who feel isolated and alienated by their working conditions.[30]

Romancelandia: A Network of Mutual Aid

In this book, I argue that the revolutionary success of romance in the digital economy rose from the unique interpersonal network structure formed by this almost entirely female community. Over four decades, Romancelandia, particularly as embodied in RWA, scored major victories for all romance writers, especially in areas of publisher contracts, payment, and rights protection, while at the same time, often failing to advocate on behalf of its members of color and LGBTQ+ members. Ultimately, I believe the story of Romancelandia holds lessons for people who might never pick up a romance.

To share these, I make a three-part argument in the chapters ahead.

1. The disparaged, scorned, outsider status of romance writers in publishing prompted them to band together for mutual aid in the 1980s in what was initially an unusually inclusive community. This network grew over four decades to include established authors, aspiring writers, readers, agents, and editors. By the twenty-first century, this sprawling network consisted of highly visible outcroppings, like RWA, as well as hundreds of other romance writing groups, associations, conferences, podcasts, and blogs, spreading and sprouting like rhizomes over time.

2. Romancelandia took on the form of a particular type of network—known as an "open-elite" network—which has long been associated with innovation and social change at widely varying times and places.[31] This type of network fosters connections between elite, established members and newcomers, making it easy to share new information across different levels of experience. During the digital disruption of publishing, this network structure accelerated information exchange, fostered rapid innovation, and allowed romance authors to outstrip other writers and traditional publishers.

3. Romancelandia, unlike most other professional communities, was shaped by historic patterns of feminized labor—unstable work, insecure pay, juggling of multiple jobs, and family labor. These patterns, inflected by race and class, closely resemble some aspects of the gig economy. Because Romancelandia was initially almost entirely made up of women, the community embodied *an ethic of care* associated with women's life experiences, a concept developed by Carol Gilligan and extended by moral philosophers including Virginia Held and Joan Tronto. An ethic of care stresses that human life is above all *interdependent*, rather than individualized, and stresses care for others as a fundamental human value. However, the model of care adopted by authors early on assumed that all authors had the same needs as the group's large majority of white, heterosexual women, and that race,

class, sexual orientation, and other aspects of social identity made no difference to women's experiences as authors. This assumption damaged the network at a time when authors needed solidarity more than ever to combat Amazon's near-monopoly in digital publishing.

Theoretical Framework: Political Economy, Networks, and Feminisms

As every romance writer knows, you can tell a story a million different ways. Three overlapping streams of scholarship help me tell this story.

Critical political economy of cultural industries. The media and messages we consume "influence our understanding of the world," writes David Hesmondhalgh. The *critical political economy of cultural industries* tries to unravel the complex relationships between economics, social structures, culture, and power, showing how they shape (and are shaped by) the messages we absorb through books, music, journalism, social media, and other forms of creative expression.

The lens provided by this intersection of economics, labor studies, and critical cultural studies helps us zoom in on the distribution of power in Romancelandia, because it calls attention to how social forces and institutions shape the experiences of creators. I draw from authors like David Hesmondhalgh, Angela McRobbie, and others to consider how micro-level decisions and the experiences of individual authors shape and are shaped by middle-level institutions and organizations, as well as macro-level forces like economic and social trends.

Recent analyses of how digital conditions impact labor conditions for creators, particularly the work of Brooke Erin Duffy and Nancy Baym, shape my analysis of romance writing as a site of feminized cultural labor. The field-defining book *Platforms and Cultural Production*, by Thomas Poell, David Nieborg, and Brooke Erin Duffy is especially useful in identifying precise ways that different technology platforms impact asymmetrical power relationships. For specific analyses of how power flows in book publishing, I find Clayton Childress, John B. Thompson, Janice Radway, and Robert Darnton's work immensely helpful. I'll draw on all these throughout the chapters ahead.

Networks and organizations. Network and organization scholars examine how webs of social relationships shape the way information, influence, and power flows in society. "In the short run, actors make relations: In the long run, relations make actors," write network scholars John Padgett and Walter Powell.[32] *Network ethnographies* (this book is one) help map those networks and reveal patterns of connection, influence, and information flow. Gina Neff's network ethnography of dot-com workers in the late 1990s, Sue Robinson's study of race-related media messages in Madison, Wisconsin, and C. W. Anderson's monograph on journalism in Philadelphia all provide important methodological and conceptual tools for understanding how a particular culture, with its philosophy and practices, can spread through a community like Romancelandia (see appendix 2 for more on this approach).

Feminisms and the ethics of care. Not all romance writers, especially in the early decades, would have called themselves "feminists." Many women distanced themselves from the term, especially in the 1980s when it threatened traditional gender roles, and again in the 1990s, when younger women assumed gender equality had been, or soon would be, achieved. But whether or not they called themselves feminists, none of the romance writers I interviewed would argue with the central tenet of all feminisms—that women should not be second-class citizens.

Feminism takes many forms. In telling the story of Romancelandia, particularly useful concepts come from *intersectional feminism*, in its identification of how gender inequality overlaps with other kinds of discrimination,[33] and *neoliberal feminism*,[34] which stresses individual choice and personal empowerment over collective reform and liberation from structural and systemic barriers.

Another strand of thought arising from feminism, *the ethic of care*, also helps reveal hidden aspects of Romancelandia. Carol Gilligan, Virginia Held, and Joan Tronto have all analyzed how women's life experiences were long excluded from the field of moral philosophy. In response, they and others developed the concept of an *ethics of care*.[35] This moral system stresses interpersonal dependence, relationships, empathy, and compassion over and alongside traditional ethical theories, which prioritize abstract principles. Vanessa Siddle Walker and John Snarney analyzed ethics of care within communities of color,[36] informing Sue Robinson's theory of "identity-aware care," which takes into account identity-based differences in people's needs and resources.[37] By examining the ethics of care within a feminized cultural labor network, we begin to see how and why romance writers formed an alternative culture of information sharing, more open than similar male-dominated networks.

Bringing It All Together

Here's how these three lenses bring into clearer focus the argument I outlined above. In the 1980s, because they were women writing about love, romance writers found themselves literary outcasts, disrespected and exploited in a then male-dominated publishing field. For mutual support, they created a network to help each other. Parts of the network, notably RWA, were surprisingly inclusive for the time, but the genre itself remained largely written by white women about white heroines. Nevertheless, and however incomplete, a certain ethic of care was "baked into" the network from its inception. A cooperative, collaborative spirit influenced patterns of behavior and mentorship, and infused future members. This led members to share information widely, to push for more diversity in publishing starting in the late 1990s, and to help authors rapidly adopt digital publishing innovations.

Unfortunately, the network's ethic of care remained largely color-blind until the mid-2010s. Without an effective, coordinated effort to care for marginalized authors, a central node of the network—RWA—began to unravel, culminating in a spectacular public meltdown in 2019 and 2020. Meanwhile, authors found they could meet their learning needs elsewhere on the internet. Throughout this long history, emerging forms of communication from the internet to e-commerce to social media played complex roles in shaping author interaction. It remains to be seen if a more loosely connected, less centralized romance community can effectively advocate for and protect writers' rights at a time when Amazon holds a near-monopoly power over the industry. Nonetheless, there remain lessons to learn from this reckoning, as a wide range of networks and organizations struggle to evolve and remain relevant under rapidly changing social, economic, and technological conditions.

How I Know What I Know

I spent eight years examining romance writers both qualitatively and quantitatively. I conducted interviews with eighty romance writers and publishing professionals between 2014 and 2023, many of whom I spoke with several times over the years. I made an effort to oversample traditionally marginalized authors, seeking out Black, Latinx, LGBTQ+, and male authors (see appendix 2 for methodological details).

My research took me around the country, to four national Romance Writers of America conferences (in New York, San Diego, Denver, and Washington,

DC) and a romance novel symposium at the Library of Congress. I also spent five surreal days at the massive Romantic Times Booklovers Convention in Las Vegas, where I enjoyed countless informal talks with romance readers, critics, and writers, some in costume.

Meanwhile, I worked extensively with several archives. At Bowling Green State University's Browne Popular Culture Library, I sifted through forty years of recordings from RWA conferences and looked at every issue on file of *Romance Writers Report*, RWA's internal magazine, as well as five years of *PANdora's Box*, its newsletter for published authors, and RWA governance records. To explore differences between romance writers and other (male-dominated) genres, journalist and research assistant Shannon Mullane and I worked remotely with the Science Fiction and Fantasy Writers Association (SFWA) archives at Northern Illinois University, and the Mystery Writers of America archives at the University of Indiana's Lilly Library, perusing newsletters dating back to the 1970s. To expand this comparison, I interviewed four leaders of SFWA, and three members of Mystery Writers of America (MWA) and Sisters in Crime (some of these authors were also members of RWA).

To gather quantitative data, I constructed a forty-nine-question survey, asking for three years of data on income, number and type of books published, years writing, experiences with self-publishing, demographic information, and much more. I asked authors to name three people they most frequently sought advice from, in order to map romance writers' advice patterns. In 2015—a critical moment following the rise of e-books—Romance Writers of America allowed me to survey their entire membership, then about ten thousand writers; 43 percent generously responded. Because my survey respondents were all RWA members, I sought to include nonmembers in my interviews. I also sought out marginalized authors, male authors, and those disillusioned by the genre, RWA, or other aspects of Romancelandia.

I shared my findings with romance writers in several ways: by sending chapters and sections to interviewees featured in those sections; through presentations at two romance writer conferences; through opinion pieces in popular media; and through scores of one-on-one conversations over several years. To help check my biases as a white, heterosexual, cisgender scholar, I worked with two different sensitivity readers: Dr. Carol V. Bell, a Jamaican-born writer, critic, and media researcher, and Laquette Holmes, a Black author and former RWA president. All these discussions and input frequently changed the direction of my thinking and enriched my analysis.

What's Missing

Despite all this research, this book does *not* try to give a comprehensive history of romance writers in the United States. Rather, it makes the argument I outlined above—that romance writers created a powerful but flawed model of women's solidarity, based on an ethics of care, which helps explain their digital success as well as their struggles with diversity. To build this argument, I don't try to document every moment of romance history, every important writer, or every talented editor—there are far too many to choose from. Instead, I focus on a handful of writers, editors, and events to illustrate major themes and building blocks for the argument.

As a result, the comprehensive history of romance writers must be left to other authors, as must the rich histories of Black romance authors, Latinx authors, and LGBTQ+ authors, which all deserve books of their own. Several outstanding writers and thinkers are working on these histories as I write. For starters, check out Jessica P. Pryde's edited volume, *Black Love Matters*; the work of Jayashree Kamblé; Julie Moody-Freeman's *Black Romance Podcast*; and the *Big Gay Fiction* podcast. In this book, I pay special attention to Black romance, because African Americans are one of the largest, most visible underrepresented groups in romance, but it's important to remember that this is not the only marginalized group, and that each group has its own story and experiences.

To trace my argument, I draw on authors' personal stories to illuminate particular themes. These stories come from my interviews and from public sources including media articles and archival material. All words in quotation marks come directly from my interviews, or from cited material, and have been cross-checked with other accounts and interviews. I've shared these narratives with those who feature in them and corrected them accordingly. I've done my best to ensure accuracy, but in the end, all interpretations are filtered by my position as a white, middle-class, abled, cisgender college professor. Others will tell these stories differently and I can't wait to read them.

Plan of the Book

You can think of this book as a story in three acts: Part I maps out Romancelandia as a site of feminized labor, explaining how writers, readers, editors, and others fit into the community. Part II flashes back to the founding of RWA and the roots of Romancelandia, exploring the origins of the network's ethic of care, the position of readers in the network, and the situation of BIPOC and other marginalized authors. Part III examines Romancelandia in the digital era, showing how romance authors were early entrants into online communities and digital publishing, and describing how publishing has changed due to "platformization," defined by Thomas Poell, David Nieborg, and Brooke Erin Duffy as "the penetration of digital platforms' economic, infrastructural and governmental extensions into cultural industries."[38] Finally, I explore Romance Writers of America's 2019 implosion. I show how social media helped expose and repair Romancelandia's failures of care and consider what comes next for the group's informal networks. I identify three possible futures for Romancelandia and summarize the lessons that romance writers offer to other creators, as well as a much broader group of independent, self-entrepreneurial workers.

Brenna Aubrey, the writer whose story opened this chapter, took a massive risk in turning down a conventional publishing contract. For her, that risk paid off (though it often doesn't): within two years, she quit her teaching job to write full time.

It's important to acknowledge that as a white, middle-class, well-educated teacher with a steady job, benefits, and domestic partner, Aubrey was well-positioned to take that risk. And yet, unlike her romance heroines, she was in no way guaranteed a happy ending. Nor are other cultural workers and precarious laborers facing digital change. But the combination of historic and economic forces that came together in her own story have broader implications, including hope and warnings, for many others.

Like Brenna Aubrey, we all live in a moment of enormous change and uncertainty. The story of romance writers shows that this generation is not the first to face precarious working conditions, social upheaval, and digital disruption. It reveals the potential of banding together to become resilient, innovative, and prosperous while pursuing creative endeavors and promoting social change. We don't yet know how this economic story will end, but Romancelandia, like its authors, holds out hope.

2

Mapping Romancelandia

IN FEBRUARY 1979, a twenty-nine-year-old mother in the tiny town of Keedysville, Maryland found herself snowbound with her two little boys. The steep mountain road to her modest house made even a grocery run impossible. Stir-crazy, she picked up a legal pad and started writing.[1] She never stopped.

Some forty years later, that mother, Nora Roberts, has published more than 240 novels, including romance, suspense, and postapocalyptic science fiction. *Time* magazine named her one of the world's most influential people. She ranks among the richest authors in the United States, according to *Forbes*.

But on that wintry morning in 1979, those accomplishments lay far ahead. At the time, she was a stay-at-home mom who married at seventeen and quit her legal secretary job to raise her boys. Creative and boundlessly energetic, she pursued crafts with a passion: needlepoint, crochet, sewing, macramé, baking, and more. She read voraciously, especially Harlequin's "category" romances— short books, about two hundred pages, each one part of an imprint sharing similar settings, characters, and themes.

"I really believe in the category romances," she told *Publishers Weekly* years later. "I was there with two young kids and the shorter format saved my sanity. I remember exactly what it felt like to want to read and not have time to read 200,000 words."[2]

When she first picked up her yellow legal pad, writing seemed like just another creative outlet. But as she filled one tablet after another, Roberts quickly realized writing would become far more than her latest pastime. When she finished, she typed up the manuscript in her kitchen, crossed her fingers, and mailed the pages to Harlequin.[3]

Years later, Roberts would cringe as she described that first story. "I took every cliché you have ever read in a novel and stuffed it in that 55,000 word book," she told a reporter. For starters, she said, "The woman had long red fingernails and he was Latin."[4] But even that first manuscript did have a few things that hinted at her future success. The story had a real beginning, middle, and end. It had characters and a setting. Even the mere fact that she typed the manuscript showed her good instincts for the business. Back then, "we were still receiving manuscripts that were handwritten," longtime Harlequin editor Dianne Moggy told me.

Few romance authors today enter the field with as little knowledge of publishing or as few contacts as Roberts had in the late 1970s. "We were going crazy for information," another writer told me about that era. In their isolation and lack of networks, romance authors in the late 1970s resembled early social media creators, who also started out alone, as home-based hobbyists, feeling their way in a new industry, needing connection with others.[5]

Between the late 1970s and the present, romance writers have grown a sprawling network encompassing readers and writers, editors and critics, formal associations and informal writing groups. In this chapter, I lay groundwork for the rest of the book by defining romance and mapping Romancelandia.

"Is This a Kissing Book?" Or, What Is Romance?

Before we go on, we should back up and ask, what's a romance anyway? Or, as nine-year-old Fred Savage puts it in *The Princess Bride*, as he glares witheringly at his grandfather who's reading aloud: *"Is this a kissing book?!"*

In 2000, author Jennifer Crusie set out to answer that very question, as part of an RWA committee to define the romance genre. Although she'd written a dissertation on women's narratives, read hundreds of romance novels, and penned dozens herself, Crusie had to admit that "defining romance is a tricky business," as she wrote in an essay describing the process.[6] Romance, she noted, is a vast and varied genre. Some novels feature scorching-hot sex scenes; others are more chaste than Sleeping Beauty's first kiss. Even the canonical "happily-ever-after" ending doesn't always exactly pan out: Some beloved romances, like Jojo Moyes's *Me Before You*, end on a distinctly bittersweet note.

"Oh, we had a high old time debating this one," Crusie conceded. "For example, there were those who suggested the definition include 'love between a man and a woman' and those who pointed out it would be a bad idea to make RWA officially homophobic, given that respected publishers like Naiad Press have been publishing lesbian romances for years."[7]

Though Crusie's essay didn't mention it, another factor complicates the attempt to define romance: mainstream publishing's long history of institutional racism. From the 1970s until the mid-1990s, white women wrote and edited the vast majority of mass-market romance, tailored to the tastes, desires, and experiences of women like themselves. (chapters 6 and 9 explore these structural biases and their impact).[8] In the early 1990s, two small publishers, Odyssey and Genesis, launched the careers of many Black romance writers, but major New York publishers released vanishingly few romances featuring people of color, or characters whose gender, orientation, religion, neurodiversity status, or abilities differed from dominant, mainstream culture. Today, that's changing. But it's important to bear in mind that definitions of the romance genre are always based on the specific set of romance novels published at the time.

Even with all these challenges in mind, Crusie's committee kept at it, figuring that the world's most widely read genre deserved some sort of definition, however imperfect. Ultimately, RWA settled on this one: *"A romance is a love story that has an emotionally satisfying, optimistic ending,"* later elaborating that the love story must be the central plot and the couple must ultimately find "emotional justice and unconditional love."[9]

Over the years, scholars have offered more academic explanations, typically focused on gender dynamics. In 1982, for instance, Tania Modleski defined romance as "revenge fantasies" where heroines subvert and resist patriarchal power structures.[10] Janice Radway, writing about historical romance in 1984, noted that the genre offers much needed escape and emotional fulfillment for women—while sometimes, ironically, reinforcing the very gender roles that made readers crave escape in the first place.[11] Pamela Regis, in *A Natural History of Romance*, defines romance based on twenty-five prominent novels from the 1980s and 1990s (all by white women, consistent with bestseller lists at the time).[12] She identifies eight narrative elements in the classic romance arc, including:

> a *definition of society*, always corrupt, that the romance novel will reform; the *meeting* between the heroine and the hero; an account of their *attraction* for each other; the *barrier* between them; the *point of ritual death*; the *recognition* that fells the barrier; the *declaration* of heroine and hero that they love each other; and their *betrothal*.[13]

Professor turned romance author Catherine Roach offers her own nine-point outline of essential romance elements, starting with the premise, "It is hard to be alone, especially as a woman in a man's world" and ending with the idea that hard work and risk lead to healing, great sex, and happiness, while also "level[ing] the playing field for women."[14] I borrow several useful elements of her definition to craft my own.

Romance Writing as a Site of Labor

All of these definitions focus exclusively on the content of romance novels: their stories, language, and subtext. But a book is never just one thing, as sociologist Clayton Childress explains.[15] For readers, a romance novel is (hopefully) a great story. For critics and scholars, it's a text casting light on popular culture and gender roles. For literary agents, Childress notes, a book is a collection of subsidiary rights to be licensed. For editors, it's the raw material of a long production process and maybe a way to advance their careers and reputations. For Amazon, books are bait to capture customer data. And so on.[16]

For writers, books are many of these things. But they're also a source of professional identity, creative satisfaction, and income. Because I study cultural production in the digital era, it's this aspect of romance writing as a livelihood that interests me most. So, for the purposes of this book, I define the *romance genre* as a category that 1) focuses on **optimistic love stories** concerned with the happiness of (still, mostly, for now) **women in a man's world**, 2) whose **themes change with the times** and that 3) provides **a site of feminized cultural labor**. Here's my thinking on each part of that definition.

1. Happiness of (Still, Mostly, for Now) Women in a Man's World

Roach writes that, in romance, protagonists "try to make up for the costs to a woman's psyche of living in a culture that is still a man's world."[17] In the United States and many other societies today, men continue to dominate leadership positions in government and business. The gender pay gap, the unequal sharing of caregiving and domestic labor, the prevalence of gender-based violence, and pervasive derogatory stereotypes all serve to wear women down.[18] As Roach puts it, romance imagines a world where encounters with patriarchy end happily—and not just for heterosexual women, as the long history of gay and lesbian small presses attests. The genre offers the same imaginary escape for people of other gender identities devalued by a culture designed by and for straight white men. If the current groundswell of romance from major publishers featuring lesbian, gay, and nonbinary couples continues to surge, romance scholars may need to remove the "women" from our definitions.[19] But for now, I'm keeping it, because the vast majority of romance from major publishers continues to focus on heterosexual women.

Romance writers themselves—among the keenest and most active analysts of the genre—note two specific paths leading to happiness in a man's world.

In a 2020 Twitter thread and later blog post, author Racheline Maltese argues that romance has "a liberation wing (protagonists *bend the world* to find their joy) and a compliance wing (protagonists *bend themselves* to find their joy)."[20] Also on Twitter, Olivia Waite, author and *New York Times Book Review* romance columnist, classified uber-romance *Pride and Prejudice* as a liberation narrative—Lizzie Bennet defies social convention and "Darcy becomes less of a jerk," she writes—and *Emma* as a compliance narrative: Mr. Knightly keeps scolding Emma and she becomes less of a jerk.[21] Maltese's compliance/liberation theory, oft cited in Romancelandia's bubbling social media discussions, explains how a single genre can include novels embracing conservative religious values, polyamory and trans love stories, and everything in between.

2. Stories That Change with the Times

The genre's countless critics disparage romance for being formulaic: "Boy meets girl. Holy crap, shit happens! Eventually, the boy gets the girl back. They live Happily Ever After," as Sarah Wendell and Candy Tan summarize in their gleefully snarky tribute to the genre, *Beyond Heaving Bosoms*.[22]

But, as Wendell and Tan point out, dismissing romance for being formulaic seems unfair. *All* genres follow familiar formulas. The detective always solves the case, the motley band of elves and dwarves always save the kingdom. The delight of romance (and other genres) is the constant reshaping of tropes to address changing circumstances. Jayashree Kamblé calls the romance novel "an evolving organism—one that therefore merits regular reevaluation rather than static labels."[23] Or as Lynne Pearce and Jackie Stacey point out, the "key to the enduring significance of romance as a discourse lies in its ability to change."[24]

Wendell and Tan highlight this adaptability by distinguishing between "Old Skool" romance of the 1970s and 1980s (brutal men, innocent young women, first-person point of view) and "New Skool" romance (gentler heroes, "kick-ass, sexually experienced heroines," a variety of points of view). As a striking example of the genre's evolution, they serve up the now-nearly-extinct rapist hero, a common character in the 1970s. Back then, rape was such a common romance trope that literary agent Irene Goodman wrote in an RWA newsletter, "It was expected there would be rape within the first 50 pages."[25] In Janice Radway's 1981 survey, readers found rape only marginally less upsetting than a story without a happy ending.[26] (That rapist-hero trope was also prominent in movies and TV: think *Saturday Night Fever* and *General Hospital's* Luke and

Laura.) Today, many readers find rape completely unacceptable in a romance. As Wendell and Tan put it, readers have "a personal line in the sand, beyond which no happy ending can be possible. Rape is that line in the sand for many readers today; it wasn't for most of the readers in the past."[27]

Romance stories, themes, and tropes mutate not only across time, but differ within the genre, and across subgenres and communities. For instance, romance written by Black authors in the 1980s focused on different themes than those of their white peers: Jayashree Kamblé notes that the "first five" commercial Black romances, published between 1980 and 1985, do *not* feature innocent young heroines and brutal men, but rather ambitious career protagonists who challenge stereotypes of Black women.[28] Not surprisingly, the rape trope appears only fleetingly and only in one of those books.

This adaptability helps explain both the genre's enduring popularity and how easily it adjusted to digital publishing, which unleashed a flourishing variety of new themes, pairings, and tropes, and pushed traditional publishing to do the same.

3. A Site of Feminized Cultural Labor

Finally, unlike most romance scholars who focus on the books' content, I like to look at the romance genre as a site where authors (and editors and readers too) perform feminized cultural labor.

What do I mean by "cultural labor"? Critical political economists, drawing from Marxist thought, define labor as the processes and relationships that allow capitalists (in this case, publishers or technology platforms) to extract as much value from workers as possible in exchange for wages.[29] But these processes and relationships look very different in an era where a third of workers are self-employed and those who aren't often have a side hustle.[30]

As I mentioned in chapter 1, today's more individualized workers look a lot like people working in the cultural and creative industries. Both cultural workers and a broader group of independent workers receive insecure pay, depend on multiple employers, "self-exploit" by working long hours, pay higher taxes, and have no health benefits or legal protections: existing labor law was designed to protect traditional employees with a single employer, not contractors.[31]

Cultural and creative workers, whom I also call "creators," stand as model workers in a culture that extols following your passion. They're often willing to accept lower—or sometimes no—payment in return for creative satisfaction or future opportunities: many hope to get "paid to do what [they] love," as Brooke Duffy puts it.[32] Rewards are vastly uneven.[33] For instance, as we'll see in chapter 8, I found that 17 percent of authors I surveyed in 2015 made nothing at all from writing that year. For those who did make money, half earned less than $10,000 (then again, 17 percent earned more than $100,000). Similarly, in 2019, more than a third of musicians earned less than $6,500, and 47 percent earned less than $13,000.[34] In 2012, 81 percent of bloggers made less than $100.[35] All these are examples of the "superstar" economics of cultural industries, where only a handful of top performers earn high incomes, and everyone else earns little or nothing.[36]

Already insecure, some cultural workers have become much more so in the age of platformization. A growing number of creators depend completely on platforms like Spotify, Amazon, YouTube, Instagram, and others, which often make seemingly arbitrary decisions about algorithms, policies and other structures affecting creators' incomes.[37] Romance writers, many almost completely dependent on Amazon's visibility algorithms, share this new digital precarity.

Is it labor, or is it fun? Nevertheless, people still flock to "cool jobs" in "hot industries," as Gina Neff, Elizabeth Wissinger, and Sharon Zukin put it.[38] Many in writing, music, freelance journalism, or social media will never make money, but they'll invest massive amounts of time and money chasing their dreams. Brooke Duffy calls this phenomenon "aspirational labor."[39] Related to concepts like Gina Neff's "venture labor" and Kuehn & Corrigan's "hope labor," aspirational labor illustrates how workers take on risk and invest unpaid work in the hope of a future payoff.[40] For romance writers, the explanation is simple: most aren't primarily motivated by money. In my interviews with eighty romance writers and industry professionals, only one, Eloisa James, told me she started romance writing specifically to make money (and frankly I'm skeptical; her prose is so vivid and joyful that I think she'd do it anyway).[41] Most romance authors I interviewed started writing because they love it. It's not just a side hustle: it's their calling. In fact, romance scholars Jennifer Lois and Joanna Gregson argue that this sense of calling helps authors persevere through long periods of rejection. They suggest that such "aspirational emotional work" is common among people pursuing creative work where "the potential for self-actualization is high, but opportunity for secure employment is low."[42]

In this willingness to work for creative satisfaction, not just money, romance writers resemble other cultural workers who feel a calling. Musicians and artists come to mind, but so do social media influencers, who work long, unpaid hours hoping for a career doing what they love. Cultural workers, then, are willing to accept creative satisfaction and hope for the future in lieu of optimizing their current pay. In this, they're different from gig workers like Uber drivers, who may drive to support their passion, but likely don't feel a deep calling to shuttle people to the airport. Professional consultants, from software developers to freelance writers to graphic designers, fall somewhere in the middle of this spectrum of willingness to forgo pay for creative satisfaction.

This blend of motives—creative satisfaction and money—also means there's a lot of crossover in cultural industries between amateur and professional, as some people make money and some don't but keep working anyway. Romance writers share these blurred professional/amateur lines with musicians, freelance journalists, and social media creators on YouTube, Twitch, Instagram, and elsewhere. This kind of professional/amateur blurring long prevailed in music and writing but became increasingly common in what Henry Jenkins calls the "convergence culture" fostered by sharing online creativity.[43]

This blurring of professional/amateur lines poses yet another barrier to traditional forms of labor organizing, because this work doesn't *look* like labor. It may or may not be paid. And much of the work is "invisible labor"—it produces economic value, as does raising kids or cooking dinner, but, like these activities, isn't paid or even recognized as labor.[44]

The specific invisible work underpinning all freelancing is the hustle—constantly making new connections, pitching ideas, drumming up new work. Communication scholar Nancy Baym describes this as "relational labor . . . the ongoing work of communicating with people over time to create structures that can support continued work."[45] Meanwhile, discussions about "digital labor" suggest that readers, fans, bloggers, and reviewers are all doing a kind of unpaid, invisible work (posting, reviewing, leaving data trails) that creates value for tech platforms. All these nuanced definitions of labor types are another symptom of the need to reinvigorate discussions around labor and protection.

What do I mean by feminized labor? The concept of feminized labor, developed by Arlie Hochschild, Angela McRobbie, Lisa Adkins, and many others, refers to work mostly (though not only) performed by women, in a context dominated by and/or associated with women. Feminized labor is usually devalued compared to "men's work", and is associated with flexibility, insecurity, isolation, low wages, caring, and managing emotion.[46] Many of these qualities associated with women's work dovetail with those of cultural labor, especially in emerging fields associated with women, like social media influencing.[47]

The US romance industry was and remains an almost-entirely female business enclave, dominated by white, heterosexual women (although less so now than in the past). All major groups in the business are women, including:

Writers: 98 percent of romance authors are women. (86 percent white; 88 percent heterosexual).[48]

Editors: Although a gender breakdown of romance editors isn't available, most editors at major publishing houses in general are white (76 percent), women (74 percent), heterosexual (81 percent), and not disabled (89 percent).[49]

Readers: Most romance readers are women (82 percent), white (73 percent, although 12 percent Black, 7 percent Latinx, and 4 percent Asian or Asian American), and heterosexual (86 percent, with 9 percent identifying as bisexual or pansexual, and 2 percent gay or lesbian).[50]

As a result of this makeup, Romancelandia's development incorporated work patterns, professional identities, social tactics, and organizational strategies associated with women, particularly white, middle-class, heterosexual women. A frame of feminized labor helps identify how wider labor tensions and contradictions play out in a feminized arena, especially tensions between isolation versus collectivism, and individualism versus care. This matters not only for romance writers today, but for emerging digital fields, like social media influencing, where most workers are women,[51] and for related fields like social media entertainment where working conditions share qualities like flexibility, insecurity, and isolation.

Three interwoven patterns associated with feminized labor recur throughout the book, informing the network's pervasive ethic of care, and its unique network structure:

Blending work and family. Although varying by race and class, women in the United States do more unpaid labor, including cooking, cleaning, and childcare, than men do.[52] Most women with families work what Arlie Hochschild called "the second shift," equally shouldering paid work and home responsibilities. Women do far more caregiving for children and other family members than men do.[53] As we'll see in the chapters ahead, Romancelandia developed into a community that always fully recognized and helped authors manage family and work expectations.

Strong ties and relationships. Throughout industrialized nations, women have long been the primary maintainers of family and friend relationships. This unpaid "kin work" includes visits, letters, telephone calls, presents, cards, organizing holidays, and all the other work that goes into maintaining relations with friends and family.[54] These gendered practices of relationship-building produce the strong ties that characterize women's networks. For instance, one study of community networks found that women provide significantly more emotional support to people in their networks than men do. Women had stronger ties with their friends. They were very likely to swap favors and do small services for others, like watching each other's kids.[55] Strong ties, favor exchanges, and a perception that women form strong, unique bonds with each other played, and play, important roles in the history and practices of Romancelandia.

Community building and networks. From quilting bees to romance writing groups to the Women's March, women have a long tradition of drawing on their strong ties in order to self-organize, defined as a process where individuals come together, either formally or informally, to collectively work toward a goal.[56]

Don't men do this too? Yes, but differently. Studies from the late 1970s, when Romancelandia was coming together, showed that men and women formed and joined distinctly different kinds of organizations: men tended to belong to large, business-oriented groups, like professional associations, while women joined much smaller, more grassroots groups, "more focused on domestic or community affairs."[57] This pattern aligns with the persistent Victorian ideal of men in the public sphere versus women in the private sphere. Women's traditions of self-organizing for mutual aid produced the nationwide "women's club movement," where mostly middle-class white women successfully lobbied for Progressive Era labor reforms.[58] Black women, excluded from white organizations, formed Phyllis Wheatley clubs around the country, as well as informal networks and church groups, dedicated to improving their communities. White, working-class women formed their own "working girls' clubs" for socializing, and sometimes joined forces with middle-class women to improve their conditions. In all these cases, both ideology and the lived realities of women directly affected the kinds of informal and formal organizations they formed, as sociologists Johanna Brenner and Barbara Laslett note. They write that "women's responsibilities as mothers and wives provided resources for, and constraints on, their capacity for collective action."[59]

Nurture, Not Nature

These three themes—family, strong ties, and self-organizing for mutual aid— recur throughout this book because they directly shaped the unique network structure of Romancelandia and its underlying ethic of care. But I want to be very clear: I am in no way claiming that women are naturally more nurturing and social than men. Instead, I'm drawing on *standpoint theory*, which argues that someone's individual experience and social position shapes their understanding of the world and informs their actions.[60] So throughout this book, when I argue that an ethic of care infused the structures and networks built by romance writers, it's based on my perspective that these women's life experiences, informed by prevailing ideas about gender, race, work, and family, shaped their actions. In the chapters ahead, we'll see how romance writers have drawn on, or resisted, these historic positions as the dynamics of gender, race, work, and family have shifted since 1980.

Nora Gets Rejected

These thoughts on labor help us see what exactly Nora Roberts was up to at the start of this chapter, as she wrote, typed, and mailed off her manuscript. She was performing three kinds of labor at once: the invisible work of childcare and homemaking; the cultural labor of writing; and the aspirational labor of investing her leisure time into doing what she loved, with some hope of a payoff. The intertwining of these feminized forms of labor would soon inform the development of Romancelandia, becoming exponentially more powerful when connected through the webs of female relationships.

For now, though, Roberts still had to break into the publishing industry—and it wasn't going well. She kept writing and submitting, but her rejection slips piled up. Harlequin politely informed her that they already published one "American author"—Janet Dailey. That was plenty, thank you very much. At the time, Harlequin didn't acquire authors—they just reprinted British romances from UK publisher Mills & Boon (which had also published Dailey's work). Neither company was in the market for more romance by US writers.

That was bad news for Nora and for a rising crop of other aspiring novelists, many inspired by the success of two bestsellers in the early 1970s: Kathleen Woodiwiss's *The Flame and the Flower* and Rosemary Rogers's *Sweet Savage Love*. A deliciously cheesy paperback from 1982 called *Love's Leading Ladies*, written by Kathryn Falk, profiled dozens of these fledgling authors who had, by then, found publishers. Under the paperback's mauve cover, sixty-five breezy profiles (all women, all white, mostly middle-aged) provided an offbeat medley of career details, zodiac signs, and favorite recipes (example: author Jude Deveraux's recipe was something called sausage cake). Reflecting the economic trajectory of postwar white America, many of these writers were born into working-class families, married in their twenties (or teens, like Nora Roberts), and worked until they had children. Like Roberts, most had started writing as a hobby, with no knowledge of the publishing industry and no network to turn to.

Fortunately, the romance publishing industry was about to change and, with it, the isolation of aspiring writers. An acquaintance who worked as a ghost writer shared a tip with Roberts: Simon & Schuster was launching a new romance line called Silhouette. Roberts packed up her latest manuscript, a novel set in Maryland's horse country called *Irish Thoroughbred*, and crossed her fingers once again.

It's fitting that Roberts found Silhouette through a friend. Isolated writers like Roberts would soon come to rely on a thriving network of relationships that would grow into Romancelandia.

Mapping Romancelandia: Three Fields, Four Components

I first heard the term Romancelandia about a decade ago, as writers described to me their sprawling network of authors, readers, traditional publishers and editors, indie editors, formatters, proofreaders, reviewers, podcasters, bloggers, and others. Catherine Roach notes that the term also sometimes describes the make-believe universe of emotional justice where all romances take place, as well as the lively social media locales—especially Twitter—where Romancelandians discuss and debate 24-7.[61] Sarah Wendell of the *Smart Bitches, Trashy Books* blog told me the term most accurately means "the romance fandom," but in this case, that includes everyone in the ecosystem, since authors and editors are almost without exception romance readers and fans too.

Occasionally, industry observers and the media have confused Romancelandia with Romance Writers of America (RWA). But really RWA has always been just one of many structures within the far bigger realm. As we'll see below, Romancelandia brings together readers, writers, editors, and everyone else devoted to the genre in a community informed by and interested in those elements of the genre I defined above—stories about women's happiness, which evolve with the times and bring women together in a site of cultural labor. Below, I outline some of the key players and provide a rough conceptual map of the realm.

In this book, I usually describe Romancelandia as a "network" or a "community," to emphasize the importance of connections. But you can also think of Romancelandia as a "field" where these connections form. In sociology, several schools of thought define fields somewhat differently, but as sociologist Clayton

Childress notes, they all agree that a field, generally, is a "social arena of attention and habituated action."[62] Within fields, various entities or actors (people, organizations, technologies, etc.) focus on a shared interest, united by a general understanding of how things should work. Fields exist at a middle level of social processes, between micro-level individual actions and macro-level societal forces. These levels mutually shape social action and the flow of power in society.

Not to make matters more confusing, but the field of Romancelandia itself is made up of three overlapping subfields: ***creation, production,*** and ***reception,*** subfields that Childress carefully documents in his book *Under the Cover*. Childress notes that, in the past, scholars typically wrote about just one of these fields, although in reality, they connect and overlap.

In Romancelandia, writers generally belong in the *creation* field, editors and publishers in the *production* field, and readers, reviewers, and industry observers in the *reception* field. But there's much crossover: writers are also readers, readers often become writers, indie writers serve as their own producers, and so on.

Within the subfields that make up Romancelandia, I've mapped four different kinds of **components** that structure relationships and interactions. These components overlap and intersect, but teasing them apart clarifies how information, ideas, and power flow through the field.[63]

1. **Informal networks** *(represented by clouds on the map)*. These are the myriad loose subnetworks within Romancelandia, like writing groups, plotting groups, reading groups, critique partnerships, and networks of indie editors and producers. These groups may come together temporarily, like the authors who launched the Romancing the Runoff fundraising effort (see chapter 9). Or they may stay together for years, like many romance writing and reading groups.

2. **Organizations** *(represented by rectangles)*. These are formal organizations, including:

    Writing associations, like Romance Writers of America, Novelists, Inc. (NINC) and The Authors Guild. Also, local chapters of RWA and regional or subgenre groups that may once have been part of RWA.

    Publishing firms and literary agencies, including the "Big Five" (HarperCollins, Hachette, Macmillan, Penguin Random House, Simon & Schuster), as well as Sourcebooks, Kensington, Harlequin, and a plethora of small and/or digital-first publishers. Amazon is *both* a traditional publisher (through its romance imprint Montlake) *and* an indie publishing service, through Kindle Direct Publishing.

Indie publishing services, like Kindle Direct Publishing, Apple Books, and
Barnes & Noble Press. These belong to larger organizations like Amazon and Apple, and are often referred to as platforms, but it's critical
to remember no platform stands alone: they're services governed by
organizations, people, and policies.

Booksellers, including chains like Barnes & Noble, independent bookstores, and online bookstores.

Note that Amazon occupies many roles—publisher, indie publisher,
bookseller—previously performed by separate organizations.

3. **Events** *(represented by pentagons).* A shifting lineup of *in-person* and
online events (e.g., RWA's national Annual Conference; Romance Slam
Jam BookCon; GayRomLit; Romance Writers' Mastermind; Romantic Times, now replaced by Book Lovers Con; and the Romancing the
Runoff auction). This also includes smaller one-off events like book
signings, regional conferences, and academic gatherings.

4. **User-created content** *(represented as lozenges)*, **including social media.**
As we'll see in chapters 5 and 7–9, major publications almost never
reviewed romance until recently. So, romance readers had to create and
share their own reviews, newsletters, and other content long before the
internet made "participatory fan culture" a common term.[64] Today,
readers generate a vast amount of text, audio, and video reviewing—
recommending, celebrating, and creating romance. A tiny sample
includes blogs, podcasts, fan fiction sites, and reviewer sites (including reader sites like Goodreads and traditional publications like the
New York Times, which began reviewing romance in the 2010s). Plus,
romance readers drive book-related social media phenomena like
BookTok, Bookstagram, and BookTubing (all terms for the use of
social media platforms to celebrate books).[65] This content doesn't
just remain in the reader world: it's in constant dialogue with authors
and the industry, shaping and creating industry trends.[66] Likewise,
writers also generate content, including discussion groups and social
media sites dedicated to storycraft and publishing. And writers,
readers, and producers all unite in Romancelandia's vigorous,
dynamic social media world.

In the chapters ahead, we'll see how these four components channel the
flow of information and resources, coming together into an unusual structure
and culture. We'll also examine the roles they play in shifting industry power
dynamics, first by helping authors improve their position in traditional

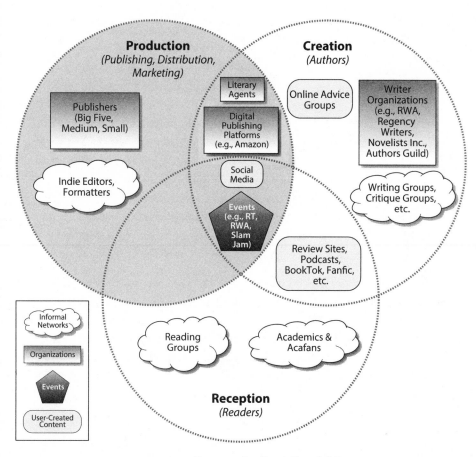

FIGURE 2.1. Romancelandia: A Rough Map

publishing, then later by spreading digital innovations, and, most recently, by pressuring both Romancelandia and publishing to become more inclusive. Above, I offer a rough map of how these components fit together within Romancelandia. It's not precise: there's a lot of overlap and intersection. You're invited to question, correct, and edit it yourself. But it's a useful thinking tool to start considering relationships and influence in romance and in other networked sites of labor.

Nora Gets Published

As the map indicates, Romancelandia today is vast and complex. But in June of 1980, it barely existed at all. That month, on a hot summer day, Roberts's phone rang. She hollered to her roughhousing boys to keep down the racket as she answered. It was Silhouette editor Nancy Jackson, offering a $3,000 advance for *Irish Thoroughbred*.[67]

Roberts later shared the moment on a romance blog:

I think I said: Huh? And I began to pace around the kitchen while [the editor's] cheerful and cultured voice buzzed in my ear, and the war in the next room reached fever pitch. My older son was, undoubtedly, pummeling his younger brother. But, you know, priorities. British-accented New York editor wants to buy my book vs. possible ER run. No contest. I listened, I babbled, and while pacing stepped on a grossly fat tick that must have fallen, sated, off the dog. There was a song in my heart, bloody footprints all over my kitchen floor and screams of vengeance from the next room. Somewhere in there I registered that she intended to pay me for my manuscript. Pay. Me. Money.[68]

The timing couldn't have been better for Roberts and her sons: by 1983, Roberts would find herself a divorced single mother. Her writing would eventually support the family.

For more than two decades, she would find community and encouragement—and later, disillusionment and disappointment—in an organization that was just getting off the ground: Romance Writers of America.

PART II

Romancelandia Rising

3

The Roots of Romancelandia

OPEN NETWORKS AND THE ETHIC OF CARE

AT AGE 47, Vivian Stephens had never worked as a book editor. But in 1978, while spending a summer in the Berkshires, she wandered into a used bookstore. In the store's cluttered back room, she picked up Kathleen Woodiwiss's *The Flame and the Flower*, an historical romance that had electrified readers with its explicit sensuality when it came out in 1972. She bought it for twenty-five cents and stayed up all night reading. "The next week, I bought five more romances. The following week I bought ten," she told me in one of three long conversations over several years. Romance editing, she decided, would be her next career.[1]

It wouldn't be the first time Stephens broke into a new field. A stylish, college-educated Black woman from Houston, Stephens had worked in textiles, airlines, education, and magazines. Gregarious and whip-smart, Stephens never found a job she couldn't master—as long as racism didn't get in the way. Early in her career in Los Angeles, she'd learned to phone companies before applying for a job, chatting up the secretaries and sharing that she was Black. "Usually if I got a young woman on the phone, she'd tell me if I wouldn't really be considered."

Fortunately, when Stephens was in her twenties, the emerging civil rights movement pushed for fair hiring practices. As part of a diversification effort, American Airlines hired Stephens, offering free-flight benefits that sent her globetrotting through Europe and Mexico. Later, living in New York City, Stephens made friends, traveled widely, and landed jobs at Saks Fifth Avenue and Time-Life Books. Her résumé was impressive.

But would it be impressive enough to launch a new career in romance editing? The predominantly white publishing industry was "the last of the genteel

WASP professions," as Black journalist Rosemary Bray wrote in *Black Entrepreneur* in 1982. The industry's notoriously low pay drove away Black workers who often had extended family depending on them.[2] The industry's pipeline had long been filled with "upper middle class white women who could afford such jobs," as Bray's *Black Entrepreneur* article put it. That trend, combined with racism in publishing, "made it nearly impossible for Black women to find jobs" in the industry.[3] In fact, according to the *New York Times*, in 1981, only six Black editors worked at major publishing houses (down from twelve in the 1970s, a decrease that editor and Nobel Prize winner Toni Morrison blamed on publisher consolidation). Three of those editors were in romance publishing, "an area that puts them generally out of touch with Black writers," according to the *New York Times*, since no Black romances had yet been published.[4]

Stephens would change that.

As Stephens began her job hunt in 1978, the book business was undergoing massive change. New technologies and distribution strategies, combined with the sexual revolution, disrupted the political economy of publishing in ways that poised the romance genre for explosive growth. Roughly thirty years later, eerily similar disruptions in book production and distribution would occur with the rise of e-books. When that happened, the foundation that Stephens and a handful of aspiring authors had laid by uniting a loyal creator community would poise romance writers for digital success.

This chapter follows the early history of romance and the forming of Romance Writers of America, which for decades remained the largest and most visible organization within greater Romancelandia. Vivian Stephens's adventures in publishing illuminate three developments in the flourishing of contemporary romance: the changing *political economy of publishing* and the proliferation of romance; the founding of RWA as an unusual *open-elite network*; and the infusion of an *ethic of care* that set it apart from other writing organizations. Along the way, we'll see how RWA developed its contradictory framework of inclusive access but unequal benefits and consider implications for other kinds of workers attempting to self-organize for mutual benefit.

The Political Economy of Publishing

To understand Vivian Stephens's job prospects in 1978, we first need to understand the political economy of publishing—the interplay of social, economic, and broadly-defined political factors that shaped book production at the time. In the 1970s and 1980s, industry consolidation led a shrinking number

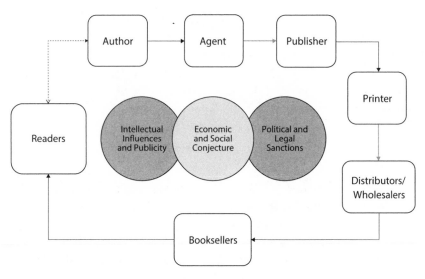

FIGURE 3.1. Book Publication Circuit, 1454–2007,
adapted from Darnton (1982)

of increasingly powerful publishers to profit from new technologies and
distribution methods—not unlike today's platform-based industries, where
a few titanic tech platforms dictate the terms of workers' livelihoods. This disrupted the distribution of power among authors, publishers, and readers.

In a 1982 essay, book historian Robert Darnton noted that book production
has followed the same basic circuit since the printing of the Gutenberg Bible.
For some five hundred years, until the rise of e-books, books traveled from
authors to editors to printers to distributors to bookstores to readers (sometimes
with exciting or nefarious detours, like book smuggling and plagiarism). Together with social, political, and cultural forces—including copyright laws,
book pricing policies, literacy rates, popular culture, and publicity practices—
this circuit determined which authors got published, which books sold well,
and who made money. Darnton captured all this in a diagram he called the
"book communication circuit," which I've simplified above (sadly, to keep it
simple, I had to remove the smugglers).

Throughout the second half of the twentieth century, books continued
to travel this route without much change until the rise of digital books. During this time, dynamics among publishers, printers, and distributors decreased
author power while setting the stage for the romance genre to explode—at the
very moment when Vivian Stephens was looking to break into the industry.

Publishers and Superstars

In the 1970s, the book trade was in the midst of change. What had previously been considered a sleepy, genteel industry where many small firms made modest profits was becoming big business.[5] An ever-shrinking number of large, multinational conglomerates replaced the proliferation of small publishing houses, increasing pressure for profits. Today, just five firms dominate US publishing: Hachette, HarperCollins, Macmillan, Penguin Random House, and Simon & Schuster.

The book industry has long balanced two competing demands: commerce and culture.[6] As large multinational conglomerates came to dominate publishing, profit pressures accelerated the "superstar economics" of publishing. In media industries including music, books, film, and other performing arts, Rosen noted that "small numbers of people earn enormous amounts of money."[7] Several realities drive this trend: First, audiences like to read and watch what their friends are reading and watching.[8] So, popular books (and movies, TV shows, musicians, YouTubers, and other entertainment products) become exponentially more popular as friends spread the word. Second, it's cheaper to sell five million copies of one item than to sell one copy of five million items, because "first copy" costs are high, but later copy costs are low.[9] In other words, it takes a lot of time, effort, and money to write a book, develop an article, create a song, or produce a movie. But once that first copy is made, making more copies costs almost nothing, especially if those copies are digital. So, companies make more money by selling a few blockbuster products from superstar creators than from pushing many more modestly selling items. In general, superstar economics work well for corporations and for a tiny handful of creators but leave most cultural producers struggling. As one editor joked to me, "If we knew which books would be hits, we'd only publish seven titles a year."

At least, I think he was joking.

Fortunately for authors, even in the age of big data and artificial intelligence, publishers, record labels, and other producers still can't predict blockbusters. As a result, publishers, music labels, film production companies, and social media platforms spread out their risk, making a few big bets on proven bestsellers and many small bets on unknowns.[10] In book publishing, that means authors like Nora Roberts receive multi-million-dollar advances, while "midlist" authors lacking a glorious track record might get $3,000–$5,000.[11] For social media creators, it means that, while most creators receive little active support from their platform, a minority of strong performers become platform "partners" with more favorable revenue-sharing agreements. Meanwhile, a few winners make unimaginable fortunes, like former Twitch streamer Félix "xQc" Lengyel, who received $100 million UDS to switch to startup streaming platform Kick.[12]

For these reasons, since the 1970s (and still today), publishers have increasingly preferred to pay ever-more-outrageous advances to a handful of proven bestselling authors, decreasing the money available for newcomers.[13] Marketing dollars that might boost sales for lesser-known authors instead go toward more expensive creators, as insurance for the massive bets publishers made on "big books."[14] As a result, in the late 1970s, it became harder and harder to break into most areas of publishing. A few authors benefited enormously, but most had so little power that an influential book on publishing in the early 1980s dubbed the authors' perspective "the worm's eye view."[15]

Printing and Distribution: The Second Paperback Revolution

While the consolidation of publishing accelerated superstar investment, new printing technologies and distribution strategies launched what industry observers call "the second paperback revolution."[16] During the first paperback boom in the 1930s, rising literacy rates drove demand for cheap paperback reprints of books previously published in hardcover. In the 1970s, three factors launched a second boom. First, offset printing and other new technologies lowered costs and increased paperback quality. Second, publishers began selling paperbacks in drugstores and supermarkets, making books an impulse item thrown in the paths of shopping wives and mothers. Third, publishers realized it might be cheaper to release original titles rather than license existing books.[17] Netflix and Amazon would realize the same thing decades later and begin producing their own movies and TV shows in addition to licensing content from other producers.[18]

Meanwhile, new social mores around sex prompted demand for more adult content. The birth control pill, the lifting of the film industry's Hays Code censoring depictions of sex, and the sexual revolution all made the chaste romances of the 1950s and 1960s feel staid and dated.

All these forces—new paperback technologies, new distribution forms, and demand for more sensual content—helped fuel the success of Katheleen Woodiwiss's *The Flame and the Flower*, a paperback original from Avon released in 1972 (the very same mass-market paperback Stephens would pick up for twenty-five cents in 1978.) Together with *Sweet Savage Love* by Rosemary

Rogers in 1974, Woodiwiss's novel revealed a reader appetite for sensual historical romance, as well as a cheaper, more profitable way to produce and sell books, by issuing paperbacks that had never come out in hardback.[19]

In 1978, as Vivian Stephens began her job hunt, American publishers were only just catching on to the new power of romance. New lines were starting to open but remained underfunded and disrespected. All this would open doors for Stephens.

Stephens's Bluff

When Stephens returned to New York in the fall of 1978, she headed straight to the offices of Warner Books, which had published some of the novels she'd devoured over the summer. She'd sent her résumé already. Now, she bluffed her way into the human resources office. Dropping by at lunchtime, when she assumed the HR director would be out, she told the office assistant she and the director had a mutual acquaintance, who suggested Stephens say hello. Stephens hoped her little ruse would bring her résumé to the top of the pile.

To her horror, the assistant invited her to sit down. The director was in.

Stephens panicked. *I've lied*, she thought. *What do I do?* After waiting a few minutes, she lost her nerve, told the assistant that she had another appointment, and that she'd come back another time.

"Oh, no, wait!" the assistant replied. "She's going to call you in right now."

And she did. Stephens barely kept her composure as she introduced herself.

"So, who is this person we both know?" the director asked coolly, her legs crossed, her eyes unreadable behind dark glasses.

On the spot, Stephens picked a friend's name out of the air.

"And where did I meet this person?" the director persisted.

"At a Time-Life cocktail party," Stephens improvised.

The director nodded. "That may be so," she said curtly. She proceeded to ask Stephens about her experience. Warner had no jobs for Stephens, but Avon, Bantam, or Dell might.

Perhaps if Stephens had come knocking a year or so earlier, before publishers began to catch on to the profit potential of romance, the director might have been less helpful. But by 1978, readers were hungry for new stories, technology had lowered costs, and distribution channels had changed. Meanwhile, American companies began to eye the skyrocketing profits of Canadian publisher Harlequin, which began to climb in 1972 thanks to a publishing model predicated *not* on superstar authors but on a very different strategy.

Harlequin's New Take

In 1957, the sleepy, family-owned Harlequin Books had started issuing paperback reprints of British romance novels from UK publisher Mills & Boon—tame love stories, often featuring nurses traveling to exotic locales. Harlequin distributed these paperback reprints, mostly in Canada, but later in the United States through a deal with Simon & Schuster. Sales marched along modestly but steadily until 1972 when the company hired a new CEO, former Proctor & Gamble executive Lawrence Heisey.

With zero publishing experience, Heisey drew on his background in consumer-packaged goods to bypass the superstar publishing model. He realized he could sell category romances the same way he'd sold detergent.[20] He could create lines of romance novels, each with its own distinctive settings and themes, and treat them like brands. He could advertise the entire line rather than promoting one book at a time.[21]

In the early 1970s, Heisey would also pioneer new distribution strategies, selling category romances on drugstore and supermarket racks, and extending distribution outside Canada into the United States through a deal with Pocket Books. He would also bypass retail outlets altogether by selling Harlequin novels directly to readers, through a mail order subscription service.[22]

Meanwhile, once Harlequin started acquiring books by American authors in the 1980s, rather than just issuing reprints, the company could avoid pricey competition for name-brand authors. In some ways, this strategy resembled the wildly successful "fiction factory" approach of the Stratemeyer Syndicate, the publisher that hired inexpensive ghostwriters to pen series like Nancy Drew and the Hardy Boys mysteries: the syndicate could promote an entire series and authors didn't gain superstar negotiating power. Harlequin would tweak the strategy, requiring most authors to use pseudonyms that belonged to the company.

Heisey's approach transformed romance publishing. At the start of the 1970s, Harlequin published 110 novels a year, mostly in Canada, all reprints of Mills & Boon romances. By the end of the decade, it sold four hundred a year (but, as Nora Roberts found it, until the 1980s, the company still published only one American author, Janet Dailey). During the 1970s, profits exploded, skyrocketing from $110,000 in 1969 to $11 million in 1977.[23]

American publishers took notice. By the late 1970s, several major American publishers, including Dell and Simon & Schuster, were looking to start new romance lines or revitalize existing ones as low-cost gambles. They put few resources into these lines, which might prove profitable but would never have prestige. Male editors handed manuscripts to secretaries to edit. With a glut of manuscripts available from homemakers like Nora Roberts, publishers could keep costs down by paying modest royalties to the thousands of women writers vying for publication.[24]

Vivian Stephens and Candlelight

As all this was happening, Stephens followed up on the leads gained from her successful subterfuge. She landed an interview with twenty-five-year-old editor Kate Duffy at Dell, who'd been hired to revive the company's old-fashioned Candlelight romance imprints.

Christened "the Julia Child of romance" by Sarah Wendell of *Smart Bitches, Trashy Books*, Duffy was a brilliant, big-hearted chain-smoker from Rochester who started out as a temp at Popular Library.[25] Over time, she'd nudged the paperback house's insipid romance line toward more contemporary, American themes. "I didn't want to be a governess or a nurse in Europe. I wanted to read about Americans," she said.[26] At the time, romance was all "women with a peignoir and a candle."[27]

At Candlelight, Duffy hired Stephens immediately for $15,000 a year to acquire and edit five manuscripts a month. Stephens became one of only a few Black women editors in New York at the time, among them Toni Morrison at Random House, romance editor Veronica Mixon at Doubleday, and Valerie Flournoy, who later became a popular children's author. Not long after hiring Stephens, Duffy moved to Simon & Schuster, where she founded Silhouette, leaving Stephens to run Candlelight. Between those imprints and other new or refreshed romance lines, American publishers suddenly needed some nine hundred new titles a year to fill the burgeoning demand.[28]

Sex and Romance

The moment Stephens stepped into her office, the low status of romance editors became abundantly clear. "They put me in a storage room," Stephens told me. "No window, no books." Just piles of unread manuscripts stacked on the floor.

Stephens, who had never bought a manuscript, somehow had to acquire five books a month. And she knew she wanted Candlelight romances to be different. One day, during her lunch hour, Stephens watched women in Woolworth's browsing romance: no one was picking up Candlelight books. When Stephens asked why, a reader pointed to a cover.

"Nobody is *that* blonde and *that* stupid, and no man would be interested in anybody *that* young and naive," the reader explained.

"That's when it suddenly dawned on me," Stephens said. "We were in the middle of the women's movement. The sexual revolution was in full tilt. I realized, 'I've got to make these books relevant.'" She sought out fresh, contemporary manuscripts, reflecting the desires and dreams of women in the late 1970s—independent, ambitious, self-sufficient women like herself. She insisted heroines have jobs and education; these characters would be happy and self-sufficient even if the romance didn't work out.[29] In letters and on long phone calls, she encouraged her writers to research the details of their characters' occupations. "Most hadn't been in the workforce unless they were teachers or stewardesses," Stephens said. She sent them off to Neiman Marcus and Saks to feel the difference between chinchilla and mink; she asked them to bestow signature perfumes on their glamorous heroines.

Stephens also wanted heroines to embrace sexual joy. She launched a new imprint, Candlelight Ecstasy, featuring voluptuous love scenes. One of the line's first titles was Jayne Ann Krentz's *Gentle Pirate*—a sensual story about a wounded Vietnam vet (which, refreshingly for its time, did *not* feature rape). Within a year, Stephens would be breaking other barriers, publishing the first contemporary romances featuring Black and Latinx characters. At the same time, she would become an indefatigable champion of romance writers, helping to launch what would become the world's largest writing network.

The Two Ritas: Creating an Open-Elite Network

Meanwhile, back in Stephens' hometown of Houston, a young mother named Rita Clay Estrada was newly in possession of a typewriter. Estrada, thirty-six, was raising four children and helping manage the family business. Like Stephens, she'd fallen in love with books like *The Flame and the Flower* and *Sweet Savage Love*, appreciating their sexy love scenes and feisty heroines. When her husband scolded her for spending too much on romances, she found a part-time job managing a B. Dalton bookstore. He changed his tune, bought her a typewriter, and urged her to start writing.

She did. When she showed her first draft to her mother, longtime technical writer and editor Rita Gallagher, her mother fell in love with the genre and started writing too. In 1978, the two Ritas attended a women's writing conference at the University of Houston.

"I walked in, and I knew this is what I wanted to do," she said.

Although most of the writers there wrote literary fiction, Estrada and Gallagher quickly befriended several other aspiring romance authors, including magazine writer Parris Afton Bonds, and Dallas-based TV reporter Sandra Brown (whose books would later sell more than 80 million copies worldwide).[30] After the conference, the group kept in touch. They continued to attend writing conferences together, gathering more aspiring romance writers and struggling to learn the ropes. As their band of writers grew, though, they soon found that few industry professionals wanted to help.

No Respect: Women Authors

"No happy woman ever writes," according to author and journalist Fanny Fern in 1855.[31] Indeed, until the twentieth century, many women writers entered literary life out of hardship.[32] One of Europe's first known professional female authors, the widowed Christine de Pizan, supported her three children by writing courtly love poetry for French nobles in the fourteenth century. In the sixteenth century, the widowed, indebted Aphra Behn became one of England's most popular playwrights. American author Kate Chopin started writing after her husband died in debt, leaving her with six children. Many Black authors drew on hardship as well, writing enslavement narratives, but also love stories. In 1892, for instance, Frances Ellen Watkins Harper, a Black writer best known for her poetry, published *Iola Leroy*, a sentimental novel featuring a romance between a mixed-race nurse and doctor in the Civil War. In 1900, Black author Pauline Hopkins published the post–Civil War romance *Contending Forces* in 1900, framing racial and gender themes with a love story where loving, educated African Americans find their happily ever after. But Hopkins's later work took a darker turn, with tragic endings. As Jim Crow laws gained momentum, Hopkins "gave up on romance because the optimism was gone," said legendary Black historical author Beverly Jenkins in a 2016 RWA keynote address.[33]

In their desire to support themselves with their words and ideas, these women writers resembled the earliest social media producers. Communication scholar Emily Hund explains that former magazine writers and editors who lost their media jobs in the 2008 recession launched blogs in an effort to hang onto their professional writing careers, paving the way for today's social media influencers.[34] Both in the digital age and long before, these struggling women met with unexpected success. In the nineteenth century, women came to write 75 percent of published fiction in America, much of it romantic or sentimental.[35] Likewise, social media influencing, a female-dominated industry, is now a coveted career path.

In another similarity to social media influencers, women writers gained little respect for work deemed fluffy and trivial by a misogynistic society. In the 1970s and 1980s, "it didn't matter what [women writers] wrote" because "all fiction written by and about women was labeled romance," reflected Rita Gallagher.[36] News outlets didn't bother reviewing romances (or most books by women). Out of the 706 books reviewed in fifteen national publications for three months of 1993, just 4 percent were romance or women's fiction (a genre focused on women's lives, but not centered on optimistic love stories).[37] Nearly two decades later, little had changed. American publications like the *New York Times*, the *New York Review of Books* and the *New Yorker* still devoted up to 80 percent of book reviews to works by male authors.[38]

In 2007, bestselling women's fiction writer Jennifer Weiner summed up the situation:

> A woman writing about domestic life can count on the word 'miniature' or 'microcosm' or some variation of 'small' showing up in even the best reviews. . . . Meanwhile, men who write about families aren't just writing about Mom and Dad; they're telling the story of America, the world, the Way We Live Now (and not in the microcosm, either).[39]

In short, American women faced a misogynist industry that devalued all women writers, but especially despised romance authors. Likewise, today, social media creators—especially fashion and beauty influencers—are often not taken seriously as professionals. "The feminized nature of the influencer industry obscures its seriousness and widespread impact," notes Emily Hund.

"Stay Away from Real Writers"

This cultural disrespect haunted the two Ritas as they and their growing band of writer friends continued to meet up at writing conferences. At one event, an agent told them, "You girls need to go start your own organization. Stay away from people who do real writing."

Indignant, the group kept searching for sympathetic editors and industry knowledge. At the SouthWest Writers' Conference in Houston in 1978, they suddenly found the person they'd been looking for—Candelight's newly hired romance editor, Vivian Stephens.

At the event's opening session, Stephens introduced herself and explained exactly what she was looking for. "They told me nobody had ever given them the same level of information about writing and publishing before," Stephens said.

One night during the conference, the two Ritas threw a party in their hotel room, inviting Stephens and every other woman writer and editor they knew.

"It was a young writer's dream of a Bohemian cocktail party," wrote one author, Kit O'Brien Jones, in an RWA newsletter years later.[40]

Writers perched on beds and windowsills in the small room. Drinks chilled in the bathtub. Charming and outgoing, Stephens quickly became the center of attention, offering advice on plots and publishing. Afterward, she promised to stay in touch. Over the next year, she fielded dozens of calls from women she met that night, seeking coaching on their writing and on publishing in general.

"I believe Romance Writers of America was founded there in that crowded hotel room, that night," Jones wrote. But really, it would take another two years.

Alone Together

For dozens of authors over the next year, Vivian Stephens became a crucial ally, an accessible link between the very separate worlds of writing and publishing. Before long, Stephens soon found herself overwhelmed with calls. She wondered if there was a more efficient way to share her industry knowledge. It might be time, she thought, for these writers to start helping each other. They needed an organization.

It wouldn't be the first-time women writers joined forces. Women authors founded the National League of American Pen Women in 1897 for "mutual aid, advice and future development."[41] The league sought to address problems including libel and copyright law, plagiarism, and gender inequality. Likewise, women journalists, excluded from the National Press Club until 1971, formed the Women's National Press Club in 1919.[42]

In the early twentieth century, other author groups were also coming together, encompassing both genders. Starting in 1912, the Authors League of America (now the Authors Guild) protected "the rights of all authors."[43] This professional organization made important gains for authors' collective interests, lobbying for fairer contracts and better information about sales, royalties, and payments. Today, emerging alliances of digital and social media producers, like the American Influencers Council, the Future of Music Coalition and a plethora of new journalism unions are similarly pushing for better conditions and more transparency.[44]

In the mid-twentieth century, other genre writers realized they needed to team up as well. In 1945, prominent mystery writers, including Erle Stanley Gardner and Rex Stout, launched Mystery Writers of America (MWA). Their motto: "Crime does not pay . . . enough." Only a few women were listed among the initial members. In 1965, Science Fiction and Fantasy Writers of America (SFWA) was founded, remaining predominantly male throughout the 1970s and 1980s.

Many women in MWA initially felt like second-class citizens. In 1986, mystery writer Phyllis Whitney wrote an open letter to Mystery Writers of America, observing that, in forty-one years, only seven women had won the Edgar Award.[45] Although women authors wrote a third of mysteries, men scored seven times as many reviews in the 1980s, according to bestselling mystery author Sara Paretsky. "Many of us encountered both fans and male writers at crime conferences who assumed we did this as a hobby, not as a serious vocation," she wrote on her website.[46]

Looking for more support, in 1986, women mystery authors formed Sisters in Crime "to plot a path toward being treated as the equals of male writers," according to the group's website.[47]

The failure of writers' organizations to serve their women members suggests the larger issue with networks and groups: they hold the power to exclude as well as include. This would prove a problem for RWA in the future, and also serve as a reminder to isolated workers in cultural industries and beyond as they seek new forms of collective mutual aid.

No Girls Allowed

As Estrada's list of aspiring and published romance contacts grew, she sought more sources of information and support. She'd heard about a coalition of mystery and science fiction writers who sent an annual delegation to major publishers to discuss business and industry trends. This sounded like just what her band of hopeful writers needed.

So, one day in 1979, she called the group and invited herself, saying she represented an organization of romance writers. *It's partially true, even if we only have five members and no name,* she figured.

The author she spoke with, a mystery author, warned her that the group might not be receptive to romance writers. Still, he invited her to make a pitch at an upcoming meeting in New York. Estrada booked a 6 a.m. flight and told her family she'd be home by bedtime.

At noon, she walked into the conference room at a Manhattan hotel, finding herself the only woman among fifteen men. They greeted her with polite distance. When the meeting started, one by one, each man stood up and reported on his genre and his own recent accomplishments. Then Estrada took the floor.

"All plots are created equal," she told them. All writers, she said, struggle to start out. All authors need insider advice about publishers and contracts. Writers should help each other, she argued. Romance writers should be part of their coalition.

She spoke for ten minutes and then the group voted. The answer was no. "We're here to discuss things you girls don't do," they said. "Romance isn't as big a thing as our genres."

The Founding of RWA

Back home in Houston, Estrada phoned Stephens and told her what happened. "Form your own organization," Stephens replied. "I'll be your guardian angel."

In December 1980, Stephens flew home to Texas for the first convening of Romance Writers of America. About forty women gathered in a bank's conference room down the block from the bookstore where Estrada worked.

Stephens brought along her sister Barbara, also a romance writer. Future bestseller Sandra Brown was there too. By the end of the day, RWA established its core leadership team, including Stephens, Estrada, and six elected board members. The leadership team included two Black women and one Latina writer (Celina Rios Mullan, author of the first Latinx romance), making it an unusually diverse group for the time. Although RWA would later drift away from this heritage of inclusion, its founders valued diversity. "Diversity is what we wanted," Estrada told me, adding frankly, "The only people we didn't really want were men."

Information Exchange

When Estrada visited the genre authors' coalition meeting in New York, she'd been struck by something odd. Here, all these authors had come together to share information—but they didn't. Not really.

> The guys . . . didn't share when they stood up. They'd say they signed a movie contract but not talk about how they did it. For some reason, they

were afraid to give information to each other. I wanted RWA to share information. When we find out information, we pass it on. We just open the door and say, "What do you want to know?"

The male writers' reticence was exactly the opposite of the romance world Estrada and Stephens moved in. As RWA quickly grew from forty to seventy members by the end of 1980, Estrada and Stephens emphasized information sharing, learning, and mentoring. One of the earliest issues of *Romance Writers Report* (*RWR*), RWA's member newsletter, solicited ideas for formalizing this sharing. The board, it said, "has been studying the feasibility of an information exchange" and had started to "solicit suggestions . . . on how such an exchange might work."[48]

As a newsletter and later a glossy magazine, *RWR* became the forum of that information exchange. In the July-August 1985 issue, 113 members responded to *RWR*'s poll, reporting income, hours worked, and more.[49] A two-page chart showed average advances by publisher and how those had changed over time. First time advances at Avon, for example, were $2,500–$12,500; at Harlequin, $2,300–$6,000; at Candlelight Ecstasy, $3,000. Previously published authors at these lines might make up to $30,000. This 1985 survey also listed contract terms, including foreign rights and print run sizes, and difficulties with publishers, like slow manuscript turnaround.

Sharing this kind of detailed payment and contract information actually violated the contract terms of some publishers. It was also, technically, illegal. As I mentioned above, US labor law considers payment and contract sharing as price-fixing. So, romance writers' widespread sharing stands as a testament to the unusual openness of romance writers. Over the subsequent decades, this tradition of sharing sensitive, competitive information would continue to skirt antitrust laws. For instance, in 2014–2018, a group of indie authors—many of them romance writers—would contribute their earnings and Amazon sales rank information to a database that helped author Hugh Howey and a mysterious figure called "Data Guy" extrapolate indie revenues on Amazon.[50]

Today, RWA's website devotes a full page to its antitrust statement, advising members not to "discuss or shar[e] company or author-specific prices, commission rates, royalty rates, advances, fees or other rates" because "a price-fixing violation may be inferred."[51] This is a clear indication of how current antitrust law works against transparency. But such concerns didn't stop romance authors in the 1980s from sharing information to protect themselves, and in the era of social media, it surely doesn't stop them now.

Creators today, including YouTubers, social media influencers, self-published authors, and Twitch streamers, often suffer from a lack of corporate transparency around payment arrangements and other contract terms. In *Chokepoint Capitalism*, authors Rebecca Giblin and Cory Doctorow urge creators to lobby for "transparency rights," including not only the right to share information, but also the right for creators to better understand how exactly their work creates value for corporations.[52] They note that the European Union passed a 2019 directive to ensure that authors and performers would receive "relevant, comprehensive and timely information" about revenues and payments due.

The fact that romance writers created a robust information-sharing network, despite antitrust laws and publishers who demanded secrecy, should offer hope for self-organizing creators today.

While all writers' groups included some degree of professional information sharing, the level of sharing in RWA seemed—and still seems—unusually high. To test that theory, I turned to the archives of Mystery Writers of American and Science Fiction Fantasy Writers of America, looking at forty years of newsletters. Neither group published a survey of author income, similar to RWA's early surveys, during any of the years I looked at (perhaps they were more fearful of antitrust implications).

To this day, RWA embodies an open information-sharing ethic unusual among professional associations. "I'm a CPA at my day job, and in that professional organization, they do not share business information. They'd see it as training the competition," said Donna MacMeans, a member of RWA's current board of directors. "With RWA, the idea has always been that a rising tide raises all boats."

Or as Brenda Hiatt wrote in a 1994 issue of *Romance Writers Report*, "When we train the competition by teaching workshops or mentoring unpublished writers . . . we are giving back to an organization that we have good cause to be grateful to."[53]

Members, in fact, even share advice *about sharing advice*. In a 2005 newsletter article called "How Much Do You Make," members recommended being vague with reporters, friends, and family—but straightforward with aspiring authors. Again Brenda Hiatt, who runs an informal survey about romance writing earnings,[54] wrote:

Nearly everyone agrees that different rules apply when the money question is asked by a writer who is hoping to break into the romance writing business . . . most authors feel that new writers deserve to know what they're getting into, moneywise.[55]

Today, RWA's long tradition of sharing proprietary information sets it apart from other groups. "It's like pulling teeth to get science fiction writers to share contract information and sales numbers," said Michael Capobianco, former president of the Science Fiction and Fantasy Writers of America (SFWA), in one of our several long phone conversations over the years. Three senior leaders of SFWA with whom I spoke confirmed his observation.

The fact that romance writers were willing from the start to share sensitive information with each other and with newcomers (and that they did it before the internet made sharing easy and ubiquitous) distinguished the group from other professional organizations from the very moment of its founding. This ethic of mutual support would establish patterns and relationships that would inform not just RWA, but the larger Romancelandia network for decades to come.

This strategy of creator transparency regarding compensation would later prove a powerful tactic for other self-organizing groups of independent workers, some of which also risked antitrust violations. For instance, one freelancer organization I belonged to put its database of publisher payments online almost as soon as the freelancer's group had a website in the late 1990s. Similarly, in 2018, Black young adult (YA) author L. L. McKinney launched the hashtag #publishingpaidme; by 2020, some 1,200 books had been posted, indicating that white authors were far more likely to receive six-figure advances than Black authors. The action elicited promises from big publishers to increase payments for marginalized authors. The power of collective sharing and transparency has continued to be a force for equity for romance writers and other independent workers today, offering a powerful example for other groups hoping to improve their working conditions.

Welcome, Everybody

Although RWA modeled itself on other professional writing groups like MWA and SFWA, its membership policy was radically different. From the start, RWA allowed anyone who had a serious interest in becoming a romance writer to join—even if they had never written a single word (for tax reasons, this changed in 2015 to a policy where members had to complete a manuscript to demonstrate their serious interest in professional romance writing—but this is still a low bar compared to other national writing associations). The policy of open membership runs directly counter to the purpose of most "professionalization projects," where members of an occupation attempt to keep other practitioners out of the field so they can "monopolize income and opportunities."[56] Such efforts usually establish boundaries like exams, certifications, licensing or other requirements to keep people out of the field.[57] RWA's membership policy, allowing aspiring and published authors to join, created ripe conditions for innovation, as members shared new ideas and practices.

Open-Elite Networks and Innovation, from Houston to Italy

The more I learned about RWA and greater Romancelandia, the more these radically open policies of sharing and networking seemed linked to the tremendous success of romance authors in the digital era. To test this idea, I ran a social network analysis of the romance writer's advice network in 2015 to determine if newcomers and elites really did connect with each other as easily as it seemed. I explain this survey in great depth in chapter 6 and the appendix. But briefly: In my survey, I asked respondents to name the three people they most frequently turn to for advice. Then, with the help of network anthropologist Elspeth Ready, I constructed a network to analyze who asked advice from whom. Typically, a network analysis will reveal that people who share certain factors like income, type of work, or race tend to seek each other out, forming cliques around certain factors. We examined five "cliquing" factors that often divide people into closed subgroups (income, length of career, type of publication, race, geography). In our analysis, *none* of these factors had much influence in who people sought advice from (with certain caveats that I explore in chapter 6). Instead, advice ties spanned diverse levels of experience and other factors, indicating an unusually open network.[58]

This openness and information sharing between elite authors and newcomers mirrored an unusual network structure observed at crucial moments of innovation across history, especially during times of great economic or social change. Network theorists call these "open-elite networks."[59] Such networks have a core of elite, relatively powerful actors (called "incumbents") who form strategic relationships with bright new upstarts, creating upward mobility for newcomers and bringing fresh ideas to incumbents. (Or, as bestselling romance author Jennifer Crusie once summed it up for *Publishers Weekly*, "RWA's strength is that it's got unpublished members. That's where all the juice comes from.")[60] In 1980, most romance writers had little experience or success, and came together for mutual aid. Over time, as some authors became published, most remained in the network—either as members of RWA, or as active mentors and guides in greater Romancelandia outside of RWA. For instance, even after Nora Roberts became one of America's most successful writers, she continued to attend RWA conferences, where she typically held a candid, freewheeling, ask-me-anything session, until 2016.

Open-elite networks have been linked to innovation in vastly different times and places. In Renaissance Florence, for instance, according to political scientist John Padgett, noble families at the very top of the Renaissance elite (the *popolani*) relied on strategic marriage alliances to maintain their financial position and social status at a time when marriage and family-controlled business were closely intertwined. Rather than seeking to stay on top by marrying at their own level, some *popolani* married far beneath them, contracting marriages with commercially successful families with no pedigree.[61] As a result, these highly elite families absorbed novel accounting systems and business methods, and opened themselves to a wider set of alliances, which helped secure their elite positions through a period of disruption.[62]

A similar open-elite network helped the biotech industry innovate during a period of disruption in the 1980s. Organizational sociologists Walter Powell and Jason Owen-Smith looked at six hundred biotech firms over twenty years, during a time of industry upheaval. They found that the group had a cohesive, highly connected core of elite firms—not unlike the Florentine *popolani*. Some of these elite firms actively cultivated partnerships with newcomers. Others "closed the palace gates" and only collaborated with other incumbents.[63] Those firms with more diverse connections became more innovative and were more likely to survive the disruption. Powell and Owen-Smith argued that this open-elite structure fostered innovation because it was both open *and* hierarchical, with members of the core maintaining close ties to each other, while also making room for fresh blood and new ideas. These two features—openness and cohesiveness—allowed new information and practices to penetrate the core elite without eroding existing industry know-how.

In these cases, high-status incumbents who reached out widely for diverse partners remained on top; those who turned inward to other established firms "faded away in a tumultuous landscape."[64] Mixing and mingling between old timers and new upstarts led to greater resilience for both groups in the face of change. Romance writers would learn this lesson multiple times in the coming decades.

Other groups of creators today, however, are struggling to create open-elite networks. For instance, the short-lived Internet Creators Guild, formed to protect the interests of YouTubers and other creators, failed in part because "creators with big audiences often don't feel the need for support from a collective voice," according to the board's statement when the guild shut down in 2019.[65]

RWA, however, did foster an open-elite network, and so did Romancelandia as a whole. Many of its informal networks prioritize mentoring and advice sharing. For instance, self-publishing phenomenon Marie Force launched the online Author Support Network as an advice forum for indie authors: eight thousand members now swap information on self-publishing.

The Woodlands Conference and the Ethic of Care

RWA's first meeting in Houston had one overriding order of business: planning a national conference. Letters and long-distance phone calls just weren't enough to keep up with authors' need for information. Authors needed live conversation.

Accordingly, the fledgling RWA began planning a conference for the following year, 1981. The group booked space at a golf resort called the Woodlands, outside Houston. With no idea how many people would come, the group booked space at the resort, committing to fill 150 hotel rooms. They spread the word person by person, writing to authors and romance book groups, expanding their network. Stephens told her writers and her editor friends about it. Conference organizing took over Estrada's life and house. Volunteers sorted paperwork on the dining room table and fielded dozens of calls.

Relational Labor

All this work represented a tremendous investment of unpaid work by a handful of women, most of whom had children, family responsibilities, and/or part-time jobs. In building this network, these women were investing "relational labor," which communication scholar Nancy Baym defines as "the ongoing work of communicating with people over time to create structures that can support continued work."[66]

Baym argues that relational labor has become more prevalent and important in cultural fields since the rise of the internet. In the social media era, she says, musicians must now engage in relational labor with fans, creating a sense of intimacy. Romance writers, too, would soon engage in intensive relational labor with their fans—long before the internet made personal contact easy. Just as importantly, however, Romancelandians invested enormously in relational labor to build networks with each other.

Such relational labor—the hard work of creating and maintaining beneficial relationships—builds on women's traditional unpaid work at home and in society, particularly the "kin work" discussed in chapter 2. In organizing the conference, RWA's founders deployed specifically feminized skills to organize a professional gathering. At the same time, they created an infrastructure that would reflect and reproduce the specific type of relational labor they had already found so professionally productive.

"It was all about sharing," Estrada said years later, at RWA's annual conference in 2015. "We didn't just want to get our own slice of the pie. We knew we could increase the size of the pie if we all taught each other. We did, and everyone got more."

Relational labor doesn't come easily to everyone. It can be especially taxing for writers, since many are introverts. "Meeting new people was difficult for me," said Linda Howard, an early RWA member who organized the first Alabama chapter and later joined the national board.[67] She and other authors wrote letters, made calls and organized meetings in return for the valuable professional and personal payoff. "I learned how to negotiate, what to look out for in contracts. . . . And the friendships you make, they last for life," she said.

Many years later, Vivian Stephens would become disillusioned with RWA because it seemed to be more of a "social club" that "wanted the camaraderie of each other more than they wanted to write."[68] This is an accusation that would come up again and again with RWA. At times over the years, the group's intensely social nature would become too familiar. This clubbiness would eventually lead to an ethics policy that was patched together informally, without sufficient legal guidance to create enforceable policies. It would also lead to the exclusion of marginalized authors.

In the 1980s, though, writers sorely needed social bonds for emotional, personal, *and* professional support. Across occupations, such bonds offer a key source of solidarity in the quest for dignity at work,[69] in part because solitary work increases the likelihood of exploitation.[70] The publishing industry has long benefited from the isolation of its writers, who only held power if their books became blockbusters.

The 1981 RWA conference would start to change all that.

Friendship as Professional Strategy

At the time I didn't know many writers and when I hit RWA, I felt like I'd been an alien all my life and found the home planet.

—JODI THOMAS, *ROMANCE WRITERS REPORT*, 2010

For me, personally, the bonus is the lifelong friendships I've made because of the organization.

—RUTH RYAN LANGAN, *ROMANCE WRITERS REPORT*, 2010

Our core writing group of eight did an in-person retreat at an Airbnb, to brainstorm and talk business and drink Prosecco.

—PRISCILLA OLIVERAS

In many professional networks, friendships might seem like a fringe benefit. In Romancelandia, women's traditions of forming strong interpersonal bonds, as keeper of friend and family ties, helped set this community apart from authors in other genres. Many of the authors I interviewed specifically mentioned female friendships as a source of the community's strength.

"We are almost all women. And a strength of women is that we tend to be maternal and like helping bring up those who want to learn. It's a very nurturing environment," said Donna MacMeans, an RWA board member who works as an accountant by day.

Of course, RWA was *most* nurturing for white, cisgender, heterosexual, and physically abled women, which led authors outside these norms to form additional networks-within-the-network to nurture themselves. For instance, as we'll see in chapter 6, Vivian Stephens started a writing group for Black romance authors that created long-lasting bonds and launched many successful careers. Decades later, in another example of networks-within-networks, a group of Latina romance authors published an anthology in 2021 called *Amor, Actually* and worked together to promote each other.

While certainly not all women "tend to be maternal," as McMeans put it, such claims highlight the social and historic context of women's labor, where women have been called on to deploy emotional and relational skills. A rich tradition of feminist labor scholarship traces this pattern, from the second-wave feminism of the 1960s through sociologists like Arlie Hochschild and media scholar Angela McRobbie to current scholars of digital-age, feminized labor including Brooke Duffy and Catherine Rottenberg.

At the beginning of the romance boom, romance writers straddled the worlds of traditional women's family work and paid labor, bringing with them caring, relationship-oriented habits and practices. Many of RWA's founders and early members, including Rita Clay Estrada, Nora Roberts, and many others, as primary caregivers for their children, wrote at nights and during soccer practice. Often, their husbands did not take their writing hobby seriously. But in the early 1980s, many of these little hobbies began earning money and these women began to have a public life.

Cultural theorist Angela McRobbie has noted similar patterns among women in other creative industries. In upstart fashion enterprises in Berlin, she notes, many small businesses work together and collaborate, bringing together "traditional women's skills" with "flexible self-organized co-working." Much like RWA, these young designers help each other, and welcome newcomers to their collectives: "What unites them in terms of ethos is commitment to providing training and support for newcomers."[71]

McRobbie sees such care-based collectives as an alternative to intense capitalistic competition ("the hard language of business plans and cash flow is muted in favor of earning a living and keeping the enterprise afloat").[72] By contrast, many RWA members relished running their own businesses. When I interviewed authors, many of them pulled up spreadsheets to show me their profit and loss calculations. Still, RWA members share many important qualities with McRobbie's fashion workers, most notably the sense that improving the fortunes of one creator improves the conditions for all.

The Ethics of Care

Why did these authors invest such vast amounts of relational labor into building their network? And why was the nature of that labor directed toward friendship and mutual support, rather than toward competition? I argue that the social, collegial spirit of romance writers in the late 1970s and early 1980s is strong evidence of a larger "ethic of care," a moral system emerging from feminist scholarship in the early 1980s. This ethic of care, focused on meeting the needs of everyone in the community, motivated the direction and style of romance authors' relational labor, which in turn helped shape the group's unique open-elite network. However, because the network lacked "identity aware" care, it did not equally serve the needs of all its members, resulting in RWA's persistent patterns of inclusive access but unequal benefits.[73]

In her studies of men and women's moral choices in the early 1980s, developmental psychologist Carol Gilligan noticed that men often based decisions on general or universal principles—a "justice ethic"—while women typically considered the specific needs of the individual at hand, informed by empathy and compassion. Gilligan dubbed this latter tendency an "ethic of care." Later scholars noted that people of color and other historically marginalized groups had likewise shared an ethic of care in allocating resources and making decisions for the common good.[74]

Since then, a flourishing literature on ethics of care has been applied to fields ranging from health care to education to journalism. In an ethic of care, "the central focus . . . is on the compelling moral salience of attending to and meeting the needs of the particular others for whom we take responsibility," according to moral philosopher Virginia Held.[75] Philosopher Joan Tronto elaborates, calling it a universal human activity "that includes everything that we do to maintain, continue and repair our world so that we can live in it as well as possible."[76] In an ethic of care, meeting the needs of everyone in the community takes precedence over individual comfort.

Although the ethic of care concept arose from feminist thought, Gilligan made no claim that the gendered differences she found arose from women's essential nature.[77] An ethic of care, she noted, could rise from socialization, life experiences. or family or professional roles related to women's societal position, rather than biological aptitude. Gilligan also stresses that men in her study sometimes demonstrated an ethic of care as well, although less often than women.

RWA's open membership policy demonstrates this ethic of care, in its intent to provide mutual aid for all aspiring romance authors, not just those who had already made it. By welcoming writers who even *intended* to pursue a career as a professional romance writer, RWA's bylaws institutionalized the long-standing porousness between "amateur" and "professional."[78] This allowed for the growth of an open-elite network where newbies and established authors could easily form ties and mentor one another.

At the same time, an ethic of care emphatically does *not* mean that everything is lovey-dovey in a community of care. On the contrary, "care is fraught with conflict," Tronto writes. As we'll see in chapter 4, an ethic of care requires a constant balancing of competing needs in an environment of scarce resources.

Despite its failings, it is clear that RWA, founded and run mostly *by* women and *for* women writing *about* women, was demonstrably more welcoming and more porous than other writing associations. And it's not the only example of an ethic of care shaping women's business enclaves. For instance, from 1999 to 2003, the *Sarasota Herald-Tribune's* newsroom boasted an all-female leadership team, including a female publisher, executive editor, managing editor, and two assistant editors. During that time, researchers found the "culture of the newsroom reflected the so-called 'feminine' traits of its leaders," including "family-friendly policies, openness, teamwork and communication" that had not been notable in earlier regimes.[79] As independent creators come together to improve their working conditions, a critical question will be whether such feminized practices as care, relationship building, elite-newcomer relationships, and mutual aid can gain equal footing with individual advancement. In RWA, and in greater Romancelandia, both were possible, and led to greater opportunities for creators.

The Woodlands Conference

The first Romance Writers of America conference in 1981 outstripped all expectations. Six hundred and seventy people registered, including six men. Roughly 60 percent of attendees had already published books.[80] Every major publisher in romance sent at least one editor; Vivian Stephens persuaded Dell to throw a cocktail party.[81]

At Woodland, Nora Roberts, whose first book, *Irish Thoroughbred*, had just come out a month earlier, finally found the kinship she was looking for. "I was fortunate enough to meet a woman who was in pretty much the same circumstances, Ruth Langan, and we've been the best of friends ever since—we still room together at every RWA conference," she told *Publishers Weekly* in 2005. "That kind of thing is extremely valuable not only for the emotional impact but for continuity, a support system, having people to talk to who really get what you do."[82]

RWA as Network Forum

The conference encouraged aspiring authors to mingle with elite, published authors and editors. In this way, it provided what communication scholar Fred Turner calls a "network forum"—a physical and/or virtual space where "members of multiple communities could meet and collaborate and imagine themselves as members of a single community."[83] Such forums allow the cross-pollination of ideas and the creation of new networks. The first—and many subsequent—RWA conferences served as network forums. The national conference encouraged the formation of regional chapters. The conferences would also serve as a place where members of different subgenres, and eventually, of different publishing types (electronic, self-published, etc.), could rapidly share information.

The network forum created by RWA established a relational infrastructure expressly designed to accelerate knowledge transfer during an industry disruption—in the 1970s, that disruption was the paperback boom, new ways of selling romance, and new consumer demand. Three decades later, that relational infrastructure would still be in place during a second disruption, the rise of digital self-publishing. By then, the organization had some ten thousand members, but still maintained robust network ties that allowed groups of different experiences to come together easily and cross-pollinate old ideas and new. The network was never completely open—but the tools of openness would continually make and remake the network, and that combination of openness and strategic relationship building would rapidly create a new understanding of publishing when e-books emerged.

The Legacy of Vivian and Rita

Founded by a Black editor and initially diverse, RWA would not always deliver on its promise of care for all its members. Meanwhile, RWA was only ever one of many actors in Romancelandia. Some authors, especially authors of color, never joined. Other authors quit as they became successful or disillusioned with the group and its many controversies and internal squabbles over the years. Nevertheless, RWA grew into the world's largest and most powerful author group, and a unique female-dominated business community that poised romance authors for massive digital success four decades later. RWA's origin story foreshadows major themes of the digital cultural economy that would later emerge, and that could help other groups self-organize now. Those themes include the value of open networks, the importance of relational labor, and the power of an ethic of care. This small group of isolated creators demonstrated how individual, micro-level social tactics could construct a much larger network, shaped by the relational values undergirding each connection. These women invested massive amounts of time and labor not only in building relationships with each other, but in creating an infrastructure to support and foster similar relationships. Those founding principles would make RWA the most powerful and effective authors' group in the world—until its internal contradictions threatened its very existence.

4

"Women Trying to Annihilate Each Other in the Name of Romance"

CARE, CONFLICT, AND THE CARING PROFESSIONAL

RITA CLAY ESTRADA heaved a sigh of relief at the end of the first RWA conference. Despite her fears, her committed band of volunteers had more than met their financial commitment to the Woodlands hotel. Membership in the new organization had grown from thirty-seven to 350 members and would reach more than 1,200 by the end of 1981.

But beneath the new organization's success, trouble was brewing. After the expense and chaos of the conference, RWA had just $700 left in the bank. "We were going broke, but we knew we couldn't take a break," Rita told me on a Zoom call decades later.

This chat—our third—took place just months before the pandemic. As always, Estrada radiated cheerful upbeat energy. She had a way of making me feel more upbeat myself, even at the beginning of a global lockdown. I could easily understand how, forty years earlier, she'd rallied a handful of fledgling authors into a nationwide group.

At the same time, I knew the organizational research. It's one thing to launch a start-up: It's another to manage its growth. As groups expand and become more diverse, social cohesion drops.[1] Nonprofit start-ups struggle to recruit and retain volunteers—and RWA's new members were all over the country.[2] Successful associations need leaders with relevant prior experience— which RWA didn't have.[3] It's especially hard to organize solo workers, who cherish their independence.[4] Above all, no similar writing association had attempted to serve both published and unpublished authors equally. Would this disparate group stay together as it grew?

The one thing Estrada and the six founding board members did know was that they couldn't invest the same time and energy into the next conference. "If we didn't delegate, none of us would write anything ever again," Estrada said.

Fortunately, scores of energetic new RWA chapters had germinated in the wake of the Woodlands conference. A California chapter volunteered to take the lead on the 1982 event, booking the glamorous Queen Mary, a luxurious 1930s luxury liner permanently docked in Long Beach. As a test run, the chapter organized a regional conference in January 1982 with resounding success.[5] The second annual conference looked like another surefire hit.

But by February 1982, relations between the California chapter and the national headquarters in Houston had soured. Members complained that the $235 registration fee was too steep. Receipts and checks went missing. The California organizers seemed to be making decisions without consulting RWA headquarters in Houston.[6]

Heated letters crossed the country as the conflict rippled out to the larger organization. Factions arose. "It was like in high school, and the mean girls [were] running the campus," a former member said decades later.[7]

It soon became clear that this conflict was a battle for the soul of the organization. Would RWA become a loosely affiliated collection of informal, autonomous clubs? Or would it become more formal and centralized? Was the growing acrimony between LA and Houston a sign that the founding ethic of care was collapsing? The dispute would become so hostile that RWA's publicist would warn them that if the dust-up went public, the media would have a heyday highlighting "a pack of women trying to annihilate each other in the name of romance."[8]

Over the next forty years, and especially during a contentious diversity-related explosion in 2019 (see chapter 9), the organization would struggle again and again with issues of who the group served and how best to serve them.

This chapter reveals how easy it is to oversimplify and romanticize the concept of "care." Often, people associate "care" with emotion, tenderness and harmony, hearts and rainbows, unicorns and sparkles. But political scientist Joan Tronto notes that "care" has another sense: a "care" is a trouble, a burden, a concern. In an ethic of care, which tries to meet the needs of all community members, "care is fraught with conflict," she writes. Meeting everyone's needs

requires the allocation of finite resources. It entails constant negotiating between competing demands.[9] As romance writers would learn again and again,
caring can be painful, difficult, and anything but harmonious.

Meanwhile, the ethic of care arising in this almost all-female network would
run into a quandary: care prioritizes the fulfilling of everyone's needs over
individual advancement and competition. But the United States in general is
a culture steeped in individualism. The business world and existing models of
professionalism especially prized individual achievement. In the 1970s, the
world understood the ideal professional to be an "unencumbered worker"
with no caregiving responsibilities.[10] That is, a man.

So, what, exactly, would a *caring professionalism* look like?

RWA was never going to be an organization without conflict, power struggles, and contradictions. No organization is. But the path to solidarity among
solo practitioners and independent contractors can be particularly thorny—as
other cultural industries have often found out. Indeed, in 1978, just two years
before RWA's founding, a group of men working in the comic book industry—
artists, writers, inkers, letterers—tried to form a Comic Creators Guild to
protest a new contract from big comic book companies. The group's initial
meeting dissolved into chaos and contention over which creators deserved
which rights. Many artists and writers didn't attend in the first place, for fear
of alienating Marvel and DC.[11] Today, other solo workers and independent
contractors in fields like social media entertainment, digitized music, and
ride-sharing are also struggling to find unity. Uber drivers have found some
success, but only by having themselves reclassified as regular employees. And,
as I mentioned in chapter 3, the short-lived Internet Creators Guild failed to
create unity between successful creators and newcomers.

Such failures highlight just how unusual it was for RWA to pull together
independent authors across the nation in the pre-Internet era. Over the next
four decades, RWA would weather fierce internal storms over the nature of the
organization and whom it would serve. By 1995, RWA would reach eight thousand members, becoming one of the world's largest writers' associations, until
it imploded in 2019 over yet another bitter conflict, this one involving race and
diversity.

In this chapter, we'll see how contradictions embedded themselves in RWA
from the start. We'll explore how in the 1980s and 1990s, RWA became *both* an
organization torn by bitter internal controversies *and* a powerful advocate for
stigmatized women writers. We'll see how RWA helped romance writers improve their position in the political economy of publishing, by 1) creating a

new model of *caring professionalism,* 2) establishing *structures of care* that embedded the founding ethic in the organization's infrastructure, and 3) becoming a forceful advocate with publishers. Throughout, we'll see the fruits and the faults of the ethic of care, including the emerging pattern of inclusive access/unequal benefits that left marginalized members behind.

As RWA grew to more than ten thousand members in 2017, in the midst of growing cultural divides in the United States, conflicts and contradictions would continue to arise and grow, making the organization, in the words for former RWA president LaQuette, "a microcosm of who we are in this country."

The Worms Turn: Authors Seek Power

At the moment when RWA came together, demand for romance writers was exploding among publishers. And yet authors, with the "worm's eye view" I referred to in chapter 3, remained the least valued part of the publication circuit. A 1985 survey published in RWA's magazine *Romance Writers Report* (*RWR*) found:[12]

- 64 percent felt they were not "treated in a fair manner" by their publishers.
- A majority of respondents wanted authors to demand fair treatment, either through a union (38 percent), regular audits of publishers' books (33 percent) or a different solution (19 percent).
- Only 26 percent were satisfied with their publisher's efforts at book promotion.

In short, romance writers recognized their lowly position in the book publishing circuit and hoped to change it. As one survey respondent put it:

I would like to see RWA become a real voice for authors—to find ways to lobby for us with management at the houses. I have a feeling that some of those guys see us as busy little beavers just whirring away for them in our little cottages (our word processors replacing the sewing machine). I'm not a mass producer of product: I'm a creative artist.[13]

Indeed, romance publishers *did* treat romance authors as interchangeable mass producers. In 1985, one Harlequin executive told a reporter that writing romance was "like producing Campbell's soup."

Romancelandia responded with outrage.

"How can we hope to better our image when Harlequin executives compare our craft to soup?" one author demanded in a 1985 issue of *Romance Writers*

Report. Already, Harlequin owned the rights to authors' pseudonyms, meaning authors couldn't maintain their brand recognition if they moved to another line. Authors nervously eyed the company as it hired ghostwriters to pen its popular Mack Bolan adventure series, after the series author left for another house (and was subsequently sued, unsuccessfully, by Harlequin for breaching a noncompete clause).[14]

Though it angered authors, the comparison to a mass-produced commodity was entirely accurate in many ways. As we saw in chapter 2, Harlequin's CEO Lawrence Heisey came from Procter & Gamble. He and other publishers insisted that all branded romance lines be uniform in quality, tone, and theme. To publish a book, romance authors had to internalize the industry's conventions as spelled out in editors' guidelines. To build a career, they needed to balance those conventions with their own original voice.

Romance and the Integrated Professional

The need to balance convention and originality is hardly unique to romance writers. As Howard Becker argued in his 1982 book *Art Worlds*, works of art, including books, "are not products of individual makers, artists who possess a rare and special gift."[15] Rather, he sees creative products as the result of an art world—that is, "all the people who cooperate via an art world's characteristic conventions to bring the work into existence." (If an art world sounds a lot like the concept of "field" that I discussed in chapter 2, that's because, although the two terms differ somewhat, they're similar enough to use interchangeably here.)[16] Becker noted that creators who regularly earn a living within an art world have to seamlessly adopt the world's conventions while still remaining original. He called this group "integrated professionals," whose work is "recognizable and understandable . . . without being so recognizable and understandable to be uninteresting." Integrated professionals contrast with "mavericks," who find existing conventions too constraining and thus find it more difficult to make a living in an existing art world. By training each other about the romance genre's conventions (and their constant shifts), RWA members helped each other become integrated professionals.

Becker notes that creators must deal with a variety of middlemen, whose interests "frequently differ from those of the artists whose work they handle . . . distributors want to rationalize the relatively unstable and erratic production of creative work."[17] At the dawn of modern romance, the interests of authors and big publishers began to diverge. At first, most romance authors were simply happy to be published at all, and publishers were happy to profit off them. But as authors began sharing information with each other, they realized their best interests were not being served—and that big publishers held all the power. Such misalignment of interests is even more true today for the many independent workers whose labor is managed by a technology platform— Uber drivers, musicians on Spotify, journalists whose work is shared more on social media platforms, Twitch streamers who have to share half their "subs" (subscription fees) with Amazon. For both romance authors and platform workers, individuals' interests in earning a living are often at odds with the firms they depend on, which seek to maximize profit and monetize data.

By coming together in RWA, authors began to see how their interests differed from those of publishers and others in industrial publishing. Because they learned as a group and shared best practices, motivated by the organization's ethic of care, these practices traveled quickly. Later in this chapter, we'll look at several specific structures and practices that helped romance writers gain an advantage when the Kindle came along in 2007. These practices developed very quickly in the early years of RWA and lasted for four decades. But before they could develop, the organization would face deep divisions regarding the purpose of RWA.

Conflicting Visions

As the Queen Mary controversies deepened, the visions of founder Vivian Stephens, still working in New York City, and founding president Rita Clay Estrada, in Houston, were growing apart. Stephens had imagined RWA as a learning organization where editors would train aspiring romance authors to become integrated professionals. After publication, she figured, authors wouldn't need RWA. But Stephens's fellow editors and publishers saw RWA differently—as a threat to the prevailing power arrangements. So, when Stephens informed her boss about the organization, she didn't get the reaction she expected.

"Vivian, do you realize what you've done?" her boss asked.

"Of course," she replied. "I've created a group to exchange information, so they don't call me on the phone all the time and interrupt my work."

"You've started a union," her boss replied. "That's a problem."

"Don't worry," Stephens said. "It won't develop into anything like that."

In one way, Stephens was right. Romance writers never did form an actual labor union: Independent workers can't unionize: maddingly, when solo contractors share salary or contract information, antitrust law considers that price-fixing.[18] RWA and professional organizations like it are "business leagues," which can't legally engage in collective bargaining. So even if authors had wanted a formal union, it would have been difficult. US labor law was designed in the 1930s with full-time, regular employees in mind.[19]

Some cultural workers do manage to unionize by arguing that they're actually employees, since they have little individual control over their creative work once they take a contract. So, unions like the Screen Actors Guild, the American Federation of Musicians, and the National Writers Union can engage in collective bargaining and push for fairer terms while protecting members from retaliation by employers. As I write this, Uber drivers and others have challenged their classification as independent contractors, New York has passed a bill offering better protections for freelancers, and some federal bills seek to grant additional labor protections to freelancers.[20]

Even if legal barriers fall, many freelancers and professionals resist the idea of unionization (as do many Americans in general, and Gen Xers and millennials in particular).[21] In the 1950s, more than third of US workers belonged to a union; now only about 10 percent of Americans are union members.[22] Approval rates for unions are at an all-time high, but most workers don't or can't join one.

So, Stephens had good reason to scoff at the notion that RWA was a union. Still, she'd been taken aback at the Woodlands conference by authors' intense interest in the business side of writing.

"I've heard people calling [writing] a business, but this is not a business. Writing is something you offer to people," she said in a 1986 interview with RWA's historical committee. Everything else—rights, royalties, marketing—should be left to editors and publishers. She'd been "stunned," she said, to see so many authors at the Woodlands conference talking to reporters and offering advice on writing. "Only editors can tell people what they want in a book."[23]

Stephens's views were shaped by the contemporary political economy of publishing, where editors served as powerful gatekeepers, wielding total control over what was and wasn't publishable. Writers, Stephens said in the 1986 interview, are "a group that has no power." She didn't intend for that to sound mean: that's just how it was in the era before digital self-publishing. Stephens herself was working hard to broaden the range of what was publishable, by acquiring authors of color, but writers themselves had little control over their working conditions.

But Stephens's boss was right to worry about the collective power of writers, even if they didn't organize a formal union. Sharing information increased romance writers' desire for better treatment. As a group, they became increasingly aware of how publishers unfairly extracted value from their labor, often playing on their inexperience. For instance, some publishers offered exploitative "work made for hire" contracts, which paid a one-time fee for all rights, rather than paying an advance on royalties. They found vast discrepancies between publishing houses' royalty statements. Harlequin insisted its authors use pseudonyms owned by the publishing company, making it more difficult for authors to switch publishers. Romance authors wanted fair treatment.

"I needed information and workshops on how to bargain and what clauses to look out for," charter RWA member Linda Howard told me. That information helped her avoid at least one bad contract. "I had a gut feeling from the workshops I'd seen and information I'd read, that they were low-balling me. I turned it down and walked away." She soon landed a much better deal.

Authors wanted RWA to push for more professional industry treatment of authors, to advocate for better terms, and to serve as a forum for sharing business information. In Stephens's view, all this was a distraction from their real job—learning to write good books.

"I would ask them, 'Why can't you be serious?'" Stephens told reporter Mimi Swartz. "I realize now that this group wanted the camaraderie of each other more than they wanted to write. They were so happy to find companionship I just let it go."[24] Soon Vivian herself would be let go when Harlequin acquired Silhouette in 1984. She went on to become a literary agent, launching the careers of many Black authors, including Beverly Jenkins, the revered pioneer of Black historical romance.

Meanwhile, authors saw their growing sense of companionship not as a frivolous distraction, but as a source of mutual aid. RWA offered a chance to bridge the worlds of amateur and professional, of social and business, in ways that would improve their lives.

"A Pack of Women Trying to Annihilate Each Other in the Name of Romance"

As the Queen Mary conference drew closer, the national board in Houston and the regional California chapter continued to lock horns. Each side accused the other of unprofessionalism. In Houston, board members panicked over the conference organizers' lack of accountability and responsiveness. In California, organizers accused Estrada and the board of using "housewife tactics."[25]

Even husbands got involved, to the outrage of one California organizer, who wrote:

> I realized that the professional organization to which I thought I belong was really, in effect, being run like a "coffee klatch" where husbands are actually allowed to open business mail and then have the nerve to complain. . . . Situations such as this are highly indicative of why women have traditionally had such a tough struggle in . . . being treated as equals in the business world.[26]

As the conference drew closer, the board in Houston met for an emergency conference call. Should they hire a lawyer and demand that the California chapter turn over all registration checks, missing receipts, and registrants' names? Should they take a gentler approach? Board members fought. Celina Rios Mullan resigned.

Back in California, the conference publicist wrote to Estrada, urging her to stop all publicity for the conference. As I noted at the start of this chapter, she believed that in the "present heated climate," publicity

> is quite likely to backfire and make Romance Writers look very bad. . . . I know that nothing would please the media more than to *record a pack of women trying to annihilate each other in the name of romance.*[27]

In fact, these struggles were not about annihilation, but survival. The organization was grappling with internal contradictions arising from its unusual form—trying to be both a nurturing organization open to all comers and a professional organization advancing writers serious about their careers. Both sides included women, most with no management experience, trying to be professional while also maintaining families. To accomplish all this, and to improve the position of romance writers in the political economy of publishing, RWA would need to find ways to live with contradictions.

Care as Conflict

Bowling Green, Ohio is not the easiest place in the world to reach. First, you fly to Detroit or Toledo. Then you rent a car and drive more than an hour to the state university, surrounded by endless farms. It's very, very flat. Still, every so often, a researcher like me finds her way to a cheerful room on the fourth floor of the Bowling Green State University library. This is the home of the RWA archives, including four decades of the *Romance Writers Report*, RWA's magazine; nearly a full run of a pugnacious newsletter for RWA's published authors called *PANdora's Box*; neat banker's boxes full of minutes and meeting notes; and years of conference programs.

The archives are housed in the Browne Popular Culture Library, a comfortable space decked with posters from *Batman*, *The Lion King II*, circus displays, and giant covers of romance novels by groundbreaking Black authors Shirley Hailstock, Donna Hill, and Felicia Mason.

The room is hushed and if you immerse yourself for days poring over old issues of *Romance Writers Report* and *PANdora's Box*, neglecting your email and texts from your family, as I did; you can almost hear the voices of romance writers from decades past. They're lively, contentious, supportive, exasperated, indignant, hilarious, and sometimes all of those at once. In some years, *every monthly issue* contains ten to twenty letters to the editor. (By contrast, the Science Fiction and Fantasy Writers' newsletters between 1980 and 1983 ran about twelve letters to the editor total during that time.)[28] The letters raise new issues, complain about old ones, and generally go about the business of care— hammering out differences, making cases for resources, calling for harmony despite divisions, despairing that RWA is falling apart, and celebrating shared purpose all at once. Sometimes those debates fill the first eight to ten pages of the magazine. Brilliantly written articles and columns by now-famous authors, including Sylvia Day, Julia Quinn, Debbie Macomber, and Jennifer Crusie, continually encouraged members to balance their own needs with those of the larger community.

It was this cacophony of voices, even more so than my interviews or data, that brought to mind Joan Tronto's note that "care is fraught with conflict." Published authors and unpublished authors battled over the organization's direction and resources. Who should judge award entries, how much the conference should cost, what counted as a romance, how to get rid of racial stereotypes in books—these and other heated debates demonstrated again and again that allocating resources and prioritizing needs is a process. At times of great dissent, members would urge each other in those pages to remember the importance of maintaining a care ethic.

"We can't all have what we want when we want it. There are too many of us and our needs are everchanging," wrote Lynn Kerstan in a *RWR* column in June 1998. She chastened members for "individual expectations which are sometimes unreasonable and nearly always impossible to satisfy." Instead, she emphasized the power of common cause: "Our size, some 8,200 professionals united in common cause, ought to empower us." She urged a "moratorium on our specifically personal concerns" in order to "direct RWA's attention to what will best serve us all," concluding "the sisterhood is alive and flourishing . . . is there another organization of writers where the members are so willing to share their knowledge and skills?"[29] Periodic reminders of this sort served to help preserve the ethic of care throughout difficult moments of conflict, rallying writers to a common cause.

A New Model: The Caring Professional

In the early 1980s, the most prominent common cause for romance authors was the quest for professionalism. In one 1985 issue of *RWR*, the words "professional" or "professionalism" appear some twenty times in just fifteen pages. In 1990, the group created a business plan and dedicated a budget to promoting the "professional image of those in the romance industry." They hired an advertising agency and produced a thirty-minute public access program about romance.[30]

But what did professional *mean*, exactly?

In everyday terms, a professional is someone paid to do a job (as opposed to an amateur), adhering to particular practices, standards, and ethical norms.[31] In academic definitions, professionals attempt to monopolize expertise in a field, through exams, licenses, and regulations designed to exclude unqualified members.[32] By any definition, though, "professional" in the 1980s meant "masculine."[33] As gender historian Thomas Winter puts it, "The characteristics associated with professional endeavors—social indifference; intellectual power; adherence to abstract, impersonal rules; mastery of expert knowledge; an emphasis on rational behavior and thought; and a premium on advancement and achievement—have been gendered as masculine in American culture."[34]

Increasingly, romance writers wanted to be seen as professionals—to be taken seriously, perceived as skilled at their craft, and respected by their industry. Yet the implicit association of professionalism with a male working style, as defined above, contradicted Romancelandia's ethic of care. As elaborated by Joan Tronto, care emphasizes attention, not indifference. It is personal, not impersonal; specific, not abstract; local, not universal. Care prioritizes the fulfilling of everyone's needs over advancement and competition. What, then, would a caring professionalism look like?

In scores of articles and conference panels, romance authors honed their own definition of professionalism.

"Shouldn't we be relishing our chance to set an example for our sisters in the business world?" wrote one author in April 1993. "If women in this female enclave cannot declare themselves as supremely different from men, where can they? . . . We are highly visible creative professionals with a unique opportunity to push the envelope in what is and is not acceptable among women professionals."[35]

Some authors even recommended dumping the whole term. In 1992, leaders of PAN, RWA's subnetwork for published authors, met with marketing executives about improving the perception of romance, later writing, "The word *professional* isn't a good word for us to use anymore. It sends an impression of grey-clad, red-tied women in pinstripe suits. What we are is *successful*."[36] Still, the word "professional" stuck, and in Romancelandia, it became increasingly connected with managing relationships and emotions.

Consider Jayne Ann Krentz's talk at the 1993 RWA conference, on a panel called "Projecting Professionalism": "To me, professionalism means the ability to survive and flourish in a tough business, a stressful business, while keeping your really important friendships and business relationships intact."

Agent Steven Axelrod made a similar point a decade later in RWA's *Romance Writers Report* magazine in October 2011, where he attributed the focus on relationships to gender. "RWA can be credited with organizing a professional group of writers who publishers would prefer to keep scattered," he wrote, adding, "The fact that the membership is almost entirely women makes it a very different organization. . . . RWA focuses on interpersonal relationships without apology."[37]

Likewise, in 1998, Lynn Kerstan wrote, "Some of us worry that RWA, by directing its focus from individual interest to the general good, will lose the treasured spirit of sisterhood (brothers included) that sets us apart from other organizations. It won't happen. The sisterhood is alive and flourishing all around us."[38]

Managing Family

For romance authors, professionalism informed by an ethic of care meant that family relationships and emotional management were never sidelined, but instead recognized as an inherent aspect of professional life. For instance, a 1990 RWA conference panel titled "Becoming a Professional" stressed family expectations:

> Establish the number of pages that you have to write during each work session and inform your family and your friends of your schedule. Begin to train them just as you're training yourself. . . . If you find that your family

and friends are ignoring what you need, remind them that you have a right to nurture your dreams too, just as you nurture your family.[39]

In my analysis of SFWA and MWA newsletters from 1980 to 2015, I found virtually no advice for dealing with family conflicts or parenting responsibilities. In the SFWA newsletters from 1980 to 1990, one issue in 1991 and another in 1992 featured husband-wife writing couples; in 2000, one woman author humorously wrote about marriage as a "roadblock to writing." Predominantly male at the time, these groups focused their newsletter stories on contract issues, selling manuscripts, story craft, publisher reports, and awards. The stark difference in topics brings to mind Gloria Steinem's observation, "I have yet to hear a man ask for advice on how to combine marriage and a career."

In 1985, 88 percent of romance writers who responded to an *RWR* survey were married, with an average of 2.3 children. Only 27 percent worked another job besides homemaking and writing. So, it's clear why many romance writers sought a definition of professionalism that encompassed family, and professional tactics that helped them balance conflicting demands.

More than twenty years later, in 2012, those tactics haven't changed much. "Most moms can have three things outside family . . . there are sacrifices to be made," wrote Marybeth Whalen in a 2012 *RWR* article. Work out plot kinks while driving the carpool and doing chores, she urged. Even better, "spend time teaching your kids to do chores properly."

Managing Emotions

Traditional assumptions around professionalism presuppose that emotions have no place in business. But RWA panels and articles insisted that professionals acknowledge and manage emotions. Through the years, *RWR* and *PANdora's Box* addressed writing through depression, grieving, divorce, and other losses, coping with guilt and dealing with author envy. These articles took for granted that emotions and relationships affected one's writing and output, so professional romance authors should incorporate tactics for managing those.

"Even while gritting your teeth, be calm and polite," Jayne Ann Krentz advised her audience at the 1993 national convention. At the same time, she emphasized managing emotional investment in relationships:

Choose your friends and confidantes carefully and well, and treasure them, for they will be invaluable to you during the bad times. And they will be the only ones with whom you can really celebrate the good times. . . . Do not try to make your editors and agents your very best friends. Keep those relationships businesslike, cordial, friendly, professional. Do not ever whine to them. . . . Turn problems over to your agent in a business-like fashion, or handle it yourself, but keep the emotional side out.

The Harlequin Baggage

No matter how much romance writers worked to project an image of feminized, creative professionalism, they were still up against "the Harlequin baggage," a term one long-time Harlequin editor shared with me to describe the persistent denigration of romance. In 1985, RWA president Maggie Osborne wrote in *RWR*, "Before the public will take us seriously, WE must. We must consider the hidden message behind our words when someone asks how we got started or why we chose romance writing." She also vowed to stop using a publicity photo of herself writing in a bathtub.[40]

Some RWA members accused other Romancelandians of cheapening the image of romance and capitalizing on stereotypes. Kathryn Falk, founder of the popular Romantic Times (RT) reader-writer convention, drew fire for giving interviews while lounging on pink silk pillows. Angry letters condemned Falk's unprofessional conduct in physically attacking a rival publisher at the 1994 RT convention in Nashville. Most egregious of all to professional authors was RT's annual cover model pageant, where a parade of bare-chested male models strutted onstage. RWA members felt this profusion of pecs "downgraded the image of the romance industry."[41] While the Romantic Times contingent of Romancelandia enjoyed vamping up the kitschy side of romance, authors wanted a more serious image. "Each one of us must become a role model . . . without stridency or histrionics, coolly, calmly building our image," wrote the *RWR* editor Sandy Huseby in 1984.[42]

By helping each other navigate the family and emotional challenges of writing, while also interacting positively with the publishing world, RWA forged a new model of what it meant to be a woman creative professional in the 1980s and 1990s. The organization's open membership policy, its emphasis on mentoring, its close-knit networks, and its recognition of family responsibilities all incorporated an ethic of care. Ultimately, RWA would "instill a degree of professionalism [that was] the envy of other writers' groups."[43]

Black Authors and the Professional Edge

For RWA's predominantly white membership, balancing work and family in a new professional model was novel. "Most of them hadn't worked before," Vivian Stephens had told me of her early writers. Unlike her writers, though, Stephens herself had a long résumé. She infused her own sense of professionalism into the organization, as did several other influential Black writers in the 1980s and early 1990s. For instance:

- Elsie Washington (aka Rosalind Welles), Vivian Stephens's friend and the author of the first Black category romance, *Entwined Destinies*, was a journalist for *Newsweek*.
- Sandra Kitt, Harlequin's first Black author, was an information specialist in astronomy and astrophysics at the Hayden Planetarium in New York City.
- Shirley Hailstock, future RWA president, worked in financial systems for a pharmaceutical company.
- Beverly Jenkins, beloved Black historical romance pioneer, was a librarian.
- Ann Allen Shockley, author of what is now considered the first biracial lesbian romance (*Loving Her*, reprinted by Avon in 1978), was also a librarian.

Though category romance was still publishing few authors of color, these authors were way ahead of many of their white peers in understanding professional culture and the challenges of juggling family, paid work, and multiple gigs. (Early RWA surveys do not break membership down by race, but it's telling that 77 percent of authors did not work outside of writing, and most were married with children.) Since emancipation, Black women have always been more likely to work paid jobs than white women.[44] Further, Black communities placed a higher value on education for women than did white communities, according to historian Shirley J. Carlson, because the ideal Black woman was viewed as a force for "uplift of the race" and a potential economic power in the house.[45]

While white women dominated in numbers, Black authors contributed invaluable professional experience early in the organization's history. As Black author and former RWA president Shirley Hailstock put it:

When I would go to places where there were huge numbers of white people and I was the only Black person in the room, I knew more than they knew.

RWA was like that. The Black people I met! Sandra (Kitt) worked at the planetarium—gee whiz! Engineers, lawyers. Then I met their [white] counter parts—a housewife with a high school education, with a husband who says you can't do this? We never got that kind of feedback from people. We got support.[46]

As the organization grew, authors of color shaped the organization and held important leadership roles. Between 2002 and 2013, RWA had three presidents from underrepresented groups: Michelle Monkou and Shirley Hailstock were Black, and Sylvia Day is Asian American.

Still, with white women making up the vast majority of members, the organization never prioritized the needs of marginalized authors. "There simply weren't enough [Black authors] to count," Sandra Kitt, Harlequin's first Black author, told journalist Mimi Swartz. Feeling outnumbered, Black authors began to feel "increasingly unwelcome and simply left or never joined in the first place," according to Swartz.[47] This scarcity of diverse voices would continue to plague romance publishing and RWA until tensions came to a head in the 2010s.

Love and Money

With few exceptions, romance authors will tell you two different things about money: 1) money is not why they write and 2) money is absolutely crucial to their ability to write. Perhaps more than any other group, romance authors take to heart Virginia Woolf's admonition: "A woman must have money and a room of her own if she is to write fiction." For many, earning money, even very small amounts, is what defines them as "real" writers.

From the start, romance writers told each other what they earned. As early as 1985, RWA was collecting information about incomes and contracts. The *RWR* 1985 author survey noted:

Writers work for themselves, by themselves. Alone. This state of solitude has distinct advantages . . . and yet that very solitude that allows us the right environment in which to create often begets professional ignorance.[48]

Understanding the financial landscape of romance writing helped empower authors and the organization to lobby for better contracts and more money. "I have a writer friend who was paid $1,000 upfront for her manuscript," with no rights to future royalties, author Gayle Callen told *RWR* in 1985. "Writers should know who to look out for."[49] Lacking information about good contracts, other new writers fell into the "work made for hire" trap, where publishers owned all rights for the books. And some fumed about sexist assumptions that influenced their pay rates.

"My biggest gripe is that most writers have two incomes in the family, and editors assume all do. They assume I have a cushion (a man to support me) when I don't. Long delays in decisions are harrowing to a freelancer who, if she has to get a job, will virtually lose her real career," wrote one survey respondent.[50]

RWA established a list of reputable publishers and pressured publishers for better pay, clearer royalty statements, prompt payment, fewer editorial delays, and better contract terms. Without exception, every newsletter and conference for nearly four decades included articles or panels on fair contracts and negotiations.

The Published/Unpublished Divide

In a 1984 poll, RWA asked its members, "What would like to see RWA do more of?" The top two answers:

- "Support unpublished writers"
- "Do more for published writers"

As I mentioned in chapter 3, this conflict between those who've made it and those who haven't yet has seriously undermined other attempts for creators to unite: as we saw, one reason the Internet Creators Guild foundered was a lack of common cause between social media stars and newbies.[51]

Romance writers at every level felt the need for a collective voice. Moreover, their strong ties, built through long investment in relational labor, created a sense of value and mutual support that tied many members together. In part, these ties formed because RWA as an organization constantly struggled to balance contradictory demands posed by its unusually open membership policy. The conflicts were often bitter and seemed unresolvable. Unpublished authors wanted guidance on craft, on pitching, on landing an agent. Published authors wanted to learn more about dealing with editors, marketing books, and running their businesses. The organization had limited resources to serve all these demands. How could it adequately apply its ethic of care—making sure the needs of all community members were met—when it served such different groups?

From the start, RWA included more unpublished than published authors: depending on the year, unpublished members often made up 50–70 percent of the organization. The mix of experienced members and newcomers helped new authors learn the ropes and helped established authors make new connections. The open membership policy also boosted the budget through membership fees. In just a few years, the organization's assets grew from $700 after the first conference to $46,000, with revenues of some $200,000, mostly from dues.

But the open membership policy also created legal and practical conflicts. To be a tax-exempt business league, the organization had to show that members shared a "common business interest" and were devoted to "improving business conditions."[52] RWA couldn't retain its tax status as just a group of hobbyists. The organization's bylaws had to make clear its business purposes, while still allowing unpublished authors to join. The group carefully crafted a mission statement defining its purpose, which seemed to accommodate both the IRS and their open-door policy: "To advance the professional interests of career-focused romance writers through network and advocacy." By 2001, RWA would require proof of "career focus"—typically, a completed romance manuscript.

Meanwhile, the group would clash internally again and again over the needs of unpublished versus published authors. Janis Reams Hudson, who joined in 1987, told me that at her first conference, "All the workshops, all the articles in the magazine, every event the organization was doing was aimed at helping unpublished writers get published. The only benefit to published authors was to give a workshop to unpublished authors," who might then buy their books.

Hudson set out to change that. Armed with a membership list from the national office, she went through all three thousand or so names, marking off those she recognized as published authors. Then she called them all and asked what they needed. Based on those phone calls, she designed a conference workshop for published authors, which led to the 1990 formation of RWA's Published Authors Network (PAN). Several years later, RWA launched another subnetwork, PRO, for authors who had completed and submitted manuscripts but were not yet published.

Many members worried these new subdivisions would cause a rift between newbies and the experts. But well into the early twenty-first century, newbies and published authors remained in constant communication and published authors continued to make a special effort to share their expertise. As one aspiring author told filmmaker Laurie Kahn in her upbeat 2015 documentary *Love Between the Covers*, "I've never seen such a pay-it-forward culture." Another chimed in, "If you're writing rock songs, you don't get John Lennon critiquing your work."

By navigating internal disputes and meeting the needs of disparate members, RWA maintained the conditions necessary for the open-elite network where old-guard know-how and new blood ideas could promote rapid innovation.

From Informal to Formal

As the Queen Mary conflict grew, it became clear that the founding board needed firmer leadership and a more formal structure. The board still relied on bylaws that Rita Clay Estrada had cobbled together based on another association's documents, which a friend had handed her in the grocery store one day. They hired an attorney to put more appropriate rules in place and to advise them on the Queen Mary situation. In 1982, the organization moved out of Rita's house into a real office with a secretary, and later an executive manager. But it wasn't until 1995, with the hiring of Allison Kelley, that the organization began to reach its potential as a well-organized, forceful industry voice.

A former bank vice president, Kelley joined RWA in 1994 as part-time comptroller. Six months later, she became executive director, and stayed for twenty-five years. Kelley centralized RWA's finances and brought its policies in line with corporate and nonprofit law: she worked closely with lawyers to make sure the organization no longer risked raising red flags for the IRS.

"She would read every word on nonprofits, everything that had to do with trade associations, so everything was done correctly. She made sure all our ducks were in a row," said Shirley Hailstock, who worked closely with Kelley when Hailstock became RWA's first Black president in 2002.

Kelley pushed for more board members with business backgrounds. Over time, she grew the office staff to ten, hiring a diverse staff of professional managers, including Leslie Scantlebury, who became the organization's first Black executive director in 2020. For the most part, Kelley stayed behind the scenes, with the notable exception of her famously stern letters to editors, publishers, lawyers, or other parties who failed to give romance writers respect and fair terms.

Before she retired in 2019, Kelley would draw criticism on Twitter for not doing more for marginalized authors during her time with the organization, and for advancing "be nice" culture at the expense of social change. On the other hand, Hailstock told me in 2022, "There's a huge group of people who think the world of her. I don't think RWA would have grown the way it did without her and all her talent."

With Kelley leading behind the scenes, the organization solidified the structures that would institutionalize its ethic of care, baking its principles into the organization.

Structures of Care

From 1982 to 1995, as romance writers were wrangling with what it meant to be professional writers, and how to expand their influence, they created structures and practices that embodied a professionalized ethic of care. These included: 1) the Golden Heart, the only genre fiction award for unpublished authors; 2) engagement groups that built trust and spread best practices among small, localized sets of authors; and 3) mechanisms to connect authors to editors and agents.

Each of these represents what I call a "structure of care"—a set of formal and informal practices that guides relations and transmits the ethic of care to new members, even if they didn't join the organization to advance care. This kind of structural embodiment of a value system supports a central argument by network scholars: "In the short run, actors make relations. In the long run, relations make actors."[53] (This is also a good explanation of how structural racism and other forms of bias can get "baked into" an organization's culture.)

Looking at these structures closely confirms that an "ethic of care" does *not* mean the selfless, self-sacrificing kind of care that women have long been expected to provide. Rather, these structures promoted mutual interests. They advanced the completion and distribution of creative commercial products. They promoted practices that would lift other writers, although it would become increasingly clear that marginalized authors reaped fewer benefits.

The Golden Heart. At the 2015 RWA conference in New York City, I followed hundreds of romance writers—some in spangled gowns and cocktail dresses, some in tennis shoes, some in both—into the Marriott Marquis's cavernous ballroom to witness the annual awards gala. I took a seat at a table bright with flowers, gift bags, and gold, foil-wrapped award statuettes made of chocolate. The lights dimmed, and best-selling author Lisa Kleypas appeared before a bright red backdrop, flanked by screens projecting her image to the back of the vast room.

"*Rewriting* is always easier than *writing*," she said, then paused for effect. "In the way that *drowning* is easier than *swimming*." The crowd laughed and applauded. Her words underscored what the audience knew well—the difficulty of finishing a manuscript, let alone publishing it. The Golden Heart award helped make it easier for aspiring writers to do just that.

Like other major genre writing associations, RWA created its own awards series for published authors. But, at the same time, the organization created an award for best *unpublished* manuscript. Established in 1981, at the very first RWA conference, the Golden Heart remained the *only* national writing association award for unpublished genre fiction until its retirement in 2019.

Over the years, the Golden Heart, and local RWA chapter contests like it, advanced countless romance authors by encouraging newbies to finish and perfect manuscripts, and by bringing winners to the attention of editors. Simply being nominated automatically admitted writers into a special sorority, as romance writer and *New York Times* romance columnist Olivia Waite explained in 2019:

> The advantages are many. . . . In the months before each category's winner is announced, every year's class of finalists picks a collective name; these names crop up for years afterward in group blogs, in book dedications, and in nearly every thank-you speech at the award ceremony.[54]

Waite noted that finalists and winners could join The Golden Network, the only RWA chapter with membership requirements, full of authors who "have become notable names on bestseller lists . . . [finalists] are able to draw deeply on others' experiences and knowledge as they move into the next phase of their careers."

Unfortunately, the Golden Heart offers an example of RWA's pattern of inclusive access/unequal benefits. The award demonstrated an ethic of care by encouraging new authors to learn industry conventions. But, like the Oscars and other major awards, the Golden Heart rarely went to authors of color.

I looked at twelve years of Golden Heart winners, from 2007 to 2019, identifying the race of 110 of 121 winners using publicly available information or self-identified data from my survey. Although 15 percent of RWA's members in 2017 identified as authors of color,[55] only 6.7 percent of Golden Heart winners during that time identified as such (three Asian American, four Black, one multiracial). Authors of color were also disproportionately unlikely to win a RITA, the awards for published novels. From 1981 to 2019, no Black author ever won a RITA, prompting a public outcry and major reforms within RWA, which I'll describe in chapters 6 and 9. To underscore the problem, in 2012, author Nicki Salcedo, who is Black, submitted a manuscript featuring Black and brown characters to the Golden Heart awards.[56] It finished in the bottom 25 percent. The next year, she removed all mention of the characters' races. She became a finalist. As with many structures within RWA and the US more generally, the Golden Heart offered important support for some groups, but not for others.

Trust groups. Another caring structure institutionalized by RWA were small, organized writing networks, including local chapters with regular meetings, online support groups, critique partners or groups, Golden Heart finalist groups, and more. Writing groups are nothing new, and certainly with the rise of the internet, they're more common than ever. But even in the days of letters and phone calls, long before email and texts, romance writers organized an abundance of groups—for writing, reading, plotting, and more—and, as we'll see in chapter 7, these would proliferate almost as soon as the internet emerged. When RWA first surveyed its members in 1985, 80 percent of authors belonged to a writing group; 73 percent attended more than one. 39 percent of authors collaborated with another author at least some of the time. When I surveyed authors in 2019, 94 percent participated in online romance authors groups and 60 percent met regularly in person with a writing or critique group.

These informal networks built trust among small groups of members who met or communicated regularly. "It was almost a three-hour drive for me to get to a chapter meeting," said Clair Brett, who became RWA president in 2022. But she went regularly all the same.

In 2006, Beverley Kendall, a Black author, joined a local chapter of Romance Writers of America in Georgia. "It's easier to not write than it is to write," she told me ruefully, but the social structure offered by the chapter helped her stick with it. Through her local Georgia chapter, she found a critique partner to provide feedback and hold her accountable. "I made friends. And the monthly meetings helped me stay focused," she said.

These kinds of structured social support and accountability groups, which former executive director Allison Kelley calls "trust groups," have been associated with increased productivity and behavior change in general.[57] The tradition helped romance writers achieve a remarkable level of productivity (many romance writers complete one to three manuscripts a year). These groups also made the increasingly vast RWA organization, and conference, feel more personal, fostering the lifelong friendships that characterized RWA.

However, not all trust groups were inclusive. "Absolutely there's racism," Kendall told me as we discussed different RWA chapters she'd belonged to, with some more racially inclusive and welcoming than others. "Being a Black person, sometimes you're so used to dealing with it, it almost goes right over your head. You just ignore it because it's so much a part of what you have to deal with."

Even when chapters aren't overtly biased against authors of color, the sheer number of white women could make it more difficult for marginalized authors to get the right kind of support. "I joined the Tampa chapter, and it was a happy place for me, but it was not diverse," said contemporary romance author C. Chilove, who is Black. "It presented challenges in terms of finding the right mentors, and peer learning. The local chapters had excellent programs and gave a lot about craft, but all that came from the dominant society's lens, so all the information was good but coming from a different lens." This serves as a strong example of how an institution can provide unequal benefits to marginalized members even if every member of the organization is welcoming and well intentioned. The dynamic led Chilove to join and eventually become president of RWA's Cultural, Interracial and Multicultural Special Interest Chapter.

Sharing connections. Romancelandia's ethic of care gave rise to a third structure that extended care through the organization—the widespread sharing of professional connections. In an industry where access to editors meant everything, RWA became a broker of what network theorists call "social capital," or the "connections among individuals—social networks—and the norms of reciprocity and trustworthiness that arise from them," as scholar Robert Putnam puts it.[58]

Ever since the Queen Mary conference in 1982, a key feature of the conference has been one-on-one editor meetings. Over time, the one-on-one sessions became a massive, highly organized event, later imitated by many other writer conferences. (A personal example: as a freelancer, I met my first *New York Times* editor at an author-editor one-on-one session at a writers' conference in 2007.) To arrange these meetups, conference organizers drew on their existing relationships and built new ones.

In 2015, I attended an RWA editor-writer one-on-one session. Like other participants at the New York conference, I'd signed up online, picking out editors and agents I most wanted to meet. I didn't have a book to pitch, but it seemed like an easy way to land interviews for this book. So, I happily joined the long line that snaked through the hotel, waiting for my turn with about a hundred other authors. I listened to writers in the line nervously practicing their pitches.

"I sold my last book this way," said a red-haired television reporter from Florida. "I came specifically this time so I could meet with one particular agent."

Once inside the door, I surveyed a sea of neatly ordered small tables, each equipped with a carafe of water and a pad of paper. Every ten minutes, cued by a gentle bell, a new set of authors filed into the vast space, finding their designated tables with one of the seventy or so industry gatekeepers in attendance. I found my designated editor and we chatted about contracts and negotiations for ten minutes until the bell signaled our time was up.

These writer-editor/agent sessions were only possible because authors use whatever pull they may have on behalf of up-and-coming writers. In an industry where few authors get published without a personal introduction to an editor or agent, this is a powerful use of social capital deployed for the good of both newcomers and experienced authors.[59]

As in America in general, though, editor meet-ups sometimes reflected hurtful biases on the part of gatekeepers. In 2013, Golden Heart finalist Piper Huguley, who is Black, was offered her pick of agent and editor appointments. Because her historical romance features Christian themes, she asked to meet with an agent well-known in the "inspirational" subgenre. "She spent my hard-won ten-minute pitch appointment [explaining] that an Evangelical audience did not want to read history centered on Black people being resilient in the face of oppression," Huguley told me.

Huguley went on to become a critically acclaimed author. Years later, she ran into the offensive agent and reminded her of their meeting. "People stop writing because of what gatekeepers like you said to me in Atlanta in 2013."

RWA had little control over what editors and agents did or said in sessions or one-on-one meetings. And many, like Huguley, never reported such incidents. But even when they did, RWA rarely took action or reprimanded editors or agents, in part because the group depended on the good will of the industry.

Despite their failings, each of these three caring structures—awards, trust groups, and editor sharing—helped many romance writers by incentivizing them to complete and refine their manuscripts. When digital self-publishing became possible after 2007, thousands of authors had polished, proofed manuscripts ready to post. At the same time, these structures also show the limits of care, in their failures to recognize disproportionate barriers faced by marginalized authors.

Regaining Our Names: RWA Advocacy

RWA's racial and cultural reckoning would come much later, corresponding with renewed national calls for social justice in the Black Lives Matter era. In the 1980s and 1990s, the organization focused its advocacy on improving contract terms and investigating and censuring disreputable publishers. A 1985 survey in *Romance Writers Report* asked detailed questions about publishers' contracts and members complaints.[60] A 1995 article urged authors to send a form letter to their publisher, asking for more complete royalty statements, some of which failed to include basic information like total copies printed or shipped—or net sales. "Why share anything? Because we benefit ourselves," explained one author in 1994. "Only by knowing and understanding the industry thoroughly can we make wise career decisions."[61]

One example makes it glaringly clear why romance authors as a group so desperately needed a stronger voice in publishing. On April 28, 1996, a seventy-four-car freight train derailed in southern Kansas, dumping ninety thousand Harlequin and Silhouette books. Although the publishers informed bookstores that the books weren't coming, Harlequin failed to let the writers know and instead let authors discover accidentally that their books were not in stock.[62] Harlequin still had so little respect for its writers as professionals that they simply failed to tell them of the train wreck.

By 1993, RWA began its annual publishers' summit meetings, holding private meetings that year with Zebra and Harlequin, which resulted in better contracts from Zebra, including better royalty statements, a shorter wait for royalties after publication, and a shorter period before rights reverted back to authors.

Not all victories came swiftly. For instance, throughout the 1980s and 1990s, Harlequin required its authors to write under pseudonyms, which belonged to Harlequin. "It meant that if an author wanted to leave for another publisher, she had to leave that name behind," said Shirley Hailstock, former RWA president, who campaigned to change the policy. "Writers who had made a particular pseudonym successful had no equity in the name they'd made popular." In the late 1990s, Hailstock, then an RWA board member, spent three years meeting with Harlequin and explaining why writers wanted their pseudonyms. Harlequin's editors were polite, but indifferent, until Hailstock, Allison Kelley, and then-president of RWA Harold Lowry sat down face-to-face with Isabel Swift, Harlequin's vice president of editorial. Finally, in November 2002, Harlequin announced that for all authors, past and present, the pseudonym clause would no longer be in effect. Authors would own their own names.

Over the years, RWA's delegations also sought improvements in foreign rights, copyright registration, and, later, digital rights. RWA's advocacy would become more powerful and more critical in the fast-approaching era of digital publishing.

The Love Boat

RWA overcame decades of internal conflict to become a staunch advocate for romance authors, even if benefits weren't always shared equally. The Queen Mary incident that opened this chapter set the organization's pattern for decades to come: intense internal strife, and harmonious and productive public events with positive outcomes for many.

RWA learned important lessons from the Queen Mary debacle. The group's newsletter, *Romance Writers Report* was refreshingly open and honest about the issues, publishing letters from various sides of the squabble, and openly discussing "bickering" and "childish emotionalism."[63] The group hired a lawyer to write new bylaws to replace those that Estrada had hastily cribbed from another association's documents. Stephens told Estrada she'd need to step aside and let others be president. Headquarters moved out of Estrada's home into permanent offices, and RWA hired a secretary.

Despite the acrimony, the Queen Mary conference in June 1982 was a hit. As 350 authors, editors, and agents mingled amid the wood paneling and polished brass fittings, "all was sweetness and bliss," according to *New York Times* reporter Ray Walters. Demand for romance was at an all-time high, as Candlelight, Silhouette, and Harlequin engaged in an all-out war for market share: Between 1980 and 1982, the number of romance titles published yearly had "increased nearly ten-fold."[64] Authors enjoyed private meetings with editors and agents to discuss their manuscripts.

Controversies Continue

Throughout four decades, RWA developed in an environment characterized by long periods of relative quiet, broken by occasional disruption and reorganization (scholars of evolution call this "punctuated equilibrium"). Internal conflicts would continue to plague RWA as it grew—some overt, others simmering under the surface. At moments, the organization would sometimes seem like a "pack of women trying to annihilate each other in the name of romance," as the Queen Mary publicist had warned.

For instance, there was the attempt to recall Harold Lowry, RWA's first male president, in 2001, over his attempts to close the divide between published and unpublished authors. There were the disastrous RITA Awards in 2005, when the organizing committee showed an intro video featuring footage of 9/11 and other world disasters, set to upbeat music. When Nora Roberts, the evening's scheduled emcee, previewed the video, she walked out of the conference, writing later, "It was appalling and offensive on every level." And there was the 2005 poll in *Romance Writers Report* that asked members whether romance should be defined as "one man and one woman" or "between two people." Roberts again took a public stand, expressing the views of many members: "It's fine to have a character fall in love with a freaking vampire, but not someone of the same sex? Bullshit," she wrote.[65] In response, RWA's then-president emailed Roberts, "explaining to me—and I am not kidding—I didn't understand that the lesbians would take over RWA. Jeez, those terrifying lesbians!"

Roberts wrote a stinging letter to the editor in the *Romance Writers Report* and RWA affirmed its commitment to a "broad and inclusive" definition of romance. But it took another eleven years for the organization to issue a formal apology, stating that "this incident was a low point from which RWA's reputation has never recovered."[66]

In the 2010s, such controversies became more frequent, more bitter, and more public. Often, they revolved around fundamental contradictions inherent in an organization based on an ethic of care. Are we a social club or a business organization? How do we represent everyone's interests? How do we make sure the needs of all our members are met, even when those needs differ according to identity?

Amid these controversies and contradictions, the power and influence of RWA, Romancelandia's most visible formal organization, continued to grow, improving romance writers' position in the political economy of publishing. The group pressured publishers to provide better contracts and, with the end of Harlequin's pseudonym clause, showed that authors could stand up to publishers. Roberts captured the history of the organization in a 2019 blog post:

> Was the organization perfect? Of course not, but I felt, certainly in those early years, it tried very hard to support, educate, advocate and offer networking opportunities. I didn't see marginalization—and fully admit I may have been blind to it—until many years in.[67]

The marginalization, of course, was there, but Roberts was far from the only one blind to it. For some members of Romancelandia, the wounds it caused would prove deep and lasting, contributing to the organization's implosion on the eve of the global pandemic.

5

The Love Train

READERS, WRITERS, AND CARE

FAST-FORWARD THIRTY-FIVE YEARS.

It's 2016. I'm in a packed ballroom at the Rio Hotel and Casino in Las Vegas, here for the thirty-third annual Romantic Times Booklovers Convention (known in Romancelandia simply as "RT"). A petite blonde in a cobalt blue velvet gown is signing autographs at a tall bar table beside me. Another author, wearing a tartan frock with hoop skirts, is greeting readers nearby. Nearby, two of the handsomest men I've ever seen—cover models—are posing with readers. One is Black, with a shaved head, wearing a Matrix-style leather coat and sunglasses; the other is white, with tangled blond locks, dressed as some variety of Regency alpha male. I'm pretty sure they're the only two men in this cavernous ballroom, where it looks like all 3,100 conference attendees have shown up.

This is the Viva La Historical party, hosted by twenty-one big-name historical writers (Collette Cameron, the writer in the blue velvet gown, is one of them). There's free chocolate (Godiva is a sponsor!). Around the ballroom's perimeter, long tables offer up every kind of swag, emblazoned with authors' names—pens, nail files, Post-it Notes, peppermints, sunglasses, lip balm, condoms, Mardi Gras masks, hand sanitizer, and much more, including my favorite—sippy cups shaped like wine glasses. And everywhere, free books. Earlier, after waiting endlessly in the registration line with hundreds of other women, I'd been surprised to find that my name tag and program didn't come with the usual conference tote. Instead, I got a wheeled canvas bag, like an airplane carry-on, to transport all the loot.

I'm here to interview romance authors—about six hundred of them attended this year. But what I'm really struck by is the readers, some 2,500 strong, from all over the country. The readers and writers will mix and mingle over the course of the six-day convention. During that time, I'll attend a costume party with fire-eaters and acrobats. People will wear satin gowns and circus attire and fairy wings and gold body paint. I'll stand in line at Starbucks with a bestselling author. At breakfast, I'll see two authors and a fan fix a defunct bagel toaster. There will be trivia and bingo and risqué prizes. Conference-goers will hurry back and forth between ninety panels on reading, writing, and selling books.

I've vowed to conduct two dozen interviews for this book while I'm here, half with authors, half with readers. But I'm feeling more than a little intimidated, both by the task, and by the sheer numbers of romance insiders. I've set up a handful of interviews in advance, but I'll need to persuade many more people to talk on the record. I'm nervous.

But as it turns out, I don't need to be. RT proves to be the easiest research assignment I've ever tackled. Readers, writers, and editors are all delighted to talk to me about romance—why they read it, why they write it, and what brought them to Vegas. I even conduct two interviews while sitting on the floor outside the Viva La Historical party, waiting for the doors to open.

RT also turns out to be one of the most important stops on my journey to explore one of this book's driving questions: why did romance authors become the undisputed leaders of digital publishing? Here, in this overwhelmingly female space, it becomes clear that the uniquely close bond between readers and writers is part of the answer, setting them apart from other fandoms explored in academic literature.[1]

At RT, I literally see reader and writer communities meld together. On one hand, RT is a massive, overwhelmingly female fan event, part Comic-Con, part bachelorette party. On the other, it's a professional networking event for authors, editors, and agents. For all present, RT is a euphoric, feminized space celebrating women, love, and happiness. At this and similar events, even the biggest bestselling writers hang out at hotel bars and restaurants, smiling when readers stop by to say hello.[2] Writers and readers frequently form long and lasting personal friendships. And all this mingling continues in Romancelandia's virtual spaces, where writers and readers constantly engage on vibrant blogs, review sites, social media, and other spaces in ways that shape the industry.

In this chapter, I show how and why the reader-writer community differs from other fandoms, tracing the roots of those relationships back to the early 1980s. I demonstrate how real friendships develop between readers and writers, and how both are willing to invest "relational labor" in forging bonds. As we'll see in the book's final chapters, relational practices that developed over decades helped lay the groundwork for romance writers' digital success. At a time when platforms control the terms of audience and creator engagement, and many producers depend on the *illusion* of intimacy and authenticity to retain an audience, romance writers and authors long ago created a community where truly authentic relationships boosted creator power.[3]

Fans and Creators

Like all audiences, romance readers exist on a spectrum of engagement. At one end are casual readers who sometimes pick up a romance at the airport. At the other is what fandom scholar Henry Jenkins calls "active" fans, who attend conventions, create videos or podcasts or TikToks, or otherwise interact with and transform texts.[4] While acknowledging this spectrum, I still use "reader," "fan," and "audience" interchangeably in this chapter, for two reasons. First, because romance readers slide around on the spectrum—today's casual reader today might be tomorrow's BookToker and vice versa. Secondly, even though active romance fans may play a more visible role in Romancelandia than more passive readers, they all contribute to an overall *discourse* of Romancelandia—a set of shared beliefs, interactions, vocabularies, and institutions that define and shape the larger community.[5]

The discourse of Romancelandia reveals itself in a multiplicity of ever-shifting reader-oriented groups and events including Romantic Times, Romance Slam Jam, and GayRomLit, and in scores of reading groups, blogs, podcasts, and social media communities today. This effervescent community helped romance authors thrive in the e-book era, and particularly in digital self-publishing.

Fandom scholars like Henry Jenkins, Matt Hills, Suzanne Scott and many others note that every fandom is unique.[6] Lady Gaga's Little Monsters engage with each other differently than *Twilight* fanfic writers, who engage differently than *Star Trek* fans.[7] Likewise, romance readers differ from other fandoms in three specific ways. First, the boundaries between readers and writers are extremely fuzzy, so readers enjoy remarkably open access to authors. Second, readers share a stigmatized social position with authors. Third—and perhaps as a result of the first two—readers and authors very often form genuine friendships, with both sides investing "relational labor" that pays off in book sales for authors and emotional satisfaction for readers. Of these three attributes, the first—fuzzy boundaries—gives rise to the other two, so we'll start there.

All aboard the Love Train

More than thirty years before my visit to the Romantic Times Booklovers Convention, a Southern California romance reader named Chelley Kitzmiller boarded a train in Los Angeles, also bound for RT.[8] Partly due to her fear of flying, Kitzmiller had spent months organizing the train trip, which would bring roughly one hundred romance writers and readers to RT's second annual conference in New York City. On a sunny day in the spring of 1983, Kitzmiller greeted her fellow passengers at a sendoff gala at LA's Union Station, sipping pink champagne to the cheerful strains of a mariachi band.

Over the next three days, Kitzmiller's Love Train would meet hundreds of other romance fans at whistle stops along the route. In Pasadena, two hundred readers showed up to say hello and collect free books. In Chicago, passengers met up with Janet Dailey, Harlequin's first American romance novelist. In New York, British author Barbara Cartland, then eighty, welcomed them at the station.[9] The trip, and romance reading itself, would change Kitzmiller and her family forever.

A stay-at-home mom until she was in her thirties, Kitzmiller typified many romance readers of the time: mid-thirties, married with two kids, middle income.[10] In the early 1980s, her kids were getting older and she felt a longing for something more. She found it on a camping trip. Snowbound in an RV, she picked up her sister-in-law's copy of Rosemary Rogers's *Sweet Savage Romance* and read until her flashlight gave out at 3 a.m.[11]

"It was the beginning of a whole new life for me," she said. Soon, she was reading three romances a week, traveling to book signings, and befriending authors.

One night in 1983, she told her husband Ted how desperately she wanted to go to the second annual RT in New York City. Organized by the flamboyant Katheryn Falk, who founded the *Romantic Times* newsletter in 1981, the event fed a hunger for connection among romance readers and writers at a time when few media outlets reviewed the genre. Over the next thirty years, until Falk's retirement in 2018, *Romantic Times* and its RT Booklovers Conference would provide a vibrant space for Romancelandia to grow and flourish. "*Romantic Times* became a voice for fans and professionals who had none," publisher Walter Zacharius told a *New York Times* reporter in 1996.[12]

But in 1983, RT was almost brand new and Kitzmiller wanted to be there.

"I really want to go," she told her husband. "But you know me. I'm terrified to fly."

"So, take the train," Ted replied.

"The train . . ." she repeated thoughtfully.

When I talked to Ted Kitzmiller in 2022, he told me he had no idea what his casual suggestion would set in motion. Before he knew it, his wife had booked train tickets and invited a few other Southern California readers and writers to come along. Then she called the many writers she'd befriended at book signings and romance events—and they decided to come along too. Not long afterward, Kathryn Falk of the *Romantic Times* caught wind of the trip and invited herself, bringing dozens more writers and readers.

Kitzmiller had never organized an event before, but soon found herself phoning and writing to famous authors, contacting publishers, and persuading Amtrak to serve heart-shaped pancakes for breakfast. Books, bags, and other swag sent by publishers quickly inundated her garage. Her teenage daughter Gina cut out construction-paper hearts to serve as name tags. Kitzmiller alerted romance reading clubs and authors in the towns where the train would make stops, inviting them to say hello. And she crafted a huge round sign to hang on the train car at whistle stops. In bold red letters, it announced "The Love Train."

As the project gained steam, the media got on board. Filmmaker George Paul Csicsery came along and produced an award-winning documentary called *Where the Heart Roams*, released in 1987. Also along for the ride was *Newsweek* journalist Elsie Washington, the first Black category romance author, who covered the journey for the magazine.

On the final night of the trip, the passengers collaborated on a romance story called "Upper Bunk Hunk," about two journalists meeting on a train.

Washington read from her notes and the crowd giggled and called out answers.

"He was tall, dark and . . ."

"HANDSOME!" shouted the crowd.

"Although he's cynical, like all journalists, beneath he has a heart of . . ."

"GOLD!"

At New York's Penn Station, they disembarked into a reception hall filled with pink helium balloons. A jewel-bedecked Barbara Cartland, swathed in rose-colored tulle, greeted them. Horse-drawn carriages and limos, arranged by Kathryn Falk, whisked the passengers ten blocks away to the Roosevelt Hotel. For the next three days, authors and readers would share meals, stories, and books, building the friendships that started on the train.

"The thing about the train was, there were big, published authors, and up-and-comers who didn't have a big name, and readers who maybe wanted to write someday," Ted Kitzmiller told me. "They all wanted to be on there to sit and chat and gain knowledge from each other."

An Open-Elite Fandom

As I mentioned above, the most notable feature distinguishing romance readers and fans from other fandoms is the extensive overlap between creator and audience, which leads to easy, ongoing access between the groups, mimicking the open-elite structure among authors themselves. Most writers start out as dedicated readers, so they deeply understand the reader community.[13] Conversely, many fans write fanfic, produce fan videos, and otherwise contribute creatively to the romance community. While this kind of fan production pervades many fandoms, in what Henry Jenkins calls "participatory culture,"[14] it's much, much easier for romance fans to cross over and become either indie or traditionally published authors than for, say, *Buffy* fans to become showrunners, or soap fans to become scriptwriters. Just a few examples of romance fans becoming authors include the bestselling author Christina Lauren; a collaboration by two women who met on a *Twilight* fanfic site; female-female romance author Radclyffe, who started out writing *X-Files* fanfic; and, most famously of all, E. L. James, who based *Fifty Shades of Grey* on *Twilight*.[15]

No velvet ropes. This extensive overlap between readers and authors manifests itself physically at romance genre events. At RT in 2016, I was lucky to share a hotel room with another graduate student, Kelly Choyke, who studies romance fandom. In her dissertation, she writes that many authors "intentionally socialize in public places at convention hotels with the intent of getting to know readers and other writers better."[16]

Unlike other kinds of fan events she'd attended, she observes, admission fees to romance conventions cover everything, without extra tickets for autographs or photo ops. Other scholars, too, have also noted that Comic-Con and similar fan conventions create structural distance between creators and fans. At such events, "the social space remains separate" between audiences and creators, according to fandom scholars Katherine Larsen and Lynn Zubernis. "Performers are protected (sometimes by convention staff and sometimes by bodyguards hired for the event) and kept in separate spaces (taking back routes through the hotels in which most conventions are held in order to avoid fan-crowded hallways and lobbies) until they are presented to the fans under highly ritualized conditions."[17]

By contrast, most of the authors I interviewed at RT were happy to meet in the convention center's coffee shop, rather than the muted, sparsely populated greenroom set aside for editors and authors. Similarly, at my first RWA conference, bestselling author Alyssa Day plopped down on a sofa next to me in the lounge and started chatting. The next day, after a session, I swapped thoughts with Nora Roberts on the importance of cute, comfy shoes. After our interview at RT, historic romance novelists (and Shakespeare professor) Eloisa James invited me along to look at antiques (I'm still sad I couldn't go).

One reason for the easy rapport between readers and writers is that they have amazing conversations. In person, on blogs, through podcasts, on Discords, readers demonstration a deep understanding of structure, story, and tropes. "Romance readers have an incredible depth of knowledge about tropes and the genre," debut novelist Chloe Angyal told me shortly after her first contemporary ballet-based romance, *Pas de Don't*, came out. "There's a level of understanding about the craft, about how the sausage gets made in terms of creating story and character that I don't think most readers have. It upped the stakes for my own writing."

The easy blending of writers and readers creates a feeling that all comers are welcome in romance, fostering the kind of open-elite network I described in chapter 3, with a central core of well-established writers surrounded by a cloud of fans and aspiring authors. Just as RWA embraced both experienced and aspiring authors, RT collapsed distinctions between readers and authors.

"Sneers and Leers": Carrying the Harlequin Baggage

Chelley Kitzmiller's grassroots "Love Train" garnered national media attention. But not all of it was flattering. In a review of George Csicery's documentary about the trip, *New York Times* critic Vincent Canby praised the film, but patronized the readers and writers it portrayed. The movie, he wrote, was "as much about barren lives as it is about living happily ever after." He added, "The site of so many people devoting themselves so earnestly to such easily parodied wish-fulfillment leaves one nearly speechless."[18]

Canby's snarky prose missed the joy, the laughter, and the delighted *self*-parody shared alongside the pink champagne. He missed the insider familiarity with romance tropes that made the passengers' collaborative story, "Upper Bunk Hunk," so much fun to write.

Instead, Canby and other derisive critics perpetuated the stigma and disdain attached to both romance readers and writers—the second quality that sets romance readers apart from other fandoms. In chapter 4, I mentioned that one longtime romance editor referred to this stigma as "the Harlequin baggage," the persistent myth that all romances are trashy novels filled with purple prose and ridiculous plot lines, and that readers and authors alike should be ashamed of themselves. Romance scholar Jayashree Kamblé dubs this false understanding of the genre "media romance," a phantom version of the genre that shapes public scorn.[19]

As author Jayne Ann Krentz put it, "When it comes to romance novels, society has always felt free to sit in judgment not only on the literature but on the reader herself."[20] As late as 2015, when romance author Maya Rodale surveyed eight hundred romance readers, a whopping 89 percent said "romance readers are looked down upon."[21]

Shame, it turns out, is nothing new for fans. "Shame about being a fan at all, shame over the extremity of 'some' fans, shame over 'certain' fan practices" is pervasive throughout fandoms, according to Larsen and Zubernis.[22] But it's not so common for creators. "Trekkies" might be labeled in a famous *Saturday Night Live* skit as geeks with no life, but Gene Roddenberry, creator of *Star Trek*, endures no such derision. Nor do musicians with massive fan bases like Taylor Swift or Beyoncé, or other creators central to major fandoms like *Star Wars'* George Lucas, *Game of Thrones'* George R. R. Martin, or *Buffy the Vampire Slayer's* Joss Whedon (at least not until 2017, when accusations of harassment and sexist behavior emerged).

But romance writers rank among the most disparaged creators in America. Whether it's Marge Simpson penning "The Harpooned Harp" or a lonely, dowdy Kathleen Turner character in *Romancing the Stone*, the media loves to satirize and stereotype romance writers. Everyday people also tend to look askance at the profession. In their aptly named study, "Sneers and Leers: Romance Writers and Gendered Sexual Stigma," sociologists Jennifer Lois and Joanna Gregson interviewed forty-four authors and found that "outsiders often made comments to writers that suggested they viewed them as oversexed women who documented their personal and sexual experiences and fantasies."[23]

So when authors and readers come together over love stories, they're united not only by shared enthusiasm, but also by the specter of the "Harlequin baggage"—the kind of common enemy and shared threat that increases group cohesion.[24] Sociologists C. Lee Harrington and Denise Bielby noted a similar phenomenon in their 1995 study of soap opera fans. Fan events with viewers, producers, and stars felt like a "family reunion. . . . because daytime TV itself was (and is) stigmatized in the larger entertainment landscape."[25]

This "family reunion" feeling between creators and readers came through most powerfully in my interviews with Black readers and writers. "In traditional publishing, you need that reader boost after a while because your spirit is so bruised and battered from all the rejection you have received," former RWA president LaQuette told me. At reader conferences, especially those geared toward diverse audiences like Romance Slam Jam, she said, "These readers actually want to read me. I don't have to convince them to try to read me. They don't walk past me as if I'm invisible. They see me."

At the same time, authors like LaQuette, or Latina author Patricia Oliveras, or same-sex author Cat Sebastian make readers themselves feel seen. For decades, readers from historically marginalized communities had to settle for white, heterosexual characters and stories filled with racial and ethnic stereotypes. Even today, only about 8 percent of traditionally published romance novels are written by Black, Latino, or Asian authors, although 25 percent of romance readers identify themselves as such.[26] And until the late 2010s, most authors of lesbian, gay, or bisexual romance were relegated to small presses with limited distribution.

For marginalized readers, it was deeply affirming to start seeing characters who look like them on the page, enjoying happy endings in a genre and a society where happily-ever-afters seemed reserved for white, heterosexual women. This drove a sense of connection and identification with marginalized authors. As one reader-writer, Allie Parker, who hosts a podcast called *Romance Ever After*, put it in the anthology *Black Love Matters*:

> One day you discover there are books where you do see people who look like you, who are seen as desirable. You're gifted this chance to be Black and happy and carefree. And—even when there's danger—at the end of the book, these characters, these Black women, are going to be safe and cared for and loved. They, like every other romance character, are worthy of love.[27]

Across Romancelandia, then, common threats like a general romance stigma, as well as specific threats like persistent rejection and exclusion, create a high degree of cohesion across fans and writers.

Friends Forever: Relational Labor and Its Payoffs

The third thing that distinguishes romance fandom is the development of genuine friendships between readers and authors, where both sides invest "relational labor" into cultivating ongoing connections that pay off in book sales for authors and emotional satisfaction for readers. These reciprocal bonds contrast with the "parasocial" relationships—where fans enjoy imaginary, one-sided relationships with creators or characters—that have long been the hallmark of music, celebrity, and other fandoms.[28] Indeed, communication scholar Nancy Baym wrote a whole book, *Playing to the Crowd*, examining how musicians in the digital age are awkwardly transitioning from parasocial to more authentic social relationships with fans. She explores the new forms of emotional and relational labor required to form these connections.[29] She notes that musicians must put up psychological barriers to protect their privacy and mental health.

While certain romance authors, too, must protect their privacy, such concerns almost never came up in my interviews with authors. Instead, authors and readers alike discussed how much they reaped from reciprocal relationships. As a result, authors were often quite willing to go out of their way to communicate with readers.

For instance, Shirley Hailstock, a Black romance author and former RWA president, once received a letter from an older Black reader who had been a romance fan since the 1950s but had only recently discovered Black romance ("Black romance" means books where both main characters are Black, as opposed to "interracial romance" or books with white characters written by Black authors). In her letter, the reader mentioned she was dying of cancer.

"I went online and searched for her until I found her phone number," Hailstock told me. After talking with the reader's daughter, Hailstock reached out to her Black author friends, asking them to them to write the sick woman a note saying how much they appreciated readers. "She [the reader] got 50–100 cards. She was getting them every day right up until the day she died."

Of course, not every fan or author invests this kind of work into their relationships, but a surprising number of authors told me about genuine friendships that developed with their readers.

"I have about fifty readers who have really become my friends over the years," said Roxanne St. Claire, a Florida author of some fifty suspenseful romances. "I've had them to my house. I visited a reader in Rome."

Even the most revered of romance authors, like Beverly Jenkins, venerated pioneer of Black historic romance, described important reader friendships.

"Many of my readers who've been with me since the beginning, since 1994, have become what I call the sisters of my heart. We text back and forth, and they have my phone number and I have theirs, and we go on trips together and just have a great time," Jenkins told me.

For decades, Jenkins has organized reader tours of Black historic sites in cities including Tulsa, Savannah, and New Orleans. When she described them to me, it was clear that these trips offered emotional support for her as well as her readers:

> There are about forty of us, ranging in age from fifties to late seventies, which is kind of cool because you see these aging women and we can't keep up with them. It's good to have those kinds of models in your life. Some of the ladies are widows like me, and some are happily married, and some are divorced.

Other authors also create their own author-reader trips: contemporary Harlequin author Brenda Jackson, who is Black, hosts a reader cruise every two years to various international locations to raise funds for her scholarship foundation. Indie author Marie Force hosts reader weekends with tours of Block Island, which inspired the settings of some of her best-loved books.

More cynical scholars than I might view such events as a ploy by authors to sell more books. And make no mistake, authors do benefit from spending time with dedicated readers who may buy dozens or hundreds of their books, and who provide all-important word-of-mouth publicity.

But in romance, attempting to untangle commerce and community oversimplifies the relationship between the two. At its best, the ethic of care in Romancelandia means commerce and community intertwine in rewarding ways. For instance, Beverly Jenkins's comments about women sharing experiences, her own widowhood, and learning from other women indicate how romance authors value the camaraderie, friendship, and understanding that result from personal relationships with readers. Most authors I spoke with considered the relationships they formed with readers as an important reason to persevere in a field where many authors cannot support themselves full-time with writing.

In cultural production fields, where rejection is high and financial compensation is unpredictable, the support offered by relationships with readers and other authors provides emotional ballast for authors. Sociologists Jennifer Lois and Joanna Gregson argue that romance writers draw on emotional resources "to manage their emotions when publication was elusive."[30] For authors, friendships with readers offered one such emotional resource. So, in a way, the relational labor authors extended to readers *was* and *is* self-serving, in that such community building enables some authors to continue writing at all.

But what about the other direction? What do romance readers get out of their relationships with authors? Why are they willing to spend hundreds of dollars going to events or on author trips, or invest unpaid time in promoting new books for authors they love? What does the genre mean to its readers?

At nearly the same moment that Chelley Kitzmiller picked up her first romance novel, a curious young scholar was heading to the Midwest to find out.

Janice Radway Visits Smithton

In the winter of 1980, a junior professor at the University of Pennsylvania named Janice Radway disembarked at a Midwestern airport near a town she would later call Smithton. She quickly spotted a cheerful woman in a lavender pantsuit, whom she dubbed "Dot," who had offered to introduce her to a group of romance readers.

As a graduate student, Radway had written her dissertation about concepts of "elite" and "popular" literature. Now, as a professor, she wanted to learn more about the readers of popular genres, especially romance. Why did they read it, even when friends and family teased them? What did it do for them? She concluded that at a time when (predominantly white and female) readers felt intensely isolated, reading romance and connecting with authors provided a missing sense of community. Her findings from nearly four decades ago still hold true today, shedding light on why romance readers felt "personally connected to their favorite authors" to the point where they would make special trips "to see and express their gratitude to the women who had given them so much pleasure." Romance, Radway concluded, created a sense of community for the readers she surveyed—one shared by the authors, who "reciprocate[d] this feeling of gratitude and seem[ed] genuinely interested in pleasing their readers."[31]

At the time when Radway was headed to Smithton, readers had been almost entirely left out of literary scholarship. But a handful of literary critics and cultural theorists, among them Stanley Fish, Jane Tompkins, and Radway herself, had begun to argue that a book's meaning wasn't entirely created by authors or the words they wrote. Readers and their life experiences and values, they reasoned, also played an important role in determining what a book meant. This approach, known as "reader response theory," argued that literary scholars would read romance texts one way because they were steeped in a particular culture of academic feminism and university politics. Mainstream readers, however, would read the books in quite another way, based on their own life situations, experiences, and ways of understanding the world. Fish called such groups "interpretive communities."[32]

In December of 1979, Radway set out to explore the interpretive community of romance readers. Why did they like it? Why did they read several category romances every week? What she discovered would change the way scholars and everyday readers understood romance and popular culture.

During her research, Radway had struck up a friendship with Dot. Effusive, warm, and welcoming, Dot worked at a chain bookstore at a mall in Smithton, loved romance, and had launched a newsletter reviewing historical romances.

So, in the spring of 1980, Radway headed to Smithton. Over the next six months, Radway visited twice, stayed with Dot and her family for a week, and spent many of her days at Dot's bookstore, conducting focus groups with sixteen white, female, middle-class, suburban romance readers and surveying forty-two readers of the same demographics.

As Radway began her interviews, she was anxious, wondering whether Dot's customers would open up to her. But Dot's enthusiastic introduction—"Jan is just people!"—quickly broke the ice.

Radway expected her conversations to revolve around the novels themselves. Instead, the Smithton readers consistently turned the conversations to the *act* of romance reading and what it meant to their own lives as mothers, wives, and women.

"It was only when the Smithton women repeatedly answered my questions about the meaning of romance by talking about the meaning of romance *reading* as an activity," Radway wrote, that she began to understand that romance reading was only partly about the text.[33] For the women she talked with, romance reading was "a Declaration of Independence," an act of liberation from a life based on the "assumption that it is women alone who are responsible for the care and emotional nurturance of others."[34] Dot herself had started reading romance when her doctor said she was on the brink of exhaustion and needed a break. The Smithton readers' focus on the role of romance novels in their daily lives, Radway wrote, "surprised me into a realization that the meaning of their media use was multiply determined and internally contradictory," she wrote.

By "multiply determined," Radway meant that romance's meaning depended not just on the stories and the writing, but also on the social position and emotional needs of the readers. That position in turn was determined by the cultural infrastructure of twentieth-century marriage and family, the male-centered workplace, and social attitudes. By "internally contradictory," Radway referred to a perplexing paradox: these middle-class, white, female homemakers, exhausted from the unrelenting care duties of marriage and family, rebelled, ironically, by reading about the search for marriage and family, in books that sometimes justified social realities that oppressed women and really needed to change (like that late and unlamented rape trope I discussed in chapter 3).[35] One of the great contributions of Radway's *Reading the Romance* is that she doesn't try to explain away this paradox but rather accepts that "resolution is theoretically impossible."[36]

Radway broke new ground in noting that romance readers, while bathing themselves in the propaganda of true love and gender roles, were also resisting negative aspects of their lives. Reading romance helped them feel better. Even though many of her subjects would not have called themselves feminists at the time, they still used romance to resist uncomfortable gender norms in "minimal but nonetheless legitimate" ways.[37]

Unbeknownst to Radway during her 1980 trip, her insights into romance readers lined up with critical-culture theories then emerging in Europe. For instance, cultural critic Angela McRobbie was arguing that academics underestimated the ability of ordinary women and girls to participate in their own liberation. A decade before, in the 1970s, Stuart Hall had proposed the theory of encoding and decoding, suggesting that audience members "decode" texts, giving them their own meanings that may be counter to the "dominant" reading or even the author's own intentions.

At the heart of all these theories was the concept of community—the way groups of people came together and developed strategies of interpretation and behavior around common issues, problems, or texts. For instance, romance readers of color became especially experienced at decoding texts according to their own interpretations. "I'd latch on to any slight mention of 'olive skin' or 'curly hair' or 'dusky nipples,' and in my mind, all of a sudden this heroine or that hero was suddenly just a super-light skinned Black person. I'd done it for years reading kid lit," writes Allie Parker, romance fan and author, in the essay collection *Black Love Matters*. Parker's habit of rewriting the characters and story mirrored those of other Black consumers of all kinds of culture. As Black feminist theorist Jacqueline Bobo put it:

> We understand that mainstream media has never rendered our segment of the population faithfully . . . out of habit, as readers of mainstream texts, we have learnt to ferret out the beneficial and put up blinders against the rest.[38]

Radway's embrace of the ambiguity of romance and its meaning for readers continues to influence romance scholars today. Rarely do contemporary scholars dismiss romance out of hand. More typical is a view like that of Jayashree

Kamblé, who notes that romance offers "a seeming compliance" with dominant cultural narratives (for instance, its heroes often align perfectly with capitalist, white, heterosexual ideals) but that "nevertheless contains reservations about them."[39] Radway was among the first to note that the real meaning of romance was complicated, contradictory, and, ultimately, unresolvable.

She was also the first to note that while reading *seemed* to be a solitary activity, for romance readers, it really wasn't. "Romance reading was a way of participating in a large exclusively female community," she wrote.[40] From the earliest days of Romancelandia that community has grown, flourished, and continued to shape the genre.

Relational Labor and Ethics of Care

Romancelandia's close-knit reader-writer community did not emerge by accident. In chapters 3 and 4, we saw that RWA's founders invested massive amounts of relational labor, through phone calls and letters and meetings, to build their author community.

Likewise, Kitzmiller poured months into organizing the "Love Train" and the grassroots author-reader community it represented. Decades later, readers would devote endless hours of unpaid work to promoting their favorite authors' books online and off, blogging and posting about the genre, its lack of diversity, and the treatment of authors, as well as many other romance-related topics. In their mutual investment in relational labor, romance readers and writers demonstrated the same ethic of care that authors had developed among themselves.

As we saw in chapter 3, political science professor Joan Tronto defines care as "everything we do to maintain, continue and repair our world, so that we can live in it as well as possible." United by a feeling of "us against the world," romance readers and writers developed a strong sense of community that demonstrated the five specific principles of care that Tronto identifies: 1) attentiveness, 2) responsibility, 3) competence, 4) responsiveness, and 5) solidarity.[41]

Authors and readers extended these qualities to each other through the relational labor they expended in building relationships. Both sides showed *attentiveness* simply by showing up at events like RT, but also through extensive correspondence (first letters, then emails, then AOL bulletin boards, and now on author Facebook sites and elsewhere). Authors showed *responsibility* to their readers by mentoring and sharing information with would-be writers and *competence* by taking part in panels and information sessions. As we'll see ahead, readers like Kitzmiller also showed attentiveness, responsibility, and competence in the many promotional activities they voluntarily undertook for writers, from sharing on social media to sending out free books and swag to other readers. All this demonstrated a sense of *solidarity* with each other as women and as devotees of a disparaged, beloved genre.

But an ethic of care is more than just a philosophy: Tronto notes that "care is best thought of as a practice," rather than "a principle or as an emotion."[42] In Romancelandia, relational labor—the regular, ongoing construction of social relationships that foster paid work[43]—became the pragmatic, central practice that made real the ethic of care, taking it from an abstract value to actual concrete actions. As it turned out, the relational practices within the reader-oriented community of RT and *Romantic Times* served marginalized authors better than did practices within the writer-oriented community of RWA. At key moments, RT, *Romantic Times*, and their sometimes outlandish organizer Kathryn Falk demonstrated more "identity-aware" care than did RWA.

As discussed earlier, journalism scholar Sue Robinson coined the term "identity-aware care" to describe an ethic of care that actively recognizes how aspects of identity that people value—like race, ethnicity, language, sexual orientation, or profession—powerfully affect their life experiences, opportunities, and values. She argues that because all members of a community are interdependent, a caring community must recognize and account for differences among its members in order to help each other appropriately. For instance, writing about journalists, Robinson notes that, for most of the twentieth century, "objectivity" meant setting aside racial, gender, sexual, or ethnic identity in order to be professionally unbiased, rather than taking these identities into account: the result was a journalism guided by the invisible hand of white privilege, inattentive to the needs of huge swaths of America. Similarly, mainstream publishing, populated mostly by white writers, editors, and publishers, considered itself unbiased and welcoming, without realizing that authors of color faced much higher and more complex barriers to entry into the publishing world. This attitude reflected much of America at the time, and today: the US Supreme Court enshrined colorblind thinking into constitutional law in 2007, ruling that "the way to stop discrimination on the basis of race is to stop discriminating on the basis of race."[44]

In Romancelandia, it was the reader community in general, and Kathryn Falk in particular, who began to extend identity-aware care to marginalized authors. As bestselling Black author Brenda Jackson noted: "It wasn't RWA that went to bat for us," she told me. "It was Kathryn Falk."

"Making Our Presence Known": RT and Diverse Authors

For Mother's Day in 1991, Brenda Jackson's husband—her high school sweetheart—surprised her with a ticket to the RWA conference in New Orleans. A successful insurance executive from Jacksonville, Florida, Jackson had recently started writing again after many years and her husband wanted her to get more serious about it. At RWA, she befriended several other aspiring Black authors, but all faced barriers that RWA didn't address. "There was no publisher buying books from and for people that looked like us," she said. RWA, she discovered, had its uses—it was good for learning craft, she told me, and making friends. But, she said, "they didn't do anything to encourage the publishers to take us seriously."

To the contrary, on occasion, RWA seemed to condone publishers' racism and exclusion of authors of color. At one RWA workshop that Jackson and her friends attended in the 1990s, a romance editor noticed the Black authors taking notes.

"I don't know why you're even here, because there's no way you'll ever get published," Jackson recalls the editor saying. "Your writing is basically inferior to the white writers."

Many authors walked out in protest. Jackson says RWA never addressed the incident and that the editor continued to attend future conferences. "That crushed us," she said, but it also fired her up. She told her friends, "We're going to go to RWA and Romantic Times, and make our presence known. We're going to sit in all the workshops and let them know we're serious about wanting to write a book."

For the next three years, that's exactly what they did. Kathryn Falk noticed their persistence presence, along with the perpetual lack of publisher interest. "Finally, she called us and said, 'This is ridiculous. People should give you all an opportunity. I'm going to talk to Walter.'"

Falk called Walter Zacharius, CEO of Kensington, a thriving mid-sized publisher with a successful romance business. As organizer of the massive romance community united by RT, Falk knew he would take her call. In fact, a few years later, Zacharius would tell the *New York Times*, "Some writers and editors are afraid of her."[45] (Perhaps with good reason: at the 1994 RT convention in Nashville, Falk got into a fistfight with a rival publisher.)

Falk successfully used her influence to advocate for Jackson and other Black writers. In 1994, Kensington launched Arabesque, with Jackson as one of its first authors. Jackson went on to become the first Black romance author to make the *New York Times* and the *USA Today* bestsellers lists. She now has an exclusive deal with Harlequin.

RT and *Romantic Times* wasn't always inclusive by today's standards. For instance, *Romantic Times* didn't review male-male romances until well into the 2000s. And some authors thought the organization should have done much more when a Hyatt hotel refused to display a male-male promotional poster at the 2007 RT conference. Still, on key occasions, the organization took steps to advance a more identity-aware form of care in Romancelandia. "Romance should be diverse," RT director Jo Carol Jones told me, "because its readership is already diverse."

Community Support

As a result of their close personal connections, readers provided very concrete types of support for authors. Perhaps most notably, they became a crucial source of publicity and promotion available to authors—a tradition that would help propel writers to digital success in the e-book era.

In earlier chapters, we saw that romance publishers like Harlequin typically promoted entire series, like Harlequin Intrigue or Regency, rather than individual authors. If authors wanted to publicize their own books, they needed grassroots publicity and marketing. Readers provided that, especially for marginalized authors who received even less support than white writers (if they could get published at all).

For instance, Brenda Jackson—the Jacksonville insurance executive turned romance author—started writing love stories in junior high school in Florida. Decades later, as a successful insurance executive, she picked up writing again because her childhood friends begged her to. When her first novel, *Tonight and Forever*, came out from Kensington's Arabesque line, she recruited those friends to help promote the book.

"You all wanted this book," she told them. "Now you all are going to help me get this book out there."

They did. With her readers' guidance and help, she alerted historically Black colleges and university bookstores to her book. Her readers helped arrange book signings at churches. When her local Barnes & Noble refused her offer to do a signing, her supporters found a mom-and-pop bookstore in Jackson's hometown of Jacksonville to host it. Local media and churches promoted the reading, and in the end, she sold seven hundred books—an astonishing number for any author's book signing. In a perfect illustration of the connection between an ethic of care and relational labor, Jackson's readers understood what she needed and showed up to provide it.

"I was only supposed to be there signing for two hours, but I was there for four. The line . . . you would think Nora Roberts was in town," she told me, with a huge grin. "When Barnes & Noble saw that, they could have shot themselves in the foot. That could have been them, but no, because I was an unknown Black author, they did not want to take a chance on me." Jackson continued to do all her Jacksonville signings at the local store until it closed during the pandemic.

In the digital era, reader promotion and support would become even more important. Indie authors quickly formed "street teams" of loyal readers to help promote their books. These teams received boxes of free advance copies, swag, and other rewards for spreading the word about their books. They also provided input into the books themselves. Today, Roxanne St. Claire has a team of about five hundred readers whom she turns to "like my private focus group." She'll ask about how much sensuality readers want in her books—more, less, the same?—and other questions about plot and character. The roots of such strategies lie in the longtime bond of romance writers and readers.

Mutual Aid

The support of RT for Black authors, and the support of readers for authors' publicity efforts, are just two examples of how the reader-writer community reflected an ethic of care where readers and writers invested relational labor to build mutually helpful relationships. In such cases, the ethos manifested itself in concrete forms of "mutual aid." Media scholar Victoria O'Meara draws on the concept of mutual aid to explain how professional online content creators, like Instagrammers, agree to "like" and promote each other's content in order to get around constantly changing and unpredictable algorithms. O'Meara explains that the term originated with Russian philosopher Peter Kropotkin in 1902, to describe practices emerging among groups of people who share common difficulties, to ease the adverse conditions they face.[46] Similarly, romance authors, readers, and members of greater Romancelandia helped each other overcome barriers in publishing, whether it was the difficulty of finding a good book, of getting published, or of finding equal treatment in an exclusionary industry.

Events like Romantic Times created and solidified bonds between readers and authors, celebrating a way of reading, writing, and viewing the world in an all-female space. These bonds provided concrete, material returns for authors, as readers like Chelley Kitzmiller volunteered enormous amounts of time and energy helping authors succeed.

The reality of mutual aid and the ethic of care that drove it didn't always live up to the underlying ethos. Many authors from historically marginalized communities told me about microaggressions—moments of intentional exclusion and institutional or individual ignorance. Nevertheless, the *ideal* of care continued to permeate Romancelandia, right up until the present day, as we'll see. During the cultural reckoning in the Trump and post-Trump years after 2016, that ethic of care would trigger a full-scale reinvention of many aspects of Romancelandia, including RWA.

The Transformative Power of Love

Over the years, many readers attending RT found themselves transformed after taking part in a female community of readers and writers, guided by an ethic of care. If romance sometimes served as an imaginary escape that made women's reality more bearable, it also served as a prompt for them to imagine new realities and sometimes bring them into being.

That's what happened for Chelley Kitzmiller. Roughly a decade after she organized the "Love Train," she published her first novel, *Touch the Dawn*, an historical romance set in California during the gold rush. Later she opened a bookstore, hosting signings with many of the authors she'd grown close with. In 2010, she founded an animal rescue organization fittingly called Have a Heart. She died of cancer in 2016.

"I love the genre; I love the authors that write for the genre. I did it all for the love of it," said Kitzmiller in the "Love Train" documentary. "I learned there's nothing that I can't do if I set my mind to it."

Seven years after her death, Chelley's husband Ted still receives royalties from her work. And the red-and-white "Love Train" sign that his wife lovingly crafted still hangs in his office today.

6

Race and Romance

FOR ALMOST FORTY YEARS, the annual RITA Awards gala was an evening of excited anticipation. Hundreds of authors would surge into a massive ballroom in the year's appointed city. Dozens of finalists shared round tables near the front, waiting to hear if they'd received the Oscar of romance, in one of a dozen or so categories. Winning a RITA boosted a novelist's prospects and sales; even more importantly, it was a rare occasion for peer celebration in a solitary job.

But in August 2019, at the Marriott Marquis, a sense of unease lurked beneath the excitement. Amid the flowers, chocolate, and champagne, a silent question hung in the air: Would this year's awards finally end decades of racial exclusion?[1] Would a Black author win a RITA at last?

For years, tensions around exclusion and diversity had simmered under the surface, in Romancelandia and the country at large. Police violence, the election of Donald Trump, and other racially charged events had sparked a long overdue nationwide cultural reckoning. Protests erupted on a scale not seen since the 1960s. Hashtags including #BlackLivesMatter and #OscarsSoWhite called for social justice. Since 2014, RWA had adopted measures to address inequity internally by recruiting diverse board candidates and convening summits with publishers to press for change.

In 2018, Romancelandia took to Twitter in outrage when not a single RITA finalist was Black—despite the 2018 publication of critically acclaimed novels by Black writers, including Alyssa Cole's Civil War-era bestseller *An Extraordinary Union*. One author analyzed eighteen years of RITA Awards data, from 1999 to 2018, finding virtually no Black finalists during that time. And of course, no Black woman had ever won a RITA.

In response to growing demands for equity, the board overhauled the judging procedures, bringing in non-RWA members from greater Romancelandia to evaluate the finalists.

The issue came to a head when bestselling author Suzanne Brockmann delivered an electrifying acceptance speech for the Lifetime Achievement Award at the 2018 RITA Awards.

"RWA, I've been watching you grapple as you attempt to deal with the homophobic, racist white supremacy on which our nation and the publishing industry is based. It's long past time for that to change. But hear me, writers, when I say: It doesn't happen if we're too fucking nice."[2]

The audience gave Brockmann a standing ovation.

Still, when the 2019 RITA finalists were announced, only three of seventy-seven were women of color—two Black, one South Asian. In protest, many white nominees declined their nominations; some authors quit RWA.

Heated Twitter exchanges broke out. "I agree 100 percent that this must change, but can't we wait five minutes for the finalists to enjoy their day?" tweeted one white author.[3]

"We can and should have this debate NOW. Not 2 weeks from now," one writer clapped back. "Voices should not be silenced as a way of letting the finalists 'have their day.' Don't tell women who are hurting to shut up and sit down."[4]

As outrage grew on social media, the RWA board promised reform: "The Board affirmatively states that there is a serious problem with reader bias in the judging of the RITAS." As the award show approached, it remained to be seen whether change would finally come.

Identity, Equity, and Care

Of all the internal contradictions and conflict RWA faced over the decades, racial inclusion was the most complex. On one hand, RWA's founder, Vivian Stephens, was Black. Two of the six founding board members were women of color (Celina Rios Mullan and Barbara Stephens, Vivian's sister).[5] RWA's *Romance Writers Report* magazine had covered racial stereotypes and discrimination in the 1990s and early 2000s, and RWA has had four women of color as presidents (three Black, one Asian American).

On the other hand, RWA tolerated overtly racist editors at its conferences and turned a blind eye when some chapters or editors were hostile to authors of color. As RWA's leadership would admit in an email to members in 2020:

RWA has failed to protect its members of color and its members from the LGBTQ+ and disabled communities and failed to offer a safe and inclusive place for all our members, because of its systemic issues with racism and bias.[6]

The contradictions between RWA as an organization that supports and celebrates all romance authors *and* a place where the advantages of membership
are unevenly distributed—that pervasive tension between inclusive access and
unequal benefits—is perhaps best summed up by Indian American author
Suleikha Snyder, who writes about "two RWAs". One is "fun and supportive
and honest . . . a sisterhood, a club, a place where people GET YOU." The
other is fraught with microaggressions toward "multicultural and queer romance," rife with exclusions and failing on representation and inclusion.[7] In
defense, underrepresented authors find refuge in their own "second RWA,
where they advise each other as they negotiated . . . the outright bigotry of the
larger organization," writes journalist Lois Beckett.[8]

This chapter examines the second RWA by exploring the history of Black
romance authors, although I also draw on the stories of other marginalized
writers. I focus primarily on Black authors because they make up a very large,
visible group marked by the residual history of enslavement in ways that made
white editors and readers doubt their capacity for happily-ever-afters. When
possible in this chapter, I try to avoid writing about "diverse" authors as a
whole, because every community has its own experiences. At the same time,
it's important to recognize that many groups experienced Romancelandia's
persistent pattern of inclusive access and unequal benefits, a pattern also seen
in broader society. ("It's not that romance is any worse than the rest of America," one Black author told me. "You see this everywhere. But you don't want
to see it in a community that's about love.")

By tracing the experiences of Black authors, this chapter shows how a pe-
culiar form of bias in the publishing industry planted the seeds of exclusion in
Romancelandia. To push back against it, Black authors joined RWA but also
formed their own support networks. Through a social network analysis, the
chapter demonstrates how complex it is to measure discrimination, then describes Romancelandia's strategies to address discrimination. As other isolated
workers seek to self-organize and gain more power against corporations and
technology platforms, the experiences of Romancelandia serve as a constant
reminder that fairness at work depends on unity among workers, but unity
among workers depends on fairness within worker communities.

Structural Racism in the Publishing Circuit

To understand the complex and contradictory issues of race in Romancelandia, first we need to understand an unusual kind of bias that pervades the
book industry, related to a strange combination of politically well-meaning

and profit-oriented impulses of white, well-educated, liberally minded editors. I call this the bias of second-guessing.

In chapter 3, I showed Robert Darnton's diagram of the publishing circuit. In the center of this diagram, three circles depict broader cultural forces. Darnton called one of those the "economic and social conjecture," which broadly represents social influences on gatekeepers at each stop on the circuit. These gatekeepers are all deeply engaged in a massive guessing game that sociologist John Thompson calls "the web of collective belief." Authors guess what readers want; agents guess what editors will buy; editors guess what booksellers will stock; booksellers guess what readers will buy. And so on.

In the publishing industry, this guessing game builds on stereotypes about Black culture and about readers. Zora Neale Hurston, the most prominent woman writer of the Harlem Renaissance, explained this in an incisive 1950 essay called "What White Publishers Won't Print."

Publishers, she wrote, care more about money than race. She believed they wanted book sales more than they wanted to exclude minority voices. But publishers' ideas about what stories (white) readers want to buy were hopelessly fixed by stereotypes about nondominant cultures:

> [Publishers] will sponsor anything that they believe will sell. They shy away from romantic stories about Negroes and Jews because they feel that they know the public indifference to such works. . . . As long as the majority cannot conceive of a Negro or a Jew feeling and reacting inside just as they do, the majority will keep right on believing that people who do not look like them cannot possibly feel as they do . . . hence the lack of interest in a romance uncomplicated by the race struggle.[9]

So, if editors believe audiences want to read about how hard it is to be Black in America, those are the stories they'll publish. They're second guessing the tastes of their audience. As literature scholar John K. Young puts it, white editors in the twentieth century only published African American writers whom they felt represented "the Black experience (necessarily understood as exotic) for the white, and therefore implicitly universal, audience."[10]

What editors failed (and still fail) to recognize was how this second guessing creates what Nigerian author Chimamanda Ngozi Adichie, in a 2009 TED Talk, called "The Danger of a Single Story": the bias of second guessing collapses the experience of an entire set of people into one monolithic stereotype. (For instance, the idea that all Mexicans are "abject immigrants," as she put it, or that all Africans listen to "tribal music," or that poor people create nothing beautiful.)[11] Cultural critic Stuart Hall argued that this sort of structural shaping of cultural narratives occurs throughout media industries: "Amongst other kinds of ideological labor, the media construct for us a definition of what race is, what meaning the imagery of race carries and what the 'problem of race' is understood to be."[12]

What Hurston described in 1950 remains true today. As Beverly Jenkins, one of American's best-known Black romance writers, put it in an interview with the *South Florida Sun-Sentinel*, "Traditionally, Black novels have been victimization books about 'the struggle.' It's important to show that Black women fall in love, go to college, have careers—not all are teenage moms living on welfare."[13]

White romance editors were so focused on the hardships of Black people that they doubted the plausibility of Black happily-ever-afters. Many editors questioned manuscripts dealing with, say, Black townships in the post–Civil War Midwest (like Beverly Jenkins wrote), or educated Black teachers and lawyers (like those in Piper Huguley's work), or Black secret agents during the Civil War (like in Alyssa Cole's Loyal League series).

No wonder romance authors of color struggled to find publishers. "My writing has always been about the idea that it's time to stop looking at what white people did to Black people. Instead, let's look at what Black people did to survive in spite of what white people were doing," said historical author Piper Huguley. In trying to publish her work, she found that "a lot of people, including Black people, are not ready for that perspective because we have so long been exposed to and taught this version of history that says all Black people were victims and didn't do anything."

Other authors of color face the same dilemma, according to India-born author Sonali Dev, author of Bollywood-influenced American romances. "If you're writing an Indian story, everyone wants you to be Jhumpa Lahiri, and write, 'Woe is me, how tortured I am as an Indian and how awful is my life.' Those are valid stories, but that's not the only story," said Dev.

Pintip Dunn, whose young-adult sci-fi romance novels feature characters of Thai descent, observed the damage the "single story" can inflict:

When I was six years old, I thought I could only write white characters. I used to read every book on the children's shelves in the library, and they all depicted a certain kind of character. I was absolutely convinced that if I wanted to be published, I had to write about white characters. I believed that until I was thirty-four or thirty-five.

Conversely, overcoming the single story and providing a wide array of positive, diverse characters can literally save lives. Len Barot, aka Radclyffe, a lesbian writer and founder of LGBTQ+ publisher Bold Strokes Books, noted, "Those who spoke to the reality of my life . . . comforted me and gave me hope that I, too, could find love."

Sadly, the political economy of publishing worked to suppress these stories within major publishing houses, leaving male-male and female-female romance to small houses like Naiad Press, which proliferated in the 1970s. Black authors would have to wait until the mid-1990s for their opportunities to expand.

Editors and Other Gatekeepers

In 1963, Langston Hughes wryly noted that Black writers "have all the problems any other writer has, plus a few more."[14] Book publishing in general, and romance publishing in particular, help illustrate how racism becomes embedded in a system, even when individuals in that system may cherish anti-racist sentiments.

In chapter 3, I referred to a 1983 story about publishing by Rosemary Bray in the business magazine *Black Enterprise*. She wrote:

> Publishing is perhaps the last of the genteel WASP professions: the long hours and low pay that are typical of entry-level jobs in the industry tended to attract upper middle class white women who could afford such jobs until they moved up the ladder. As the number of Blacks willing and able to forego short-term rewards for long-term career satisfaction has increased, traditional racism has reared its ugly head and made it nearly impossible for Black women to find jobs in trade, or "mainstream," publishing.[15]

With few Black editors in New York publishing, stories about ambitious, successful, and happy Black women earning their happily-ever-afters attracted little interest. Even when Black editors like Vivian Stephens and Veronica Mixon did acquire Black stories, bookstores proved to be another kind of gatekeeper. Professional buyers typically shelved romances featuring Black couples not in the romance section, but in the African American section, or Black history shelves. Only recently have booksellers started shelving Black romances in both areas. Similarly, today, search algorithms on Amazon often make it difficult to find Black romance.

The single-story bias of publishers and the shelving choices of booksellers are just two of those "few more problems" Hughes mentioned. Both are prime examples of institutional racism, defined as "customs and practices which systematically reflect and produce racial inequalities in society." This definition, by British judge William Macpherson in 1993, goes on to explain that:

> If racist consequences accrue to institutional laws, customs or practices, the institution is racist whether or not the individuals maintaining those practices have racial intentions . . . [this includes] organizational structures, policies, processes and practices which result in ethnic minorities being treated unfairly and less equally, often without intention or knowledge.[16]

While RWA institutionalized an ethic of care, it also, like much of America itself, unwittingly institutionalized racism and other exclusions, which proved extremely difficult to root out later.

Networks within Networks

With higher barriers to publishing and entrenched institutionalized discrimination, how did authors of color or authors of same-sex romance get published *at all?*

Much of it had to do with the same ethic of care that brought RWA together in the first place—but this time, an identity-aware care expressed in identity-based networks. Small lesbian or gay presses published female-female or male-male stories. Authors of color built their own networks, which operated both within and outside of RWA, starting with the efforts of Vivian Stephens.

From her first year as a romance editor, Vivian Stephens had published authors of color, beginning with her friend Elsie Washington who worked at *Newsweek.*

"Elsie mentioned she was going to London to buy Christmas presents," Stephens told me. "I said, 'While you're there, take in some information and write me a romance.'" She did and Stephens promptly acquired it.

When Stephens told her editor-in-chief and the head of sales she was publishing a Black romance, "I didn't get any pushback at all," she told me. "How could they tell me, a Black woman making money for them, that I can't do a Black book?"

Washington's book became the first category romance written by a Black author and featuring a Black couple (this is the definition of "Black romance"). Stephens went on to acquire books by Joy Wu, Celina Rios Mullan (writing as Marisa de Zavala), and Jean Hager—the first Asian, Latina, and Native American category romance authors writing about romance heroines who shared their authors' ethnic backgrounds.

"I bought them because those are the real people who make up America," Stephens said. "They're happy in their job, they meet someone who returns their affection and love, they have a family. You can own your own home, educate children, take vacations, and die a quiet, peaceful death." Her tip sheet for authors addressed ethnicity, encouraging authors to write characters with authentic ethnic details, as long as they represented contemporary America. "You can do that for any extraction, but everybody wants to shop at Saks," she said.

Stephens's vision of upward mobility, middle-class consumerism, and the American melting pot might seem dated today, but it was au courant in the 1980s (think *The Cosby Show*). For Stephens, the burgeoning romance genre in the 1970s and 1980s represented the expansion of opportunities for Black women like herself.

"I Realize Now How Racism Can Work"

After Stephens left Dell for Harlequin in 1981, she continued to acquire diverse authors. But at Harlequin, unlike Dell, Stephens's choices came under the scrutiny of several layers of white, male managers. So, when Stephens published Sandra Kitt's *Adam and Eva*, Harlequin's first Black romance, upper management balked, worrying their readers would complain. Stephens dismissed their worries. In the end, the company received only four letters about the book.[17]

No longer flying under the radar, Stephens began to notice overt racial bias in book publishing for the first time. At one focus group, a white, male moderator asked a roomful of white, female readers about their perception of the novel's Black hero. Stephens and her bosses watched from behind one-way glass. Initially, the women all said they liked the book. But as the moderator pressed them about the Black characters and choices, their tone began to shift. "When he finished, the women had changed their attitude about the book altogether. I was so mad, I was screaming at my bosses," Stephens told me. "I realize now how racism can work. [The moderator] might not even have known he was doing it. But it didn't have to be that way."

When Harlequin fired Stephens after just two years, she moved on to work as a literary agent and book packager (an editor who works with authors to develop and write manuscripts). A few other Black editors, including Veronica Mixon, were also publishing Black authors, but the market largely dried up after Stephens departed from Harlequin. One study of 15,000 romances published in the 1980s found that only ten featured Black characters.[18]

Even Sandra Kitt turned to writing about white couples after Stephens left. "For the next 10 years, from 1984–1994, I wrote for Harlequin, they never published another Black romance from me."[19] Harlequin and its readers loved Kitt's fluid prose and well-developed characters—as long as they were white.

Responding to the lack of outlets for Black romance, a government worker in Washington, DC named Leticia Peoples decided to change things. She took classes in publishing, withdrew $10,000 from her retirement savings, and, in 1990, launched Odyssey Books, with moral support and advice from Kathryn Falk of *Romantic Times*.[20] A shoestring operation (Sandra Kitt designed her own cover for one of their books),[21] Odyssey would publish just eleven novels by 1994 and be out of business by 1996.[22] During that time, though, the company launched the careers of successful authors including Donna Hill, Francis Ray, Eboni Snoe, and others.

"What she did woke people," said Donna Hill. Peoples's books showed that "Black people can write them, and Black people read them."[23]

Meanwhile, another Black author was proving that white readers, as well as Black ones, could love Black stories too.

The Relational Labor of Terry McMillan

Terry McMillan hit the bestseller list in the summer of 1992 with *Waiting to Exhale*, her third novel.[24] The book, which centered on the friendship between four Black professional women, resonated with readers of all races. The *New York Times* called it "hilarious" and "irreverent," as well as "thought-provoking, thoroughly entertaining and very, very comforting."[25] Although not a romance, since it doesn't center on one couple's love story, romantic themes weave through the book. The novel broke through racial stereotypes by portraying its heroines in their full humanity, finding joy, frustration, sorrow, and happiness in love.

Also during the summer of 1992, Toni Morrison and Alice Walker had hit the bestseller lists. The success of three Black women authors at once became a hot news topic. By 1995, *Waiting to Exhale* had sold some 3 million copies, and the movie version starring Whitney Houston, Angela Bassett, and Gregory Hines grossed some $87 million worldwide.

Waiting to Exhale broke through white editors' desire for stereotypical Black struggle stories, as *New York Times Magazine* writer D. T. Max observed:

The majority of [Black authors'] books have been consciously literary efforts, or novels in which ideology is at least as important as character development or plot . . . McMillan, by contrast, writes about the lives of essentially conventional [B]lacks, who have up to now received little attention. Her success has opened publishers' eyes to a growing Black middle-class readership.[26]

To many, even her own publisher, McMillan's breakout success seemed an inexplicable bolt out of the blue. But her secret was this: in addition to being a brilliant storyteller who tapped into the zeitgeist, McMillan excelled at relational labor. Through her extensive networking and promotion efforts, McMillan bypassed laissez-faire publicists at her publishing house and created her own network of buyers. As a pioneer of self-promotion, she wrote the blueprint for future Black romance authors and a generation of indie authors decades later.

When McMillan's first book, *Mama*, came out in 1987 from Houghton Mifflin, it received only a small print run and a modest publicity budget. So, McMillan, then a typist at a law firm, took the book's promotion into her own hands. She sent letters to thousands of booksellers and reporters describing her book. She contacted campus associations, often of Black students, around the country, offering to give readings.[27] Some two decades before Facebook or Twitter hit the scene, McMillan handcrafted her own social networks, largely among Black readers and book lovers; as a result, that first book sold five thousand copies—far more than the publisher expected—and laid the groundwork for the monumental success of *Waiting to Exhale*, which she also promoted vigorously through her network.

These individual relationship-building tactics foreshadowed the relational labor that would enable self-published authors of all races to outperform other authors after the dawn of e-books. Since the rise of social media, such personal contact with fans and customers now characterizes many creative and cultural fields.[28] But romance authors had been building interpersonal relations with fans for decades. McMillan's tactics, specifically aimed at her target readers—Black women—drew on this tradition, establishing a pattern that would characterize romance authors in the future.

Seeds of the Second RWA

At the same time that McMillan was demonstrating the power of relational labor in selling books, Vivian Stephens was continuing to work to advance Black authors, helping them create their own informal networks. This relational labor by Stephens and an early band of Black romance authors whom she mentored were the earliest manifestation of the "second RWA" described by Suleikha Snyder—that shadow network of marginalized writers, enduring micro-aggressions and discrimination within the predominantly white institution.[29]

Shirley Hailstock, who would become RWA's first Black president in 2002, was an early beneficiary of Stephens's efforts. An irrepressibly cheerful Howard University graduate with a chemistry degree, Hailstock started writing romance on a bet in the early 1990s and found she enjoyed it. Researching publishers, Hailstock came across an item in *Romantic Times* magazine mentioning a New York-based romance writing class specifically for Black women—run by Vivian Stephens.

"It was just a small little item, saying they were going to meet at the New York planetarium, where Sandra Kitt worked. It was just a train ride away, and that was where I met Vivian and many others," Hailstock recalled. To Hailstock, accustomed to being the only Black author in the room, the group of twelve writers felt like home. She attended for three years, even when the meetings moved to a public library on Long Island. "It was an hour and a half there, and it met once a month. But it was worth it because I got to talk to Black writers."

At the end of the first year-long class, Stephens edited the manuscripts and offered advice about which publishers to approach. By the early 1990s, ten of the twelve group members had been published, among them Rochelle Alers and Donna Hill. Sandra Kitt, also a member, had already been published.

Stephens's writing program gave these authors something that RWA often did not: a community of peers who looked like them and understood the deep merits of their stories. When Hailstock had walked into her New Jersey RWA chapter meeting for the first time, she was the only woman of color in the room. Even for the indefatigably outgoing Hailstock, it felt awkward (and this is a woman who's so good at networking, she once asked her agent if it's possible to be "*too* well connected").

Nevertheless, the group turned out to welcome her. "There wasn't any noticeable difference" in her treatment due to race, she recalls. "They just liked that you were intelligent enough to do the work." Hailstock went on to serve as president of her local RWA chapter three times, and eventually became president of the national organization.

Hailstock told me she rarely encountered overt racism. But when she did, it felt like a slap in the face. One writer sent her an ostensible fan letter that revealed deep and naive racism, later quoted in a *Guardian* story:

Dear Shirley, I'm writing to let you know how much I enjoyed *Whispers of Love*. It's my first African American romance. I guess I might sound bigoted, but I never knew that [B]lack folks fall in love like white folks. I thought it was just all sex or jungle fever I think "they" call it.[30]

This comment perfectly exemplified Zora Neale Hurston's observation that some white readers imagine "that people who do not look like them cannot possibly feel as they do."[31]

The Summer of Black Romance

Stephens's group, and other Black authors, rode the wave of Terry McMillan's success. Almost immediately after *Waiting to Exhale* hit the *New York Times'* bestsellers list, publishers began snapping up Black authors.

"In the past year, more than 30 Black authors have concluded contracts with large and small publishing houses, compared with only a handful since 1980," the *Dallas Morning News* reported.[32]

In 1994, Avon published Beverly Jenkins's *Night Song*, the first Black historical romance by a Black author, featuring a schoolteacher in a Kansas township and a dashing sergeant with the Buffalo Soldiers. That same year, romance publisher Kensington launched Arabesque, its first romance imprint featuring Black protagonists (see chapter 4 for details). Even then, though, Black authors were paid lower royalties than white writers. "Everyone else got 8 percent" as their royalty. "We got 4 percent," Jackson told me. "We knew this going in, but we didn't care. We figured, give us a chance and we'll prove to you there is a market."

They did. In 1994, Arabesque published twelve books by Black authors. Francis Ray, Rochelle Alers, and Donna Hill (the last two from the Stephens writing group) together sold more than a million copies.[33]

Meanwhile, in 1993, two Black lawyers in Columbus, Mississippi, launched Genesis Press, run by their daughter Niani Colom. Like Odyssey before it, Genesis helped launch or further the careers of Black authors but struggled to make a profit. (As its publisher Wilbur Colom told researcher Ann Yvonne White in 1993, "Nothing in publishing is lucrative.")[34] In 2004, the line contracted with Kensington to distribute its books.

Around this time, some Genesis authors began to notice problems with their payments. In 2006, *Publishers Weekly* reported that thirty Black authors were issuing a public complaint against Genesis, alleging that Genesis had withheld or delayed payment, failed to issue royalty statements, and filed inaccurate tax data.[35] In return, the founder sued several of the authors for some $6 million in damages, charging slander and defamation.[36] RWA intervened, funding an audit of the publisher's royalty payments.

The incident highlighted the huge power imbalance between authors and even the smallest of publishers. Authors were almost entirely dependent on publishers to reach their audience. They often lacked complete and accurate information about sales and royalties. In the event of a dispute, authors' only recourse was to leave their publisher and find a new one. For Black authors, with limited outlets for their work, this option rarely existed, which constrained their negotiating power in an industry that already paid them less than white authors.

But by the late 1990s, publishers had caught on to the profit potential of ethnic markets. In 1998, Kensington sold its Black-oriented Arabesque line to BET for a huge profit, then launched a Latinx line in 1999 and a new African American line in 2000.[37] In 2001, Simon & Schuster struck a deal with superstar Black erotica author Zane, who had built a huge online following on the early Internet. In 2005, Harlequin bought Arabesque from BET, renaming it Kimani.

Even with the rise of African American lines, authors of color continued to find it more difficult than white authors to find outlets for their work. Largely disregarded by publishers, they were also invisible to RWA.

"I didn't think the RWA people were excluding us. I think they just didn't think of us," said Shirley Hailstock on an RWA video panel in 2020.[38]

"The problem I had with RWA, even though it was good for teaching craft to authors, was that African American women came to the conference every year, but RWA didn't do anything to encourage publishers to take us seriously," said Brenda Jackson, the former insurance executive. As we saw in chapter 5, Jackson built her success through relational labor, reaching out to African American bookstores, HBCUs, churches, colleagues, and individual readers.

RWA did provide some support for Black authors. A short-lived African American RWA chapter, formed in the 1990s, survived only a few years (one former member told me this was due to ineffective chapter leadership, rather than lack of support from RWA). RWA defended Black authors by funding the audit of Odyssey publishing. A pointed, sarcastic article by Deb Smith (a white writer) in a 1997 issue of *Romance Writers Report* shamed fellow authors for prolific, egregious stereotypes of Black characters in a wickedly satirical send up.[39] "This subgenre is a real money machine for publishers," she notes. "Not to mention an easy sell for us white historical writers. And it makes us feel good too—we're so open minded." Another *RWR* article in 2008 drew attention to the shelving issue, where bookstores failed to classify books by Black authors as romance.

Despite these occasional efforts, racism was apparent. Year after year, Black authors were shut out of the RITA Awards. Sometimes white members at the RWA conference would simply not talk to authors of color. "I've heard horror stories from other authors [of color] about sitting at a table at the RWA national conference and people who are there will get up and walk away from them," South Asian author Alisha Rai told NPR in an interview in 2018.[40]

"I'd go to the conference, but not even go in," said Beverly Jenkins. "I'd sit outside and smoke and hold court. I'd meet with my editors and publisher, and network with a lot of writers." And indeed, at the national conference in Denver in 2018, I found her perched on a concrete planter in the sweltering heat, right outside the doors of the convention center.

Many Black authors, including Jenkins, refused to enter the RITA awards; the registration fees seemed a waste. "I knew I wasn't going to be tapped," Jenkins told me. "So why take myself through that?"

Love Is for Everyone

Other diverse authors also struggled to tell their stories. LGBTQ+ authors, disabled authors, Asian American authors, Latinx authors, neuro-atypical authors—most were excluded from mainstream romance publishing and marginalized within RWA.

For instance, although gay and lesbian presses like Naiad and Bold Stroke Books had published rich and varied LGBTQ+ stories for decades, mainstream presses only published books with heterosexual couples until very recently.[41] Indeed, if you judged the world only by category romance, you'd be forgiven for thinking lesbian, gay, queer, or trans people didn't exist at all. Even bestselling author Suzanne Brockmann couldn't persuade her publisher to keep a gay character in a 1992 manuscript.

"This was a *secondary* character," Brockmann stressed, during her 2018 acceptance speech for RWA's Lifetime Achievement Award, describing the exchange.

> [My editor] told me that traditional romance readers were very conservative, and they did not want to read books that included even the briefest mention of gay people. She said, "You have to make the sheriff straight."

I said, "You can't be serious. It's 1992. The real world is filled with gay people." . . . But this was non-negotiable.

"We'll get letters," she said. I remember that so clearly. She said, "Readers will be offended, and they'll write angry letters." . . .

As my silence dragged on, the editor said, "Other publishers won't let the sheriff be gay, either. That's just the way it is."[42]

Nearly a decade later, in 2001, Brockmann introduced gay FBI agent Jules Cassidy in her novel *The Defiant Hero*, who became one of her most beloved characters. Nevertheless, she still felt silenced by her peers in RWA. In 2008, conference organizers asked her to remove a line from an RWA speech in San Francisco celebrating the recognition of gay marriage in California. This was an especially joyful occasion for Brockmann, whose son is gay.

"I was stunned when I was informed I could not say that. I was told the issue was divisive and some RWA members would be offended," she said a decade later.[43] (The RWA board claims that the members in question did not act or speak on behalf of the organization.)

Such exclusion ran directly counter to an ethic of care, which seeks to meet the needs of everyone in the community. Such contradictions increasingly troubled a growing portion of RWA members, who sensed an expanding social divide in Romancelandia, reflecting the growing polarization of America itself.

Bicultural Networks

Given the lack of support from the dominant network, relational labor turned out to be even more vital for marginalized authors than for the predominantly white, straight RWA membership. Drawing on tactics remarkably like those of RWA's founders, marginalized authors formed their own networks within greater Romancelandia.

In my author survey and interviews, I asked about networks and organizations that authors belonged to. White authors typically said RWA and, maybe, Novelists, Inc., an association for published authors. Authors of color mentioned these mainstream networks, but also belonged to networks focused on historically marginalized aspects of their identity. For instance, gay authors often attended GayRomLit, an annual retreat for authors and fans of gay romance. Several Black authors mentioned Romance Slam Jam, an annual gathering founded in 1995 to celebrate authors of color. Women of Color in Romance and Building

Relationships Around Books were also mentioned as sources of information for marginalized romance authors.[44]

Marginalized authors, in other words, belonged to multiple networks—the mainstream network of RWA and other identity-focused groups. Management research suggests this kind of dual membership is common among marginalized groups. One study found that career-oriented Black women have "bicultural" network patterns, belonging to both predominantly white professional networks and also smaller, predominantly Black networks.[45] Another study pointed to racially concordant interpersonal networks as a valuable defense against race-based microaggressions in the workplace.[46] Other research shows that identity-based networks can make an important difference within some major corporations. IBM, for example, launched a multicultural women's network in the mid-1990s, along with a recurring symposium to bring these leaders together; between 1995 and 2003, the number of multicultural women executives at IBM more than quadrupled.[47] Studies on "affinity groups" and "employee resource groups" suggests the power of relationship building between peers, which expands opportunities to find mentors among one's own affinity group.[48] In this way, some organizations have successfully instituted policies promoting the relational labor of connection-building between colleagues.

In a very clear example of the power of identity-focused networks, Vivian Stephens's romance writing group for Black authors had a trailblazing effect. Almost all members became beloved and widely respected authors; among them are Donna Hill, Rochelle Alers, Shirley Hailstock, Sandra Kitt, Doris Johnson, and others. Some twenty years later, they're still helping each other. "I just went over to Doris's house to help her with self-publishing," Hailstock told me during one of our chats. In this way, relational labor and the long-term trusting relationships it produced helped authors like these stay in the game.

Elusive Exclusion: Measuring Bias

The more stories I heard about RWA from authors of color, as well as white authors, the more I wanted to explore the concept of inclusive access and unequal benefits—starting with whether access to advice really was inclusive or not. The attempt didn't yield definitive results but does shed light on why many white people can sincerely believe their organizations or neighborhoods aren't racist.

Here's an overview of what I did (see appendix 2 for details). In 2015, I surveyed 4,270 romance authors who belonged to RWA. My forty-nine survey questions included a "name generator" question, where I asked respondents to name three authors they most often asked for writing advice. I also asked how often they asked or gave advice, and what kind of advice they asked for. Working with network anthropologist Dr. Elspeth Ready, I constructed a network of advice relationships (more about the brilliant Dr. Ready in chapter 8).

Network theory predicts that similar people tend to group together into cliques, in a phenomenon called "homophily," or the "birds-of-a-feather effect."[49] So we expected to find that authors of color and white authors would form separate advice cliques to some extent. But we didn't find that. It seemed like race, income, geography, and genre played only a small role in clique formation.

We figured this out by analyzing a factor called "assortativity," which measures how open groups are to associating with other people, based on specific factors.[50] An assortativity coefficient of one indicates an entirely closed clique (like, say, popular high school girls). If white authors and authors of color formed totally separate advice cliques, the race assortativity coefficient would be one. Conversely, a coefficient of zero would mean white authors and authors of color were equally likely to share advice with each other. (A negative coefficient would mean that authors avoid writers like themselves.) So we expected to find coefficients closer to one than to zero for "cliquing factors" like race, income, local chapter, and so on.

Surprisingly, *none* of the factors we tested played a big role in forming cliques. For every factor, the assortativity coefficient was much closer to zero than one. Race and income were the least influential factors of all (see table A.3 in the appendix).

So, at least on the surface, the data seemed to support what most of my interviewees told me. RWA did have surprisingly open advice networks, where authors of many levels of experience and different types of identity—including race—could easily share advice with each other (this supports the open-elite idea that I described in chapter 3).

But we *knew* that discrimination and bias existed, because authors of color told us so. And because not a single Black author had ever won a RITA at the time when we collected our data. What was going on? Were the data gaslighting us? In the end, we came up with three compelling explanations. Together, they indicate just how elusive racism can be, and explain why many people live in a bubble where they think it doesn't exist.

The first explanation is survivorship bias. It's likely the people who felt most hurt and excluded by discrimination weren't members of RWA and didn't take the survey. This would make RWA (or a neighborhood, or school, or association) *look* like a totally open and welcoming advice network, because everyone who's not welcome leaves. Case in point: Beverly Jenkins, the queen of Black historical fiction, didn't join RWA until 2017, when she received the Lifetime Achievement Award. On a related note, even if authors of color did join RWA, they might have felt less invested and less willing to devote time to a long survey.

A second explanation is that certain local chapters were more inclusive than others when it came to advice sharing. Even if some chapters or groups developed strong race-based advice cliques, those might not show up because our analysis calculated an average across a large network, including 145 local chapters. Averages tend to smooth things out, so they can hide spikes and valleys in the data. My interviews supported this idea. For instance, Black author Beverly Kendell told me she thought her Georgia chapter was more welcoming to her as a Black author than a northeastern chapter she'd joined.

A third possibility is that authors of color actually *did* have equal access to the advice network. As Shirley Hailstock told me about her first visit to a New Jersey RWA chapter in 1990s, "They were very welcoming. . . . They just liked that I worked hard and was intelligent enough to do this work." But maybe that easily available advice, shared equally across racial divides, wasn't equally useful to everyone. This would explain the exclusion of authors from the RITAs—maybe advice networks weren't biased, but the judging process was. Or maybe, as C. Chilove found, advice was plentiful, but based on a genre created by and for white people.

All these limitations and explanations underscore a larger truth in US society. Many white people, like me, want to believe our own communities or organizations aren't racist. We may honestly not see that racism for a variety of reasons, well documented in books like Ruby Hamad's *White Tears, Brown Scars*. My own mixed success in measuring exclusion suggest that survivorship bias and localized incidents are two more factors making it easier for white people to see what we want to see.

Social Media and the Second RWA

During the early decades of RWA, internal conflict usually remained internal, out of the view of media who would love "nothing more than to see a pack of women trying to annihilate each other in the name of romance," as RWA's publicist put it during the Queen Mary controversy described in chapter 4.[51]

But the rise of social media meant that RWA, and many other organizations, had to fight this battle in public.

"Where RWA ignored us back in the 1990s," said Beverly Jenkins, "these young people—you're not going to ignore them, because they have social media on their side. They will put your business out there, [and] then everybody knows there's a problem within your organization."

Romancelandia's move toward social justice began in earnest around 2015. The previous year, a nonprofit called We Need Diverse Books began pushing for diversity in children's literature, and the movement spread to other genres. By the time I attended the 2015 RWA conference, dozens of authors were wearing "We Need Diverse Romance" t-shirts and buttons. #WeNeedDiverseRomance joined media activist hashtags like #OscarsSoWhite, #MeToo, and #BlackLivesMatter, which had started to demonstrate the power of decentralized social movements.

At about the same time, Chinese American author Courtney Milan joined the RWA board of directors, becoming a powerful voice for equity in romance. During her tenure, the board launched a diversity committee. The organization began recruiting more authors of color and LGBTQ+ authors as board candidates and committee members. In 2016, RWA convened its first diversity summit with publishers to advocate for marginalized authors. In 2017, the organization created two grants, funding underrepresented authors' attendance at the annual conference. Avon Books followed suit, instituting the Beverly Jenkins Diverse Voices Sponsorship, awarding $2,500 and a one-on-one meeting with an Avon editor to a marginalized author.[52]

Meanwhile, RWA turned its attention to a huge structural problem in publishing. Most editors break into publishing through unpaid or low-paid internships. RWA created a grant to pay for a publishing intern's summer living expenses, as an effort to move economically disadvantaged students into the editorial pipeline. These were meaningful, albeit nascent, attempts to address the greater political-economic forces working against diverse authors.

Many, but not all, RWA members welcomed the organization's measures. Some felt diversity efforts were consuming too much of the organization's attention and resources. On an internal RWA online forum in 2017, one founding member, Linda Howard, who is white, called the diversity focus divisive and discriminatory, saying that it was driving some longtime members to quit.[53] A Twitter uproar ensued and Howard resigned, later explaining, "I wasn't against diversity. I was against the way the board was handling it . . . I thought it could have been handled better and gotten better results."[54]

Amid the controversies, RWA president HelenKay Dimon, who is white, chastised white members, pointing out that they "have always had 90% of everything available, and now all of sudden they have 80%. Instead of saying: 'Oooh, look, I have 80%' they say: 'Oh, I lost 10! Who do I blame?'"[55] (In fact, white authors had not lost 10 percent. At the time, authors of color wrote only about 8.3 percent of romance from traditional publishers.)[56]

Among the many measures RWA took to provide more equal benefits to marginalized authors, the most visible were reforms to the RITA judging process. Observers noted that when previous winners judged categories, they perpetuated unwritten criteria that might have biased expectations. The organization brought in non-RWA members from greater Romancelandia, including critics and librarians, as judges. All received antibias training.

But would any of these efforts make a difference? The 2019 RITA Awards offered the chance to find out. Three authors of color had made it to the finals—but would they win?

The 2019 RITAs

Diversity was on the minds of the night's award presenters as well as recipients. The evening launched with a peppy film short about romance "trailblazers," highlighting titles from Black, Asian, Latina, and LGBTQ+ authors as far back as the 1970s. Out of fifteen presenters and speakers, seven were authors of color or LGBTQ+ authors; among them were Sandra Kitt, Rochelle Alers, and many others. Out of thirty total speakers and winners, more than two-thirds mentioned the long fight for diverse authors or pointed to a diverse author as a role model.

Diversity was also on the mind of the evening's emcee, Sarah MacLean, a white author who was president of the New York chapter. "Some of you are nervous," she said, referring to the political tension, the Twitter storms, and the anger and passion that had arisen over the past few years. She gave a mischievous grin. "Don't worry. I'll be so, so gentle."[57]

A wave of relieved and knowing laughter swept the crowd. After jokes about Spanx and sex, she concluded, "What better way to smash the patriarchy, to combat hate, racism, and bigotry, what better way to change the world than to live our triumphant happiness in love?" The room resounded with applause.

For the next ten minutes, almost every presenter and winner referred to the need for equity. The first winner, J. R. Ward, a slender blonde who won for best paranormal romance, spoke through tears. "I urge the organization to hear the people who need to be heard," she said, her voice trembling.

Then it was time for the award for best long contemporary novel. After a series of bawdy double entendres, the presenter, Lexi Ryan, opened the envelope and tearfully announced the winner.

Kennedy Ryan, author of *Long Shot*. The first Black author to win a RITA.

Weaving her way through the standing ovation, Ryan was crying too. A self-published author who had written an acclaimed novel with domestic violence themes, Ryan laughed through her tears, sharing that she'd just accidentally deleted her speech. So, she spoke from the heart.

"This moment is so much bigger than me and my book. It's been thirty-seven years, waiting for someone who looks like me to stand here. It is spectacularly overdue."

The applause was long and heartfelt. The awards continued. To the crowd's delight, another Black author, M. Malone, won for *Bad Blood: Left at the Altar*. It was a moment of celebration and of relief. But not one to rest.

"We won't stop asking," Kennedy Ryan told the crowd. "We won't stop agitating until everybody's represented."

PART III

Romancelandia in the Digital Age

7

Virtual Romancelandia and
the Electronic Frontier

IN 1993, I was working in the book department at *Cosmopolitan* magazine in New York, fetching coffee and making copies. I planned to work my way up the ladder as countless aspiring writers had done before me. But one fall day, a friend called me over. He popped a shiny silver disk into his Macintosh and changed my career plans forever. The Mac (with its state-of-the-art *full-color* screen!) opened up a game called *Myst*, displaying vivid interactive landscapes and captivating steampunk graphics. Suddenly, I felt as if I'd glimpsed the future of media. It wasn't magazines! It was . . . CD-ROMS! They would change the world of publishing forever!

CD-ROMS, of course, eventually went the way of 8-track tapes and Laser-Discs, but what was then called "interactive multimedia" still offered plenty to be excited about. Suddenly books, magazines, and other publications didn't have to be the static, paper products they'd been for nearly five hundred years. Text could be interactive. Audio, video, photos, and text could converge. Tech companies and publishers began to experiment. In 1994 and 1995, Mosaic and Netscape suddenly transformed the all-text internet into the visual, clickable World Wide Web. Microsoft published an interactive multimedia encyclopedia called Encarta with audio and video entries. An upstart media firm called Voyager released an interactive version of *Maus*, the graphic novel by Art Spiegelman.

For twenty-something creative types like me, huddled in Manhattan working low-level publishing or design jobs, the possibilities of interactive media seemed magical, limitless, and intoxicating. Venture money was everywhere, funding new kinds of media companies and "innovation" was the magic word of the day.

Romance writers, too, immediately saw the possibilities, publishing e-books a full decade before the Kindle launched. From the earliest moments of digital culture, Romancelandia migrated online, rapidly extending its open-elite practices and ethic of care. Romance authors and readers came together on bulletin boards and dial-up online services, mixing as freely as they did at physical events. They adopted the language and mindset of New Economy entrepreneurs, sharing ideas about self-promotion and e-book publishing that would prime them for digital success a decade later, when e-readers finally became widespread. Meanwhile, their long practice at forming remote communities meant they'd already built, and now grew, support structures for solo work that would provide community, solidarity, and greater security at a time when other creators and workers at large were adjusting to a new, more precarious economy.

Romancelandia Online

Since the days of electric typewriters and the earliest word processors, romance authors have been the first to experiment with new communication technologies.

"Romance writers were very fast to take up personal computers," literary agent Steven Axelrod told me. "They were very early adopters of technology relative to other writing groups. These were authors who had the money to buy word processors and early personal computers, and they used them to great effect and with great relish."

I speak from experience when I say that authors and editors will try anything—*anything*—to make writing easier. It's no coincidence that the first successful ballpoint pen was invented by a Hungarian newspaper editor in 1931. Or that in 1833, Mark Twain typed the first book manuscript written on typewriter.[1] Anne Rice, Amy Tan, Stephen King, and George R. R. Martin all adopted computers early.[2] Within a month of ChatGPT's public release, authors were already self-publishing books written by AI.[3]

So, it should be no surprise that romance authors came early to technology. In 1984, *Romance Writers Report* was already reviewing word processors and computers. In 2003, fully seven years before iPads debuted, the publication was reviewing portable word processors.

Even more importantly, at a time when most long-distance contact still relied on letters and phone calls, online communities suddenly supercharged the open-elite network practices and ethic of care that Romancelandia had already established. By the late 1980s, services like CompuServe, Prodigy, and AOL allowed ordinary people to email each other and post to bulletin boards. GEnie, an online service launched by General Electric in 1985, even offered free accounts to professional writers.

The Falling Costs of Relational Labor

Online communities offered the perfect place for romance readers and writers to come together. The internet was already proving a fertile space for other fandoms, like soap opera viewers. Then-graduate student Nancy Baym based her 1990 dissertation on soap opera fans' electronic discussion groups on Usenet.

"The more time I spent reading and posting," she wrote, "the less the collection of written messages seemed like lines of glowing green text. I saw in them instead a dynamic community of people with unique voices, distinctive traditions and enjoyable relationships."[4]

She argued that online, "fans create an ongoing social space in which the shows and their fans are legitimized, and their pleasure enhanced rather than shamed . . . [they] are legitimizing the emotional concerns traditionally associated with women."[5] She noted that many users formed close and lasting friendships that extended into the real world.

Online Romancelandia wasn't just a fan space though; it became an open-elite forum where published authors freely mingled with readers, and the two groups continued to blend and overlap. For instance, when Terri Brisbin, a dental hygienist in New Jersey, first logged onto Prodigy's romance bulletin boards in 1994, she expected to find other fans. But almost immediately, she found herself chatting with historical romance author Samantha James, whose book Brisbin had just finished. Soon, Brisbin was spending eight to ten hours a month on the bulletin boards, talking with other fans and authors like Jill Barnett and Susan Wiggs. This was a time when only about 14 percent of Americans were online, and some 40 percent had never even heard of the internet.[6]

It's important to note that the racial divide in technology may have meant fewer authors of color participated in these communities. At the time, white households were three times as likely to have internet access as Black households, and four times as likely as Hispanic households, even when controlling for income.[7] So, as Romancelandia moved online, many marginalized voices were structurally excluded from the community.

As we saw in chapters 3 and 4, Romancelandians had previously organized themselves entirely through phone calls, letters, and in-person meetups. These time-consuming efforts paid off in friendships, a sense of community, more sales for authors, and more mentors for aspiring writers. The payoff was high, but so were the costs—phone bills, travel expenses and the sheer emotional energy required to connect. With early dial-up connections, the human costs of relational labor plummeted, as technologies suddenly made it easier and cheaper to connect with others, build relationships, and extend Romancelandia's practices of relational labor and its ethic of care.

As with other networks and communities, the more people who joined online romance networks, the more valuable the networks became, in a classic example of *network effects*.[8] As virtual Romancelandia grew, more aspiring writers could find mentors, and more published authors could find new readers. The community's ethic of care and open-elite access would expand dramatically.

A Virtual Ethic of Care

Like so many other readers before her, Brisbin had toyed with the idea of writing a novel herself. And here, online, was a readily available community happy to teach her how to do it. Thanks to the community's ethic of care, authors coached new writers and moderated writing forums for free. Published authors on Prodigy and AOL, including historic romance novelist Lorraine Heath, would offer critiques and conduct informal workshops. Brisbin joined a group led by Colorado author Sharon Mignerey, who conducted asynchronous text sessions on character development and plotting. Brisbin found these threads so valuable that she printed them out and saved them in binders. "In my group of ten, two of us were later published. I've heard that many of these [groups] continued even after Prodigy shut down," she said.

Online, Romancelandia offered another example of how an ethic of care does *not* mean altruism or selflessness; it means that a community's top priority is making sure everyone's needs are sufficiently met to advance everyone's mutual interests. Published authors didn't mentor and build relationships online strictly out of altruistic generosity—they received intangible compensation in many ways: burnishing their reputation, increasing readership and loyalty, and, of course, the benefits of friendship and fellowship in a difficult field.

In this two-way exchange of benefits, Romancelandia's ethic of care dove-tailed with an emerging digital culture that valued the generous and reciprocal exchange of information, which journalist Howard Rheingold described:

> Reciprocity is a key element of any market-based culture, but the arrange-ment I'm describing feels to me more like a kind of gift economy in which people do things for one another out of a spirit of building something be-tween them, rather than a spreadsheet-calculated quid pro quo. When that spirit exists, everybody gets a little extra something, a little sparkle, from their more practical transactions; different kinds of things become possible when this mind-set pervades. . . . In the virtual community I know best, elegantly presented knowledge is a valuable currency.[9]

Of course, not all communities in the 1990s were oases of gift exchange and care. Negative features of online life—toxicity, flame wars, trolls—were al-ready disrupting community interactions in Romancelandia and elsewhere. For instance, the science fiction forumSFF.net became so nasty that "at some point, the reputation among members was that it was a cesspit of bad people," according to Michael Capobianco, a past president of SFWA.

Controversies and arguments also broke out in virtual Romancelandia, evoking admonishments in *PANdora's Box* like this one from 1992, regarding a public online spat about PAN, the professional author's network within RWA:

> Grow up! These boards are PUBLIC. Decide who is the LAST person you want reading your posts and write every single message as if they were beaming their way straight to that individual. . . . This is a free country, and you can do what you jolly well please, even commit professional suicide. I'd hate to see you take PAN and RWA down with you . . . I'm not suggesting you never mention PAN or RWA in public again. What I am suggesting is that we keep family business in the family.[10]

Partly to avoid public squabbles, RWA launched its own private email loops and forums in the late 1990s and early 2000s. These discussions sometimes became heated, too, but in general, "family business" stayed in the family rather than spreading outside Romancelandia. While this allowed RWA to avoid appearing like a "pack of women trying to annihilate each other in the name of romance," an emphasis on harmony may have helped the organization ignore the inclusive access/unequal benefits tension and other issues. As one author observed in August 1992, "Things are often swept under the rug for the sake of our harmonic image in this organization, which is part of what breeds,

I think, long-term problems." This comment turned out to be prescient, as we'll see in chapter 9.

Despite these issues, virtual Romancelandia in general offered a collaborative and mutually supportive community for its participants, where the group's ethic of care extended dramatically.

For instance, when Terri Brisbin sold her first manuscript in 1997, she sought out other first-time authors on AOL, and they united to help each other. "I noticed a handful of people saying they'd just sold [manuscripts], so I approached a number of them and said, 'Hey, can we talk amongst ourselves about this?' And we started our own little group."

The group—christened "The Sold and Yet to Be Published," or the "ToBeez" for short—allowed authors to share information gleaned from their various publishers, editors, and other writers. Even after they published, they remained in the group, which started as thirteen people and grew to two hundred. Members included future bestsellers Eloisa James, Sylvia Day, Brenda Novak, and Carly Phillips. Demonstrating an ethic of care, these writers continued to help other authors with questions about contracts, publicity, and more.

They also teamed up to publicize each other. In 1998, the ToBeez produced a brochure called *Rising Stars of Romance* to distribute to bookstores. Each page featured one of the authors and her new book.

This collaborative effort gave each author more visibility than she would have garnered through her own individual efforts. For instance, Kathryn Falk of *Romantic Times* was so impressed with the group that she invited them to give a whole day of workshops at her conference. Meanwhile, RWA copied the brochure idea, creating its own promotional handout for bookstores featuring RWA members. Collaborative promotion efforts like this presaged the kind of publicity groups and "engagement pods" that social media creators would later pull together to promote each other's work.[11]

The online extension of Romancelandia coincided with a major expansion of RWA. Between 1990 and 2000, RWA's membership swelled from about 4,700 members to eight thousand. The growth in membership meant more financial resources for the organization to use in promoting members' interests.

Exploring E-Books

In 1996, RWA board members sat down with a group of New York publishers. As the group discussed contract terms and rights, one RWA board member posed a question.

"What happens," she asked the publishers, "when books are no longer physical?"

Allison Kelley, longtime executive director of RWA, attended the meeting. The publishers, she said, were dumbfounded by the question. "I thought their heads were going to explode," she told me years later.

The publishers had no answers. But romance writers did. They were already experimenting with e-books.

As early as 1945, the influential engineer and policy maker Vannevar Bush described a knowledge machine called a "Memex . . . a device in which an individual stores all his books, records, and communications."[12] In the 1960s, technology firms including Xerox, IBM, and RCA began acquiring publishers, as they envisioned a world of electronic books (selling them again soon after).[13] In 1980, Michael Hart, founder of Project Gutenberg, distributed a digital version of the Declaration of Independence on an early computer network, in what some consider the first distribution of an e-book.[14] Very early e-readers, like the Sony Data Discman, appeared in the early 1990s, along with books for PDAs (portable digital assistants) like the PalmPilot.[15]

Despite all this innovation, e-books remained barely a blip on the radar for big publishers. Even in 2012, when sociologist John Thompson published *Merchants of Culture*, his extensive study on the publishing industry, digital technologies had affected internal production processes, but little else. The publishers he interviewed understood technological change was coming—but what it would look like, "no one knows," he wrote.[16]

But, in fact, romance writers *did* know. By the time Thompson wrote those words, romance writers had been selling e-books for more than fifteen years. In 1996, RWA member Madris DePasture launched the first all-digital romance publisher, New Concepts Publishing. Other tiny independent e-publishers like Dreams Unlimited and Hard Shell Word Factory quickly followed. These companies weren't exactly high-tech innovators: readers ordered them by phone or email, then received PDFs via email or through the mail. But these publishers paid royalties and promoted the books, just like traditional publishers.

From the moment e-books emerged in the mid-1990s, Romancelandia became deeply divided over whether they counted as real books. RWA would not accept them for consideration in the RITAs. The romance blog *All About Romance* refused to review them, noting in 1998 that they were "poorly (if at all) edited, and among some of the worst books [the reviewers] had read."[17] One *All About Romance* contributor called e-books "unedited, first-draft quality, unprofessional piles of pyrite"—that is, fool's gold. *Romantic Times* also refused to review digital books, maintaining that their audience was only interested in print books.[18]

E-publishing, then as now, had many bad actors. Some so-called electronic publishers exploited unpublished authors who had been rejected by mainstream publishing. Some never paid, and some only paid a one-time fee, not royalties. Some were vanity presses that charged authors exorbitant fees for publication and often paid little or no royalties.

Nevertheless, romance authors instantly understood that e-book publishing would give them more freedom and power. "Electronic publishing opens up a whole new world of artistry. Authors are not restricted to a particular word length; genre-crossing is the norm rather than the exception; and characters do not have to fit a formalized mold," wrote romance author Angelica Hart in 1998.[19] By 2000, RWA's magazine *Romance Writers Report* was running articles about the pros and cons of e-publishing. "I still write print books," wrote Jane Toombs in the January 2000 issue of *RWR*. "But when electronic book publishing began, I decided to venture into this new book medium because I could see its potential." The article included advice about e-publishing associations that protected authors through an approved list of e-publishers who paid royalties.

Most early e-publishers didn't last long. But one, Ellora's Cave, launched the careers of bestselling authors Bella Andre, Sylvia Day, and others. Started in 2000 by RWA member Tina Engler, whose erotica-heavy manuscripts had faced constant rejection, Ellora's Cave began publishing in 2000.[20] The books were hot—much steamier than those published by mainstream romance. Ellora's Cave paid royalties and developed new authors, offering romance writers real opportunities to earn money and build their following through e-books. The venture offered an important outlet for authors who had difficulty getting past traditional publishing's gatekeepers, including LGBTQ+ authors. Although Ellora's Cave went out of business by 2016, plagued by accounting problems and payment delays, the company proved for some sixteen years that electronic publishing could open up new markets and expand the genre.

Meanwhile, higher profile authors were starting to experiment with e-books. Simon & Schuster created an e-book imprint in 1999, and the following year, put out a Stephen King novella called *Riding the Bullet*, available exclusively as a downloadable file for $2.50. Some 600,000 copies sold within two weeks.[21] King's successful e-book experiment brought some credibility to what still seemed laughably distant to most authors. Nevertheless, it would be a decade before e-books represented even 1 percent of the overall book market.[22]

Romance writers, especially aspiring ones, continued to experiment. Many remembered how changes in distribution and production had produced the mass market paperback revolution, opening the market for American authors back in the early 1980s. Maybe, they figured, changes in technology would help them again now. Certainly, they appreciated the changes that Jeff Bezos had made to book publishing since Amazon launched in 1994. Physical bookstores had stocked only the most recent romance novels, but Amazon could offer any book still in print. Romance authors' backlists became accessible to fans who wanted to buy them. Grateful for the expanded market, RWA gave Bezos its prestigious industry award in 2000.

As writers kept track of publishing innovations, the broader working world was also starting to change, moving toward workstyles that resembled those of romance writers.

Welcome to the New Economy

At the time when I left the magazine world for multimedia development, tens of thousands of my peers were doing the same. Between 1995 and 2000, some eight thousand new media firms created 140,000 new jobs in New York's Silicon Alley, a sprawl of hipster neighborhoods abutting Soho and Little Italy.[23] Young media workers like me fled quiet, corporate cubicles for airy, sundrenched lofts at interactive development firms like Razorfish and Rare Medium, which produced websites and interactive marketing communications for big companies. Suddenly, creative, well-paid jobs seemed to be everywhere, if you were willing to leap off the corporate ladder. Those of us who did worked twelve-hour days and weekends, but we *wanted* to—our colleagues were also young, hip, and creative. If we needed a break, we could drop in on the lavish tech parties inevitably running at a bar nearby.

Welcome, we were told, to the New Economy.

Here in the new media world, venture capital dollars flowed freely. Innovation was the future! Change was good! Or so said best-selling business books in the late 1990s and early 2000s, like *Who Moved My Cheese*, *Free Agent Nation*, and *The Rise of the Creative Class*. Taking risks and crafting independent, creative careers would bring fulfillment and financial rewards. We could all work the way artists and musicians did—guided by our inner creativity and passion, working flexible hours, free from the constraints of the old-fashioned corporate world. As sociologist Mark Banks later wrote, "the future of all work is now widely assumed to be adopting a cultural industry model."[24]

The New Economy rhetoric resonated with romance writers and spurred many to see themselves in a new light. For more than a decade, romance writers had fought to be perceived as professionals, even though they didn't fit the conventional professional mode—they worked at home, held multiple jobs, set their own hours, and blended family and work. Now, suddenly, qualities like flexibility, self-enterprise, and gig work, which they'd incorporated into a new version of professionalism, were glorified by the New Economy mindset.

Romance writers readily absorbed the entrepreneurial rhetoric; as a group, they'd already been working as creative entrepreneurs for years. As the New Economy discourse spread, romance authors leaned more and more heavily into the start-up metaphor. "Each of us is an entrepreneur with a small start-up company and a staff of one," wrote one author in 1998.[25] In the 1990s, compared to the 1980s, *RWR* ran fewer and fewer articles about how to be professional, and more and more about how to run a business and promote yourself.

For instance, during the 1990s and early 2000s, romance authors increasingly complained that publishers did too little to publicize their books and began to promote themselves. As we saw in chapter 5, Black authors like Terry McMillan and Brenda Jackson had already shown the way. "We did not get any promotion," Brenda Jackson told me. "They didn't know how to promote Black authors. We had to beat the bushes. I sent books to bookstores and wrote letters introducing myself. It was up to you to let people know about the books."

Other authors quickly followed suit, focusing more intently on promoting themselves as brands, improving their own marketing and publicity and negotiating better contracts. These entrepreneurial innovations might be small grassroots measures, like putting information stickers about forthcoming books onto current novels—a tip Terri Brisbin gleaned from her mentor Shirley Hailstock. Or they might be much bigger endeavors, like hiring an independent publicist or creating a collaborative brochure for bookstores, as the ToBeez group did. Either way, romance writers increasingly adopted the view that they could not depend on publishing companies to promote and market their books. Instead, they themselves had to become the entrepreneurial engineers of their own success. This attitude and the experiences it motivated would equip romance writers with skills, attitudes, and habits that became exponentially more important when the e-book revolution finally exploded in 2010.

A few prescient authors questioned the wisdom of taking on promotion and publicity. "Are we cutting our own throats?" one author asked in the March 1994 issue of *PANdora's Box*. "If we keep going on as we are, romance writers are going to be given more and more of the responsibility and the cost of promoting our own books. . . . We are the only genre that takes on any of these costs as individuals. . . . [Publishers] will over time step back and allow that burden to be assumed by most if not all of these writers. Can we have a debate in these pages, please?"[26]

Looking back, these few authors who raised such concerns seem prophetic. As the New Economy boomed along, few romance authors—or dot-com workers like me—realized that this new willingness to shoulder more responsibilities and work longer hours for uncertain compensation signaled a much larger, long-term shift in the political economy of work. In the 1970s through the 1990s, US corporations started moving toward smaller, more flexible networked forms of organization, away from huge hierarchical structures.[27] By the 2000s, these trends would power the gig economy.

Political scientist Jacob Hacker called this change "the great risk shift."[28] As firms downsized, they also ended "no layoffs" policies, curtailed benefits, and replaced full-timers with part-timers and contractors. For authors, that meant doing work that publishers once did, like line editing or book promotion. Meanwhile, government policies cut back on rules and requirements regulating corporations and industries, on the principles that too much regulation hampered the free market. A better, more efficient economy, the reasoning went, would help everyone. A costly social safety net would no longer be necessary because the rising free market would float all boats. Following this logic, federal and state legislators rolled back rules that protected consumer and worker well-being.[29]

British scholar David Harvey called this philosophy "neoliberalism," an ethic that assumes that "human well-being can best be advanced by liberating individual entrepreneurial freedoms and skills."[30] While scholars differ somewhat on the term's definition, they generally agree that neoliberal systems prioritize a free market, individual responsibility, and self-reliance. This ethic contrasts directly with an ethic of care, which prioritizes caring for others' needs and promoting mutual aid.

New Economy thinking and the rise of Silicon Alley fit neatly into neoliberalism because they both fostered a mindset of "self-enterprise" that resonated with young tech workers, romance writers, and a much larger group of workers in many fields. Even corporate employees were encouraged to pursue "intra-preneurism," the generation of new business ideas and product innova-tions. "Self-enterprise" meant seeing yourself and your career as a mini-entrepreneurial venture, but it also meant seeing work itself as an enterprise of self-fulfillment, especially if one looked inward to "follow your passion" as so many self-help books and articles urged. Finding this kind of fulfillment required workers to pursue self-improvement, cultivating "energy, initiative, self-reliance and personal responsibility," as organization scholar Paul du Gay put it.[31]

All this New Economy discourse encouraged the development of a flexible, risk-tolerant worker.[32] Sociologist Gina Neff studied the connection between neoliberal discourse and the way dot-commers thought about risk and reward. She observed that the way magazines, newspapers, and the media *communicated* about risk created a cultural discourse that made risk seem glamorous, adven-turous, and cool, as well as a smart career strategy. Jumping from job to job, freelancing, gig work, risk-taking, remote working, and self-reliance now seemed like résumé-building moves that increased workers' long-term employ-ability.[33] In fact, *not* being able to do all these things, and relying on corporate job security (or even federal social security) seemed risky.[34]

Romance authors' publications and events mirrored this shift. *Romance Writers Report* ran its first article on self-promotion in 1993. Within a few years, *every* issue of *RWR* included content about advertising, publicity, and promotional strategies. The image of writer-entrepreneur pervaded Romancelandia just as the image of the self-as-entrepreneur pervaded larger American society.

From New Economy to Gig Economy

Then, suddenly, in early 2000, the dot-com bubble burst and the downside of working like an artist suddenly became clear—insecure employment, long hours for uncertain pay, no benefits or safety nets, and a lack of social support. Some dot-commers, like me, moved to freelancing and consulting; many turned to blogging and evolved into social media influencers, as Emily Hund describes in her history of the field.[35] Even if the self-employed life could sometimes be more lucrative and more creatively satisfying (as I experienced), it brought with it constant anxiety. Ulrich Beck called this political economy of insecurity and uncertainty "the risk regime."[36]

This new way of working depended on independence, self-reliance, and "individualization," where "people increasingly have to become their own micro-structures," wrote Angela McRobbie. "They have to do the work of the structures themselves."[37]

Further, Mark Banks argued, this lack of support structures among many knowledge workers in the gig economy wasn't likely to change, due to "a general antagonism" among cultural workers "toward collective forms of action which remain symbolically linked to the tired and pedestrian climate of the 'old' economy."[38]

But none of this was true of romance writers. Romance writers had *already* spent a decade creating support structures for themselves that other new entrants into the New Economy lacked. Romancelandia's ethic of care created mentoring and learning structures where authors could help each other succeed. Further, RWA had developed industry clout. During the 1990s, RWA successfully pressured publishers for better terms, achieving real benefits for writers. At a time when the government-secured social safety net was contracting, and self-employed workers were excluded from many benefits enjoyed by full-time workers, Romancelandia offered the next best thing—structures of care to promote the success and fill the needs of its citizens. These structures gave romance writers an important advantage when digital publishing suddenly burst on the scene after 2010.

Romancelandia's networking differed from that of Silicon Alley workers. In a network ethnography, Gina Neff shows that Silicon Alley's much vaunted networks simply weren't diverse enough to make workers resilient enough to survive the dot-com crash of 2000. Everyone did the same sort of work, in the same sort of industry, and had the same sorts of skills and qualities (young, ambitious, educated, white, and so on). But romance writers with their rapidly expanding open-elite networks—both online and offline—*did* develop ties across different levels of experience, different subgenres, different income levels, and different races (even though the latter was never enough). The openness of the network to diversity would help romance writers be remarkably resilient in the face of a publishing industry disruption just around the corner—the rise of e-books.

The Writer as Entrepreneur

For now, though, in the early 1990s, the pervasive New Economy discourse helped romance authors see themselves in a new light. Throughout the 1980s, they'd fought to establish themselves as professionals. As the 1990s began, romance authors came to see themselves more and more as entrepreneurs, running their own businesses. Published authors began to focus more intently on promoting themselves as brands, improving their marketing and publicity, and negotiating better contracts. As their focus shifted from "how do I get published" to "how do I advance my career," published authors developed new needs, separate from those of unpublished authors. The question began to arise: how could one network, one association, fulfill such different demands?

"This was a big issue, and a divisive one," wrote one past RWA president in an internal RWA history of PAN. "Were we a Big Sister organization or were we a professional writers' organization?"[39]

Where and how to draw the line between professional and amateur in many types of media work would become increasingly unclear as the digital revolution continued.[40] But for romance writers, the question loomed large because its unique power stemmed from its open-elite membership, with its distinctive mix of newcomers and seasoned practitioners. Maintaining such a network requires constant readjustment. "An elite faces a balancing act," write network theorists Walter Powell and Jason Owen-Smith. "Too much attention focused on other elite members produces a rich-get-richer dynamic that leads to consolidation and eventual stagnation." On the other hand, they add, too much attention to newcomers and novel information "can lead to elite disintegration" as the network's powerful core loses cohesion.[41] In Nancy Baym's study of an online soap opera community, she found this balance was tested over time. The newsgroup she studied "maintained its welcoming attitude toward newcomers," she wrote, but the "relationship between old-timers and newbies is more strained than it once was."[42]

> Too many new posters neither understand nor care that this is a group with long-standing traditions which are highly valued within the community . . . these violations and challenges to convention, once treated with gentle reminders, now result in flame wars that make the "rules" explicit . . . there is ongoing tension between the old ways of doing things, exemplified by the old-timers and the attitudes of the new people, who either do not know these traditions or do not like them.

Significantly, Baym noted that even the flame wars over conventions had "value in community preservation" because they led to community agreement and enforcement of acceptable behavior. In Romancelandia, too, controversy and debate caused bitter division more than once, but typically these rifts led to clearer understanding and definition of the network's values.

Because RWA allowed unpublished authors join as full members, unlike other writing associations, the unpublished often outnumbered the published members. In 1988, about 52 percent of 3,600 members had never published.[43]

But as the organization grew with the rise of virtual Romancelandia and the institution of new local chapters, the proportion of published and unpublished shifted quickly in favor of the unpublished, with unpublished authors sometimes representing as much as 70 percent of the membership.

The open membership policy filled the organization's coffers and allowed it to hire lawyers and provide other support to defend authors' rights. However, as the balance tipped toward newbies, published authors felt their needs weren't being met. Author Janis Reams Hudson wrote later:

> Once you got published, there was nothing more RWA could do for you, so you were expected to teach the 'how-to' workshops at conferences, mentor new writers, judge unpublished manuscripts—everything anyone could think of to help the unpublished. But there was no help for the published, because who was there to help them?[44]

Thus, the coming of a new, more entrepreneurial spirit also brought Romance Writers of America to a critical juncture: Would published authors split off and create a new organization, a more elite branch of Romancelandia? Or would RWA find a way to fill the needs of both groups?

As it turned out, both things happened. In 1989, a group of published RWA members formed Novelists, Inc. (NINC), an association for published authors. (To join NINC today, you need to publish at least two novels of thirty thousand words each, with earnings of at least $2,000 for each title, or $5,000 on each self-published title, in the past year.) NINC became a thriving authors' organization. Today, some 68 percent of members are bestselling authors.[45] (An interesting note: In my 2015 survey, about 9 percent of respondents belonged both to RWA and to Novelists, Inc. Among those with dual membership, about 8.2 percent were authors of color—almost exactly representative of the percent of all romance novels published by authors of color at that time.)

Shortly after, in 1990, RWA launched the Published Authors Network (PAN), an internal group "meant to help guide the organization as a whole," wrote Robin Lee Hatcher, a past RWA president.[46] Joining PAN required authors to have published a "commercially available" title with an approved publisher, and to have earned a certain amount of money. By 1992, 15 percent of RWA's members were PAN members (again, when I did my survey, about 8 percent of PAN members were authors of color—strikingly similar to the percent within Novelists, Inc. and the percent of romance novels written by authors of color in general).[47]

At the annual RWA conference, PAN set up workshops for published authors only. "Things were shared in these PAN workshops that have not been shared in public," wrote romance author Margaret Brownley in an unpublished history of PAN provided to me by RWA.[48] Frank information was also shared in the PAN newsletter *PANdora's Box*, which had an uncensored, no-nonsense edge that "got the job done," wrote Brownley.

While PAN added a new boundary between elites and newcomers, the group also benefited authors who hadn't yet published. For instance, PAN launched a member survey and issued ratings on what publishers did or didn't do well. "We sent each publisher a report card based on the survey. . . . We'd say things like, 'You got an A for distribution but an F for royalty statements,'" wrote Brownley. "This led to many tangible changes." PAN demonstrated that one publisher was using the same cover on different authors' books. The group also persuaded Harlequin to pay writers' travel expenses when the company asked them to fly in for meetings. "It has always been my belief that what is good for the published members is good for RWA," wrote Hatcher.[49]

The existence of PAN made some unpublished authors feel excluded, but it also gave them a goal to shoot for. And discussions about who should or shouldn't be allowed into PAN, though often bitter, eventually identified more needs among specific groups of writers. For instance, in 2000, RWA founded PRO, for authors who had finished a manuscript and were in the process of submitting. By identifying the specific needs of groups within RWA, the organization continued to place an ethic of care at its center, even as entrepreneurship, self-promotion, and New Economy rhetoric permeated the organization and the greater culture of work.

This kind of network-within-a-network may serve as a helpful model as other self-organized communities come together. The Internet Creators Union shut down after only a few years because established YouTubers didn't see the value: an open-elite network, in other words, must offer value to the elite, as well as newcomers, or they won't stay. Likewise, groups hoping to create solidarity and mutual aid for larger, more disparate groups—say, social media creators, or freelancer writers, or gig workers in general— would be wise to focus on the separate needs of the elite and newcomers, the dominant and nondominant subgroups. It's not easy to achieve such a balance, which may be one reason open-elite networks are rare. But especially in industries where platforms or distributors hold all the power, it's worth the effort to try.

Changing Forms of Feminism

While neoliberalism and the New Economy were changing the attitudes and realities of the workplace, feminism and the status of women were changing in ways that might threaten Romancelandia's solidarity.

By the early 1990s, women represented almost half the labor force, up from about 33 percent in the 1950s.[50] Most of RWA's original members worked as homemakers (about 27 percent of respondents in a 1985 survey worked outside the home). By 2009, 60 percent of members had a job besides writing. The gender wage gap had started to close for women of all races, although gains were unequal and white men still earned the most after adjustment for age, education, and experience.[51] For many young women in the 1990s, it seemed things could only get better, with women's education rates skyrocketing from 1970 to 1995, while men's stagnated.

As I mentioned in chapter 2, not all of RWA's founding members would have called themselves feminists, but all believed that women should not be treated as second class citizens. Similarly, by the 1990s, many young women avoided the "F" word (feminism).[52] By the late 1990s and early 2000s, a "post-feminist" mindset disavowing the need for feminist activism was competing with other forms of feminism, like Black feminism and intersectionality, which continued to call for social justice, equity, and liberation.[53] Increasingly, white feminists stressed the idea that "any remaining inequalities were not the result of sexism but of natural differences and/or women's own choices."[54] This version of feminism, which Catherine Rottenberg calls "neoliberal feminism," stressed individual self-enterprise and choice, and downplayed the need for structural change.[55] "Millions of women," wrote feminist scholar Shani Orgad, "feel that they are to blame if they cannot manage to rise up the ladder as fast as men and also have a family and an active home life (and be beautiful to boot)."[56] This fetishization of personal and individual power worked against marginalized authors, since many white writers embraced a color-blind version of feminism that assumed all women had the same choices.

With many Romancelandians embracing the can-do, self-enterprising energy of neoliberal feminism, would the spirit of mutual aid fall by the wayside? It did not. As we've seen, romance authors and readers continued to bond in a spirit of mutual aid throughout the new media/New Economy era. In fact, many authors parodied the demands of neoliberal feminism, particularly in a romance-related genre dubbed "chick-lit," (until the publishing industry retired the term as derogatory and dismissive). In chick-lit's founding text,

Bridget Jones's Diary, a novel published in 1996, author Helen Fielding documents the humorous struggles of a young British heroine to become the ideal self-enterprising young woman—career-minded, sexy, organized, healthy, and thin. "Must not sulk about not having a boyfriend, but develop inner poise and authority and sense of self as woman of substance, complete without boyfriend, as best way to obtain boyfriend."[57]

Not all chick-lit was romance, not all centered on a single romantic relationship, and not all had the traditional happily ever after ending. Allison Pearson's *I Don't Know How She Does It*, for instance, features a harried, married mother trapped by the crazy career-family juggle. The heroine of Jennifer Weiner's blockbuster debut novel, *Good in Bed*, enjoys a happy-for-now ending. But the heart of the book is the heroine's personal development as she seeks career happiness, finds success as a writer, becomes a single mother, and accepts herself as a size sixteen.

Readers themselves often found it a hilarious and comforting depiction that resonated with their own experiences: "The fact that I was reading a beautiful, fun, sexy story about a woman I could see myself in was a game changer," wrote reporter Maggie Fremont in 2019, nearly twenty years after reading the book at age eighteen. "What was even more ground-breaking, the thoughts and feelings I had been having my entire life and couldn't put into words were suddenly staring back at me on a page written by a complete stranger. It was incredible."

Not surprisingly, "chick-lit" was written off by many critics as "a mouthful of cotton candy," as Jennifer Weiner noted.[58] But romance publishers jumped on the bandwagon, rushing to add imprints like Harlequin's Red Dress Inc., with brightly colored covers and screwball heroines. In the 2010s, the term "chick-lit" gave way to "rom-com," adapted from the film term. But whatever you call it, this newly popular flavor of romance offered a powerful example of romance writers wrestling with emerging social and feminist themes in their own typically playful, ambiguous ways.

Throughout the 1990s and early 2000s, romance writers felt the pull of evolving discourses about work and female empowerment. Even as a new emphasis on entrepreneurial success and even as technology supercharged their traditions of relationship building, an ethic of care—however incomplete and imperfect—remained at the center of Romancelandia. And although emerging, problematic forms of feminism, like neoliberal feminism, influenced their work, a strong sense of female solidarity continued to influence writers like Terri Brisbin. "This is going to sound very sexist," she told me, "But this is a group of women. We have our good parts and bad parts, but the good thing women do for each other—we do mentor and help each other. I've been in professional organizations that are largely men, and their view of power is, 'I control, I keep, and I hold.' With women, I see a different idea of power. It's about helping each other succeed so we can all benefit."

Prime for Disruption

For Terri Brisbin, stumbling into virtual Romancelandia and its ethic of care led to a new career. Eventually, she joined the New Jersey chapter of RWA and discovered mentors like Shirley Hailstock and Debbie Macomber. Her first novel came out in 1998, followed by many more publications through Harlequin, which published her Scottish historical novels, and Berkeley, which published her time-travel fantasy books.

Like many of her fellow authors, Brisbin held onto her "day job" as a dental hygienist for many years. A large majority of romance writers never support themselves on their writing alone, but many—like Brisbin—have found the income to be a comfortable addition. "At first, it paid for family trips, and then it paid for cars and insurance for the kids. And then it moved up, to be equal or more than my dental hygiene money," she said. In this way, romance authors perfected the "side hustle" long before the coin was termed. Their working styles and support networks offered them powerful support in the coming gig economy. And their rapid move online, bringing along their relationship building traditions and ethic of care, would soon give romance writers an advantage in the brave new world of digital publishing.

8

The Self-Publishing Gold Rush

WHEN RANDOM HOUSE DROPPED Bella Andre in 2010, the contemporary romance author was crushed. In the past six years, she'd published twelve books with four publishers, and though none of them ever made more than $21,000, her writing provided a dependable, if modest, income. Without the Random House contract, "I was hanging on by my fingernails," she told a reporter in 2014.[1]

But as it turned out, she couldn't have picked a better time to be dropped by a traditional publisher. Hoping to make ends meet, she self-published a few manuscripts through Kindle Direct Publishing. Though the Kindle had offered self-publishing since its debut three years earlier, few established authors had bothered to try it. Now, hoping to make ends meet, Andre uploaded a few old manuscripts. Then a few more. To her astonishment, by the end of the year, she was earning nearly $20,000 a month as an indie author—far more than traditional publishers ever paid her.

"Every day, as the numbers ticked by, my husband and I were floored," she told the Washington Post in 2011.[2]

The indie gold rush was on.

Disrupting the Publishing Circuit

For Andre and others, the e-book era unleashed the full power of Romancelandia's open-elite networks and its ethic of care. The solidarity and cooperation of romance authors set the stage for phenomenal indie success for romance authors—particularly for underrepresented authors—as information and advice about self-publishing rapidly spread through the network. As the e-book revolution picked up steam from 2010 to 2015, romance authors saw dramatic income increases, while other authors saw only declines. The income gap between authors of color and white authors closed. The romance genre became more popular than ever before. Traditional publishers were forced to change contracts and adopt practices they learned from indie authors, like featuring diverse characters. E-books in general, and digital self-publishing in particular, nudged power away from big publishers, and toward romance writers.

But it soon turned out that Amazon gained the most power of all. As romance publishing became "platformized"—that is, dependent on a single technology platform for the creation, production, distribution, and consumption of products—Andre and others faced new power asymmetries with big corporations. From 2010 until the present, Amazon.com would infiltrate every aspect of the book industry. As with many other cultural creators and gig economy workers, the platformization of publishing would both enable new business models and advance new forms of precarity, making creator solidarity more important than ever.

This chapter examines the impact of e-books on the five-hundred-year-old political economy of publishing, showing how Amazon and Kindle Direct Publishing bypassed many of publishing's middlemen. This boosted romance author income and powered a proliferation of stories by underrepresented authors, who could finally give long-denied happily-ever-afters to a much wider range of characters—Black, gay, lesbian, bisexual, full-figured, middle aged, neuro-divergent, and more. This chapter also probes Romancelandia's advice network more deeply, detailing how open-elite advice patterns fostered innovation. Finally, the chapter explores how a new set of gatekeepers—technology platforms—have given creators new power while also creating new inequalities, demonstrating the ever-growing need for mutual aid among a broad range of platformized workers.

The Rise of E-Books

I bought my first Kindle as soon as it came out in 2007. It was simple—lightweight, white, and gentle on the eyes, thanks to its e-ink technology. The navigation was clunky. No touchscreen, just a curious little thumb-wheel for scrolling. Still, I was completely enchanted. The device had a free internet connection, so I could download anything, anytime, anywhere. Suddenly, books were in the very air, just waiting to be summoned.

That first magical Kindle began as a secret project launched by Jeff Bezos in 2004, who hoped to disrupt publishing the same way Apple had disrupted music.[3] If the project succeeded, books would no longer be passive paper bricks: they would become connected interactive devices, pocket-sized bookstores that could collect customer data, serve up recommendations and advertisements, and offer subscriptions. As a result, Kindles would create far more business opportunities for Amazon than online book retailing ever could.

Other companies saw the possibilities too. Between 2006 and 2010, Sony, Barnes & Noble, and Kobo all released e-readers. In 2010, when Apple launched its iPad, the e-book market finally took off, growing from less than 1 percent of US book sales in 2008 to nearly 10 percent in 2010, reaching almost 25 percent by 2014.[4]

Today, Amazon dominates e-books and much of publishing in general. The company sells 82 percent of all e-books.[5] Some 90 percent of indie e-books are published through KDP (although they may also be published through other services as well).[6] Amazon's own publishing imprints release about a thousand books a year.[7]

E-books transformed romance publishing in two ways. First, authors like Andre and hundreds of others began to self-publish their own books, relying on their historically close relationships with readers to move the books. From 2007 to 2010, KDP authors received 35 percent of each sale, already a huge increase from the 8–10 percent typically offered by traditional romance publishing.[8] Indie authors' cut doubled to 70 percent in 2010 when the iPad debuted, paying indie authors that rate, and prompting Amazon to follow suit. Second, as romance writers pioneered new tactics and gained power in indie books, traditional publishers began to create "digital first" imprints that mimicked self-publishing schedules and began to publish more diverse stories.

Publishing's New Political Economy

For the first time since the invention of moveable type, Amazon and e-readers changed the publishing circuit sketched out by Robert Darnton back in 1982 (see chapter 3). At first, as traditional publishers began to issue e-books, e-readers bypassed printers and bookstores (not entirely, of course, since print books would remain popular). Gradually, as authors like Bella Andre began to publish their own e-books, self-publishing replaced literary agents, editors, and publishers too.[9] Digital self-publishing now gave authors *two* potentially viable business models to choose from—indie or traditional—instead of one (see figure 8.1).

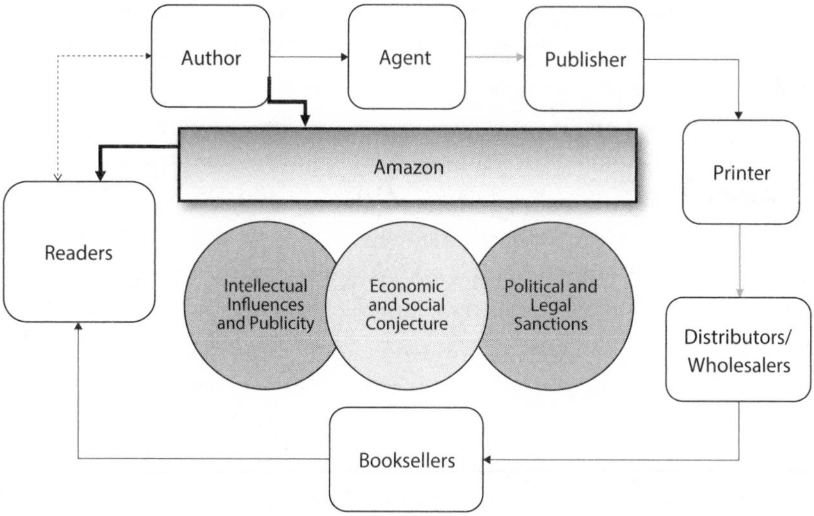

FIGURE 8.1. Indie Shortcut in the Book Publication Circuit,
2007–present, adapted from Darnton (1982)

Romance: The Kindle's Killer App

Every new device needs "a killer app"—an indispensable game or piece of software that people want so badly that they'll go buy new hardware to make it run. In the 1970s, "Space Invaders" drove sales of Atari game consoles. In the 1980s, spreadsheets and word processors were the killer apps sparking personal computer sales. Streaming music spurred iPhone sales. For e-readers, romance novels were the killer app.

Romance readers purchase far more books than most Americans. Almost half of romance readers finish a book per week (the average American reads one book a month).[10] Traditional bookstores had never had enough shelf space to keep up with the demand for new romances, or to stock a wide variety of older ones. As a retailer, Amazon had already made romance much more easily available (in fact, RWA gave Bezos its Vivian Stephens Industry Award in 2000). Now the Kindle promised to give romance readers as many books as they wanted, whenever they wanted.

"It's quite difficult for a bricks-and-mortar store to stock the range and selection these passionate readers want," said Michael Tamblyn, CEO of e-reader maker Kobo, in a 2016 interview with the *New York Times*. "These customers have come much more quickly to digital."[11] He noted that 75 percent of Kobo's most active readers were middle-aged women and proclaimed e-readers to be "the first technological revolution being driven by [those aged] 45 and older."

Initially, there weren't enough e-books available for voracious readers. When the Kindle launched in 2007, it offered only about ninety thousand titles. That may sound like a lot, but it represented less than 4 percent of the 2.5 million print books for sale on Amazon around the same time.[12]

"Here were these brilliant new Kindles and publishers weren't putting enough books out in digital at that point," said author Terri Brisbin, the New Jersey author of Scottish romances and time-travel novels we met in chapter 7. Romance authors like Brisbin, Andre, and thousands more were ready to fill the void.

As we saw in chapter 4, romance authors had spent thirty years developing specific strategies and structures, like the Golden Heart award for unpublished manuscripts, to help them write, finish, and submit polished manuscripts. So, when KDP launched, hundreds of authors had unpublished books already proofread and ready to go. In addition, the sheer volume of romance published every year meant that many books went out of print, with rights reverting to the authors. In 2011, Terri Brisbin uploaded four of her out-of-print novels. None had ever earned more than $4,000. That year, those books made $80,000.

By 2011, a whopping 60 percent of romances sold were e-books.[13] Physical bookstores, and even Amazon, had vastly underestimated demand for romance.

Still, book publishers weren't convinced that e-books fundamentally threatened the age-old book cycle. Even after the proliferation of e-readers in 2006 to 2010, "many people in the industry were happy to take a back seat and wait to see what happened," according to book scholar John B. Thompson.[14]

Untapped Demand: Happily-Ever-Afters for All

In 2008, the year after the Kindle's debut, Harlequin offered a life-changing deal to Brenda Jackson, the Florida insurance executive turned romance author we met in chapters 5 and 6. If Jackson would write for Harlequin exclusively, forsaking all other publishers, Harlequin would pay her enough that both she and her husband could quit their jobs. In negotiating the deal, Jackson made a brilliant move. She retained her rights to self-publish books that Harlequin didn't want.

"I said, there are books my readers want that you all don't want to publish, because they don't fit your guidelines," she told me. Harlequin wanted young, slim heroines. Jackson's fans had been asking her for older characters, full-figured protagonists, and a much wider range of stories than traditional romance gate-keepers acquired. Harlequin agreed, and she launched her own self-publishing venture. "I had many stories I wasn't allowed to write until I started my own company," she said.

KDP and other digital platforms put self-publishing in the hands of authors without the means to start their own companies as Jackson did. They discovered a lucrative market for more diverse stories that "would not have met the approval of traditional, pre-digital gatekeepers," as media economist Joel Waldfogel put it.[15] For years, romance writers had begged publishers to allow a much wider range of characters to enjoy happily-ever-afters: women of color, trans people, lesbians, gay men, queer people, fat people, disabled people, and many others. At long last, indie publishing allowed authors to break the mold. Between 2009 and 2015, the number of romance subcategories, issued by the Book Industry Study Group, grew from eighteen classifications (including African American, historical, and paranormal) to twenty-four classifications. No other fiction genre saw as much growth and change in categories during that time. These categories continued to proliferate, growing to fifty subcategories in 2023, including trans, polyamory, bisexual, and later-in-life.[16]

Long excluded by mainstream publishers, authors of diverse stories experimented early with indie publishing. According to my survey, authors of color were already earning money from self-publishing in 2009, but white authors were not. Even more importantly, as we'll see in the next section, authors of color did so well in this new market that they closed the income gap between themselves and white authors between 2009 and 2014.

Indie Author Income

By 2015, everyone knew that indie romance authors were crushing it. But nobody could prove it. So, in my author survey, I asked fifteen detailed questions about romance-related income for 2009 and 2014 (just before and after e-books took off). I asked how much they made from traditional publishing, indie publishing, and their day jobs if they had them. I asked about their household income, and how much came from writing. I was unbelievably nosy, and hundreds responded anyway.

The Authors Guild, a national writers association, was equally nosy in a similar study at the same time, which included authors of all kinds of books—fiction, nonfiction, and even academic books. I conferred with the Guild's research firm, The Codex Group, and adopted the same methods and analyses so I could compare romance writer income with other authors. Both studies examined authors who reported any book-related income in 2009, even one dollar, even if they didn't earn book income in 2014.[17] This filter left me with a subsample of 668 romance authors. I compared them to the Authors Guild sample of 1,095 fiction and nonfiction authors.

The analysis revealed dramatic differences between romance authors and other writers during the dawn of indie publishing.

- Romance authors' median income from their books **grew an astounding 73 percent** between 2009 and 2014 (see table 8.1).
- Authors Guild respondents' median income from books **decreased 40 percent** at that time.
- In romance publishing, the **racial wage gap was no longer statistically significant** (see table 8.2).
- All of romance authors' increased income can be explained by the introduction of indie publishing: **traditional authors did not see a rise in median income.**
- The authors who saw the greatest income increase were those who published in *both* formats, traditional and indie.

As we've seen time and time again, romance writers do things differently than other authors. They share more information. They're remarkably open about earnings and strategies. They try to bridge gaps between established authors and newcomers. They build unusually strong bonds with their readers. All this correlates with growing income for romance authors.

Above, I mentioned that some authors of color (about 8 percent of the 645 respondents who provided *both* income *and* race data) reported self-publishing income in 2009, while no white authors did. Their success closed the racial income gap. In 2009, white authors' median income from romance publishing was *four times* the median income of authors of color—a statistically significant gap. After the indie revolution, a gap still showed up, but was no longer a statistically significant one (that is, there's no way to tell if the difference in income is real or due to statistical error and to random chance). Authors of color saw their median income increase 150 percent between 2009 and 2014, while white authors' income grew far less—just 63 percent. In short, the e-book revolution helped diverse authors in my survey more than it helped white authors.

What's more, the income gap closed largely because of changes wrought by digital publishing. A closer look at the numbers showed that white authors' median incomes from traditional publishing *dropped* (from $8,000 in 2009 to

TABLE 8.1. Romance Writers' Income Compared to Other Authors' Income, 2009 vs. 2014

Median Income	Median Income, 2009 *	Median Income, 2014	% Change
Romance writers (n=668)	*$5,828*	*$10,100***	*+73%*
Authors Guild (n = 1,095)	*$6,924*	*$3,750*	*−42%*

* 2009 figures are adjusted to 2014 dollars.

** Statistically significant difference; p < 0.001. (Note: I did not have complete access to Authors Guild data so could not run my own significance tests on their figures, but Codex assured me this difference is significant.)

TABLE 8.2. Romance Author Book-Related Median Income by Race, 2009 vs. 2014

	2009*	2014	Increase
Authors of color (n = 51)	*$2,000*	*$5,000***	*150%*
White (n = 594)	*$8,000*	*$13,000*	*63%*
GAP	*x4*	*x2.6*	
Significance	*p < 0.05 (statistically significant)*	*p = 0.11 (not statistically significant)*	

This analysis examines the same authors as Table 8.1 but leaves out twenty-three authors who did not report race / ethnicity.

*Adjusted to 2014 dollars.

$6,100 in 2014), while authors of color held steady, moving from $1,750 to $1,950. Meanwhile, in self-publishing, authors of color saw their median self-published income grow from $2,500 in 2009 to $3,750, while white authors grew from zero to $3,500. (All figures are adjusted to 2014 dollars.)

Why did income from traditional romance drop for white writers? It may relate to the fact that e-books and indie publishing dramatically undermined the mass-market paperback market, with revenues declining some 43 percent in 2020 alone.[18]

The drop in income reflects the impact of indie publishing on publishers, as indie books replaced mass market paperbacks in romance. Because authors of color had enjoyed less opportunity in traditional publishing, they had less to lose from its decline.

Like all research, this analysis has limitations. It relies on authors' self-reported data and only includes RWA members, not all romance writers. As

TABLE 8.3. Median Income from Traditional and Indie Publishing by Race, 2009 and 2014

	2009 (Median)*	2014 (Median)
Traditional publishing income (white authors)	$8,000	$6,100
Traditional publishing income (authors of color)	$1,750	$1,950
Indie income (white authors)	$2,500	$3,750
Indie income (authors of color)	0	$3,500

Adjusted to 2014 dollars.

I discussed in chapter 6, it's possible that less successful or engaged authors did not belong to RWA or did not fill out the survey.

Even so, these are the best existing figures on romance writer income. And the results are very clear: during the e-book revolution, romance authors did better than all other authors. Among romance writers, marginalized authors gained more than white authors.

Romance and Resilience

Bella Andre was just one of many romance authors who benefited from indie publishing. By 2015, she'd sold 4 million e-books, often making $500,000 a month (yes, you read that right: $500,000 *a month*) primarily from her contemporary romance series about the Sullivans. By 2020, she'd sold 10 million books. She'd hit the *New York Times* and *USA Today* bestseller lists ninety-three times. She'd ranked as the #1 author on Amazon and been named one of Apple iBooks' all-time bestsellers, along with Nora Roberts and Nicholas Sparks.

Very few romance authors enjoyed the superstar success of Bella Andre, Barbara Freethy, or other indie sensations. In my survey, 25 percent of respondents earned less than $1,200 from their books in 2014 (conversely, the top 25 percent earned more than $52,800). The *Washington Post's* profile of Bella drove this home with a cheeky aside in all caps: "WE NOW INSERT THIS PUBLIC SERVICE ANNOUNCEMENT BECAUSE WE DO NOT WANT YOU CALLING US WHEN YOUR E-BOOK TANKS."[19]

These unevenly distributed income patterns, where a few make huge sums and most make nothing, are exactly what make romance authors a strong example of most creative and cultural workers. Furthermore, even romance writers with low or modest incomes saw clear improvements from 2009 to 2014. For instance, I found that between 2009 and 2014, the percentage of romance authors earning more than $100,000 nearly doubled, from 9 percent to 17 percent. Similarly, in 2009, only about 22 percent of romance authors in my survey met or exceeded the median income for women (about $34,000). By 2014, 31 percent were meeting or exceeding that benchmark.

With a viable economic alternative to traditional publishers, romance authors found they held more negotiating power. As romantic suspense hybrid author Beth Yarnall told me, "Now my New York publishers are competing with me. What can they do better that I'm not already doing?" As a result of her indie books, her traditional contracts improved. "They tried to say, 'You cannot self-publish in this genre for six months after we publish one of your books,' and I said, 'Nope. That won't work.'"

Traditional Publishing Catches On

Unlike romance authors, most of the traditional publishing world observed the indie phenomenon with vague curiosity, until three events caught the attention of major publishers.

First, in March 2011, the twenty-five-year-old self-published romance author Amanda Hocking struck a four-book deal with St. Martin's Press for more than $2 million. In 2010, Hocking had posted a few unpublished paranormal, young adult manuscripts online, hoping to make $300 so she could attend a Muppets convention in Chicago.[20] One year later, she'd sold a million copies of nine titles, landed an agent, and sold her next series to St. Martin's at auction. Second, in 2012, Random House offered E. L. James $1 million for the rights to publish *Fifty Shades of Grey*, which started as *Twilight*-inspired stories released online by a small Australian publishing website.[21] The book sold 70 million copies, boosting Random House's profits by a staggering 75 percent that year.

Third, in 2014, indie author Barbara Freethy proved that you didn't have to move to a big publisher to get your books into retail bookstores. That year, US book distributor Ingram agreed to distribute Freethy's self-published romances to bookstores.[22] Now readers didn't have to go online to buy her work.

These three authors all proved that romance writers and indie publishing could fundamentally change parts of the traditional publishing industry. Their success drove even more readers to the genre. In 2005, romance represented 17 percent of the overall US fiction market; by 2015, it held an astounding 39 percent of the market, according to a 2016 report by Nielsen.[23] From 1994 to 2008, romance never represented more than 9 percent of books on *USA Today*'s bestseller list. By 2012, romance made up 25 percent of the list.[24] During the indie boom, romance became wildly more popular with the rise of e-books and self-publishing, while other genres, including mystery and sci-fi, lost market share.[25]

Protecting Authors

While most large publishers ignored indie authors for several years after the Kindle's launch, Harlequin closely monitored their success. It seemed even the industry leader had underestimated the public's appetite for romance, especially for diverse stories. In 2009, Harlequin announced a deal with Author Solutions, a self-publishing company with a sketchy reputation. Authors rejected by Harlequin would be offered the option to self-publish under the imprint Harlequin Horizons.[26]

To established romance authors, this smacked of vanity publishing, where authors pay presses, rather than vice versa. Putting the Harlequin name on such a venture would cheapen the significance of being a Harlequin author—an honor that authors already had to defend to skeptics outside Romancelandia. "The whole mess is one big stinking pile of conflict of interest," wrote one commentator on the *All About Romance* blog.[27]

RWA came down hard on Harlequin. "With the launch of Harlequin Horizons, Harlequin Enterprises no longer meets the requirements to be eligible for RWA-provided conference resources," the organization announced.[28] RWA banned Harlequin from editor meetings, book signings, and publisher spotlights at the annual conference where Harlequin had always had a major presence (the company's annual dance party, with free dance socks included, was a perennial favorite). Mystery Writers of America and the Science Fiction and Fantasy Writers of America also issued statements and removed Harlequin from their approved publishers list, meaning that Harlequin authors wouldn't qualify to join either organization.[29]

Harlequin quickly abandoned the deal. But the internal dialogue it prompted in-house led to a new concept: The "digital first" imprint, which would operate more like indie publishing. In 2009, the company launched the first digital imprint from a major publisher—Carina Press—which released e-books only, with the option to add print editions later if the book did well electronically. Unburdened by printing and physical distribution costs, Carina sped up its book publishing schedules. Realizing that romance authors enjoyed indie's higher royalty rates, Carina changed its contracts to offer low or no advances but high royalties. All this lowered the risk associated with acquiring new, unproven authors, allowing Carina and other digital-first imprints to acquire far more diverse authors than other mainstream publishers, including trans romance, male-male, female-female, polyamory, and other themes.

The Self-Publishing Stigma

Despite all this, many authors, both within and outside of Romancelandia, continued to disdain self-publishing, tainted as it was with the stigma of vanity presses. Most publishing insiders continued to view self-publishing as the hack's last resort. Most writers cared deeply about the prestige game of New York publishing, where landing a fancy agent or a big publisher meant they could call themselves "real authors."

"When you talk to other groups like Mystery Writers of America or Sisters in Crime, they were like, 'Self-publishing? That's vanity publishing.' They feel they're not truly a writer unless someone in New York validates it," said author Beth Yarnall, who belonged both to RWA and Mystery Writers of America.

As longtime literary outcasts, romance writers cared far more about what their readers thought than anyone else. "Romance as a genre is stigmatized anyway, so we're used to it. We're just like, 'Eh, self-publishing is just another thing other writers will think is weird. That's OK,'" Yarnall said.

Unlike writing organizations such as Science Fiction Fantasy Writers, which admitted self-published authors as members in 2015, and Mystery Writers of America, which admitted them 2017 (as long as the author had earned at least $5,000 for their indie publication), indie authors had always been accepted as RWA members, since they'd all completed a manuscript. Still, it took RWA a few years to fully embrace self-publishing.

"At first, RWA just didn't recognize self-publishing at all. Self-published books weren't eligible for the RITA contest, and didn't make you eligible for PAN membership," recalls former RWA president Shirley Hailstock. "They viewed it as vanity publishing."

Since 1980, the organization had focused single-mindedly on improving its members' chances of success in a publishing industry that had existed for centuries. Although romance authors at all levels could join, a clear line still existed between published and aspiring writers. In fact, RWA was founded to help authors cross that line. So naturally, some traditional writers looked askance at indie publishing.

A suspicion of new outlets is common in cultural industries. "Participation in the established distribution system is one of the important signs by which art world participants distinguish serious artists from amateurs," wrote Howard Becker.[30] "People who use alternative systems created for those rejected by the regular system, whatever their reason, may mark themselves as non-serious."

Further, romance authors who cared about craft feared self-publishing would open the floodgates to horrifically dreadful prose. Indeed, there's no shortage of ghastly writing in indie romance. (Or in traditional published romance: as *Smart Bitch*'s Sarah Wendell and Candy Tan write, "some romances are utter fucking crap. Complete, utter shittastic fuckcakes of crap with a side order of 'How in the world did I pay actual money for this?'")[31]

The wonder of indie publishing isn't that bad writing exists. It's that so many sparkling stories never would have made it to the bestseller lists otherwise. "No one wanted these books except my readers," said Marie Force at one RWA conference. She became an indie phenomenon with contemporary romances rejected by major publishers.

While RWA members continued to pioneer indie publishing, RWA stayed on the fence. From 2008 to 2011, RWA's national conference program didn't include *any* mention of self-publishing. In 2012, only six out of 144 workshops focused on self-publishing. But by 2014, RWA had fully embraced self-publishing—perhaps because the numbers were hard to argue with, and perhaps because several board members were now either indies or hybrids (authors who publish both traditionally and independently).

In 2014, fully 25 percent of national conference workshops addressed self-publishing issues, ranging from cover design to publicity, from foreign rights to self-published audiobook production. Over the next few years, Bella Andre, Barbara Freethy, and other well-known indie authors became regular speakers at the conference. As Andre cheerfully told the crowd at one session I attended, "I've lost tens of thousands of dollars screwing up foreign translations, so you don't have to!"

Learning Together

The public loves an overnight success story and as the indie boom exploded, the media churned out breathless stories of superstars. But as we've seen, in reality, Romancelandia spent some thirty years building structures and practices that fueled this success. In interview after interview, authors told me how much Romancelandia's tradition of advice sharing and mutual aid helped them succeed in the new indie world.

"Today, there's a lot more information out there about how to do this," Andre told me. "Back then, it was like making fire with sticks. We had to figure everything out ourselves."

But in Romancelandia, nobody's ever alone for long. Soon Bella started swapping notes with other indie authors. "RWA had connected me with a network of really intelligent, experienced women," Andre told me. "My brain trust became Tina Folsom and Barbara Freethy"—two other Northern California authors.

As interest grew around self-publishing, both experienced and aspiring indie authors would gather in person whenever possible. Before big official conferences like RWA or Novelists, Inc., indie authors held their own "unconferences," booking a hotel ballroom and discussing indie issues. "We had one in San Francisco, and Bella talked about the importance of metadata in book blurbs to make books show up in search algorithms," Courtney Milan told me. Another author explained how a newsletter link in the back of her books dramatically increased her marketing reach. Theresa Ragan, an indie author near Sacramento whose books had been rejected for nearly twenty years, flew to a Mexican resort with nine authors she'd never met in person to brainstorm how to get on bestseller lists—which they all managed to do within the year. The Author Support Network, an indie-advice Facebook group started by Marie Force, now boasts more than eight thousand members.

Almost all the writers I interviewed pointed to Romancelandia's generosity in helping them adapt to the world of e-books.

"Maybe it's because we celebrate relationships and love," Roxanne St. Claire told me. "The whole sense of giving a hand-up to each other and sharing what we've learned just never changed."

Andre agrees. "The networks of female authors are very strong. I think this is a reason you don't see the same success with mystery and thriller writers. Men are like, 'I hold my cards close to my chest.' Women are like, 'Whatever. Here are my secrets. The biggest is you just have to work really hard.'"

And work hard she did. Andre started looking for new markets and new ways to find readers for her rapidly growing backlist. She entered the audiobook market, hiring a Broadway star to record her books. She broke into foreign markets, after figuring out how to release translations in Germany, France, and Italy. Along the way, she constantly turned to other authors for support.

"I have a group of six other writers, and we'd go away every six months or so together, and work out plots and talk about marketing," she told me. She started a series called the Maverick Billionaires with a writer friend, Jennifer Skully.

Other indie writers also started exploring the benefits of collaboration. Some launched multi-author miniseries where each author writes one of the books. Others teamed up on anthologies in order to share their readers. For instance, four Latina authors—Alexis Daria, Priscilla Oliveras, Sabrina Sol, and Mia Sosa—launched a Facebook group about romance called 4 Chicas Chat and helped promote each other's books. The four Chicas, plus three other authors (Adriana Herrera, Diana Muñoz Stewart, and Zoey Castile) self-published an anthology in 2021 called *Amor Actually*.

All these strategies helped indie authors produce content at a faster rate. The more books they had, the more money they could make—and the more fun they had, as *Romance Writers Report* noted in a 2012 article.

> Self-publishing has become an attractive option, but it takes a lot of time, research and energy if you do it alone. But do you have to do it alone? No. You can create not only wonderful stories, but also work with other authors toward the common goal of earning a good living from those stories and boldly go into brave new publishing worlds.[32]

Even with help from her indie colleagues, Bella Andre knew she couldn't keep up her twelve-hour days forever. Like many other indies, she recruited other people to take on tasks once filled by traditional publishers, including editing and marketing. In fact, an entire shadow publishing industry of freelance editors, proofreaders, cover designers, and marketers has sprung up to serve indie authors.[33]

In my survey, 20 percent of indie authors and 28 percent of hybrid authors (who had published both as indies and with traditional companies) employed at least one paid assistant helping with formatting, social media, or marketing, compared with roughly 15 percent of traditionally published authors. Some of these assistants work freelance, others for production groups run by romance authors themselves. Marie Force, for instance, launched a service called Formatting Fairies to help authors with cover design, editing, and uploading. Others, like Kathryn Le Veque, started their own publishing companies to publish other authors. These ventures provide another way for romance writers to promote mutual aid, helping others while helping themselves.

Networking Down

Throughout the book, I've argued that romance writers' unusual open-elite networks helped spread information and foster innovation. I've supported that claim through interviews, archival research, and comparisons with other writing organizations.

But all this evidence is anecdotal. For a more systematic look at the network, I set out to analyze romance authors' advice networks to see if newcomers and established authors really were sharing information as fluidly as they said. I described the first step of this analysis in chapter 6, where I examined cliquing patterns based on race, income, geography, genre, and other factors. With important caveats, the network appeared to be surprisingly open, with advice shared across all these attributes. To find out if open-elite practices correlated with innovation, I would need to do a more complicated social network analysis. Inspired by Romancelandia, I reached out for advice.

Seeking Advice on Advice

On a sunny day in 2016, I sat in an outdoor cafe on the Stanford campus, drinking coffee with anthropologist Elspeth Ready, whom I mentioned in chapter 6. Ready, an outdoorsy blonde from Canada, is the Indiana Jones of social networking. For her dissertation, she'd spent nearly a year living in an Inuit community, studying how climate change affects food sharing networks. She'd lived with an Inuit family, learned handicrafts, and spent days foraging and fishing. I'd sought her out because she knows more than most people on earth about communities and sharing.

What do romance writers and Inuit fishing villages have in common? They both trade in valuable resources that promote well-being—advice and food, respectively. These commodities can be shared widely in the community. Or they can be hoarded for personal advantage.

I told Ready about my data. In my survey, I'd asked respondents to name the three people they most often asked for advice. (I discussed this in chapter 6, where I explained just one part of our network analysis, which dealt with race and cliquing factors.) As I mentioned earlier, 749 people had answered that question (about 64 percent of survey respondents). They provided 4,615 advisor names. About a quarter of those advisors had also responded to my survey, so I knew a lot about them, including age, income, race, type of publishing, and more. Ready seemed intrigued. She agreed to help explore the data, looking for advice patterns that might explain romance writers' success at innovation. (For more on our methodology, see the appendix, and also the paper she and I published in 2022.)[34]

We set out to find whether newcomer authors and elite, published authors really did form advice ties. Would the network's elite core (in this case, authors who had already established themselves in traditional publishing before the rise of e-books) form strategic ties with newcomers in ways that help them both?

The answer was yes. We found that:

- Although we expected that newcomers would ask the most advice, in fact, all groups were equally likely to ask for advice.
- The most active advice seekers were elite authors who published both in traditional and in indie formats. Their active advice seeking correlated with innovation.
- These innovative, elite members were more likely to ask advice from newcomers than from traditionally published elites.

Birds of a Feather, Fresh Blood, and Innovation

Here's an overview of how we explored the network.

We started out with three basic facts well-explored in the social network literature. First, networks tend to have "structural holes," an absence of connection between people who have different knowledge and might be able to help each other.[35] Second, creating "bridging ties" that span structural holes is "notoriously difficult,"[36] according to communication professor William Barley, because people often don't share a common vocabulary, communication style, habit of mind, or mutual trust.[37] In other words, as I mentioned in chapter 6, birds of a feather flock together—it's easier to form cohesive ties with people of similar backgrounds and experience. It takes a lot of effort to overcome this tendency toward homophily.[38]

Third, it's often worth the effort to invest the relational labor to form such ties, because the most innovative networks include an evenly distributed balance of cohesive and bridging ties. The cohesive ties extend the community's values and practices (like the ethic of care), while bridging ties introduce "fresh blood" and new ideas (like indie publishing). For instance, one study of Broadway musicals from 1945 to 1989 showed that productions achieved more "artistic success" when the production team included a mix of longtime collaborators and new members with new ideas.[39]

All this suggests that the secret to romance writers' success in digital self-publishing related to the balance of cohesive and bridging ties within the network. A network that valued mentoring, meeting all members' needs, and forming relationships would lower the relational labor costs involved in creating diverse ties. At conference hotel bars, on message boards, and on author

Facebook pages, it would be easier to acquire diverse advice if elites and newcomers were already in the habit of sharing information back and forth. That would explain why information about an innovative form of publishing would spread so quickly in this unusual network structure.

To test this theory, we compared two groups. We called the elite core *established authors*. This group included all writers who had already published before indie publishing exploded in 2010 (some of them had also started self-publishing since). Our newcomer group we dubbed *aspiring authors*. They hadn't published before 2010.

Within these two groups, authors fell into one of three categories: Established authors could be either *indies* (meaning they'd self-published as well as traditionally published), or *traditionals* (who only traditionally published). Newcomers might have published as either *indies* or *traditionals,* or they could be *unpublished*. Even though they might have some publishing experience, they were still newbies compared to the elite group.

We examined how often these different groups sought advice. In most networks, you'd expect newcomers, who need to learn the ropes, to ask advice more than anyone else. Surprisingly, this was not the case. *All* published authors, aspiring or established, were equally likely to ask for advice (see table A.2 in the appendix).[40]

Then we looked at who sought advice from whom. We hypothesized that established authors who formed bridging ties with aspiring authors were most likely to give self-publishing a try, because they'd be exposed to new knowledge. On the other hand, they might have already tried self-publishing and be seeking advice on doing it better.

We found that established indie authors were *much more* active in asking for advice than any other group. They hadn't stopped asking for advice just because they'd already successfully published. And they were more likely to ask for advice from newcomers, rather than their established, traditionally published peers, even though they had "come up together" over the years.

We called this pattern where elite, established authors ask newcomers for advice "networking down." Elite authors who networked down reminded us of the high-born Florentine families I described in chapter 3, who strategically married into upstart families with no social standing and bolstered their illustrious positions by absorbing new accounting and business strategies.[41]

Fittingly enough, in 2015, a group of indie romance authors self-published a book about self-publishing. Coauthor Jane Graves summed up the value of open-elite networking: "It's a wake-up call when you realize you don't know the first thing about self-publishing. . . . Suddenly I was the newbie, hanging on the words of successful indie authors and hoping some of their wisdom and experience rubbed off on me."[42]

All this work by established Indies—building bridging ties, offering advice, proactively building community—paid off. Established indies saw their income more than double between 2009 and 2014, while established traditionals saw no change.

This analysis shares all the caveats I've mentioned earlier. It's self-reported information and it only describes the subset of authors who answered the advice question. In addition, we only asked for three names, so advice networks might look different if we'd left the question open-ended. Plus, social network analyses in general tend to be a little shallow: they offer one snapshot of a set of relationships at one moment in time. For deeper information about the kind of advice people asked for, how often they asked, and what they learned, I had to rely on the interview data and archival research I've presented in earlier chapters.

Even so, it's clear that a great deal of advice and information sharing circulates among romance authors with different levels of experience. The network's open-elite structure made a two-way exchange of information easy, lowering the relational labor costs of bridging structural holes. As historical romance author Donna McMeans put it when we talked:

> Self-published authors teach me about advertising, promoting myself, how to time my release dates. I'm learning from newer members about technology, and I teach them about craft. It's a two-way network.

The Platformization of Publishing

By 2015, indie publishing had become a legitimate, accepted route to success for romance authors, on par with traditional publishing. This gave authors more choices and more negotiating power, while also pushing traditional publishers to offer stories with characters of a wide array of ethnic and racial backgrounds, sexual orientations, gender identities, abilities, and body types. Authors became more secure and less precarious, earning more, writing a wider array of stories with a broader spectrum of protagonists, and capable of choosing indie or traditional routes.

But while authors gained more power against publishers, they faced a new and different power imbalance with Amazon. By the late 2010s, Amazon's influence in publishing had grown inexorably. Its massive collection of consumer data gave it a huge advantage in publicizing its own books from its publishing line. It also used that data to sell ads to publishers and authors. For instance, authors could buy ads on the opening screen of the Kindle and Kindle Fire for about $35,000. Amazon also sold ads on its retail site, displaying sponsored items before products better fitting the consumer's search.

Through these and other means, the Kindle helped Amazon become the world's largest, and most secretive, clearinghouse of data on book buyers and sales. Every purchase or online interaction provided Amazon with more data about how to market books, while also powering related businesses, like ad sales and book promotion. Other Amazon initiatives—like Kindle Unlimited with its automated narration feature that undermined indie audiobook sales and its no-questions-asked return policy for audiobooks—threatened to take money from authors' pockets. RWA met with Amazon over important issues, lobbying for algorithms that don't obscure Black authors, for instance, but the company still responded sluggishly to complaints of plagiarism and book stuffing (a scam to game Amazon's pay-per-page-read payment system for Kindle Unlimited). Many indie authors said it was impossible to get a person on the phone to repost books that had been erroneously removed.

Meanwhile, the book industry struggled to make sense of Amazon's impact on publishing revenues, because the company refused to share sales data. There's no reliable way to estimate the size of the indie market, or to glean many other important statistics about the book industry.

"The primary reason we do not have deep data and transparency about e-book sales, in both units and dollars, is because of Amazon," wrote Michael Cader, founder of industry newsletter *Publisher's Lunch*. "They keep their data private for competitive advantage in the marketplace, plain and simple." He argued that the lack of transparency should be a "rallying cry" for authors and publishers alike. "In this digital age, we don't see why authors should have to be in the dark about real sales on the site that works so hard to secure their trust as the *exclusive* venue where their product is sold."[43]

Romance authors' complaints echoed those of other platformized creators, like YouTubers, Instagram influencers, and Twitch streamers. For instance, in the 2016 YouTube "adpocalypse," major advertisers bailed out when they discovered their ads running alongside controversial or offensive content. YouTube changed its ad policies and algorithms to be more family friendly, and many content creators lost ad revenues as their streams became demonetized. They had no easy resource for reinstatement if YouTube erroneously defunded them. Such incidents demonstrate how platform businesses generate many conflicts of interest. Authors may be interested in making their books easy to find, but Amazon is also interested in selling advertising, so it benefits from the clutter. Because Amazon has its own e-book imprints, including the Montlake romance imprint, indie authors and publishers are competing against Amazon—which holds all sales data about all books from all publishers on its site, a huge marketing advantage. Amazon wants to sell its streaming book service Kindle Unlimited to customers, generating regular monthly revenue, which can devalue books and dissuade readers from buying individual books (a better deal for authors). Through all this, Amazon collects, uses, and resells "astonishing levels of data" from different customer groups, according to the Association of American Publishers.[44] It also controlled the algorithms that made books—including its own products—visible to readers.

The potential for conflicts of interest in a platform model were immediately apparent to authors. For one, Amazon's secrecy about algorithms gives its books an advantage over authors and publishers. Even hugely profitable indie authors with their own Amazon reps don't know how the search algorithms work. "The reps are good for certain things," Tina Folsom, superstar indie author of vampire romance, told me. "But trying to get information about algorithms? Their eyes glaze over like they didn't hear you. If they told us, they'd probably have to kill us."

All this puts romance authors, like other platformized content producers, in a position of what communication scholar Brooke Duffy calls "algorithmic precarity,"[45] a dependence on platforms that could decimate their visibility and income with a single algorithm tweak. Algorithms, like AI, tend to reinforce preexisting cultural patterns, so they often make it harder to find marginalized authors. "As a Black author on Amazon, it's harder to find my books," LaQuette, former RWA president, told me. "If you type in my name, you'll find three or four books by white women before you actually see a book of mine," she said. I did. She was right.

Amazon's recommendation function posed the same problem, LaQuette told me: "In the recommendations, white authors appear on my pages. I don't appear on theirs." Research by Safiya Noble and others confirms how search engines could reinforce and reproduce racism.[46] Biased algorithms, in essence, were playing the same role as bookstores that shelved Black romance authors in the African American section rather than the romance section. Both made marginalized authors less visible.

Streaming Books

By the late 2010s, authors were becoming increasingly disillusioned with Amazon's tactics that worked to devalue books. In 2014, the company launched Kindle Unlimited, a streaming service that allowed members to borrow a virtually infinite number of books for $9.95 a month. Rather than receiving 70 percent of sales, indie authors are paid "per page read," dividing a monthly pool of money allocated by Amazon from its subscription fees. Each author's share of the pool depends on how many of their pages are read (generally, payment adds up to about half a penny per page).[47] To participate, authors have to list their books exclusively on Amazon, rather than "going wide" and selling on all e-book platforms.

Some authors love Kindle Unlimited because it helps them find new fans. "These are readers who are on a budget and who love to read," said indie author Kathryn Le Veque. "I've been able to do what I call double-dipping, because people find my books in Kindle Unlimited and love them, and then go and buy them."

Still, even authors who do well with Kindle Unlimited sometimes view it with suspicion. They worry that an all-you-can-read approach trains readers to think of books as free media, like music or movies have become. They worry that Amazon will drive other booksellers out of business, then pay authors less. Even more, they worry that the streaming model gives more power to the service than the writer. On Kindle Unlimited, Amazon makes money from attracting subscribers, not selling books. Authors *might* make more money through Kindle Unlimited if subscribers read books they wouldn't have bought otherwise. But with more than a million books available on Kindle Unlimited, visibility has become a fierce battle, making advertising a necessity for many indie authors (and another revenue stream for Amazon).

Meanwhile, authors also have to worry about system gamers. Some unscrupulous authors boost their "pages read" count by inserting many, many pages of unnecessary text, so that their readers have to flip through to get to the material they want. One book stuffer, for instance, offered to enter readers in a drawing for diamonds from Tiffany & Co. if they paged through all the excess content.[48] Because Kindle Unlimited authors all receive a share from a common pool, successful book stuffers take money away from legitimate authors. Ironically, Amazon benefits from all this clutter. The more books they offer, the more attractive the service looks to customers and the more important it becomes for authors and publishers to buy advertising—from Amazon.

Gorilla Hugs

Amazon's market dominance is characteristic of platform businesses, which tend to become monopolies because of "network effects"—the more people who join a network, the more valuable that network becomes. When there are benefits to everyone using a single platform, that platform often becomes a monopoly.[49] Not surprisingly, Amazon has been embroiled in multiple antitrust lawsuits.[50]

All this leads romance authors to see Amazon as an untrustworthy ally—one that gives thousands of authors the chance to publish and earn money, but one that can just as easily vaporize their incomes with a single algorithm tweak. In my interviews, authors called Amazon "a horrible monster," "spreading rot," and "completely untrustworthy."

"It feels like you're a tiny kitten adopted by a giant gorilla," Courtney Milan told me. She was quoting her friend, romance author Bree Bridges (who writes with Donna Herren under the pen name Kit Rocha). "You're happy that it's petting you, but it could crush you at any time."

At the same time that Amazon opened up exciting new opportunities for romance authors, it also created new kinds of precarity.

Happily Ever After?

Bella Andre's reinvention, from musician to blockbuster indie author, would have made any economist proud. And in fact, it did: her father, Alvin Rabushka, a well-known economist at Stanford, came to my dissertation defense, where I presented many of the facts I've just discussed.

"I'm pretty sure I've never had a research subject's father show up at a defense," one of my committee members mused.

Andre did many things right. She's a terrific writer; she asked for and gave advice; her long days and prolific pace gave her customers more and more books to purchase. She also excels at relational labor. A naturally social person, she's quickly built warm relationships with near strangers (like readers, or, say, researchers like me). And her easy accessibility and eagerness to share information attests to Romancelandia's ethic of care.

But she *also* succeeded because she was in the perfect place at the perfect time, at the convergence of several major long-term social changes, including the digital disruption of cultural production, the rise of new communication forms, and evolving political economies of work and gender. The pieces of the puzzle came together at just the right moment for her, and for hundreds of other romance writers in my study.

Many cultural producers in other media experienced similar patterns. Social media influencers, YouTubers, Twitch streamers, and others suddenly found income and careers based on technology platforms that connected them to audiences. A broader group of platform workers including rideshare drivers also found that platforms could provide an income.

At the same time, along with romance writers, many creators have encountered precarity because of the lack of transparency offered by these platforms, their seemingly arbitrary policy changes, the difficulty in reaching a human being to solve issues, and other frustrations resulting from power asymmetries. At a time when platforms have created unprecedented opportunities for creators to reach fans and make money, they also threaten to make creators' livelihoods ever more precarious.

Romancelandia's success in building alternative, caring forms of self-organization offers a compelling alternative not just to the way authors work, or cultural producers work, but to the way we think about business, careers, and work life. But as we'll see, without identity-aware care that addresses the needs of everyone in the group, not just the majority or the successful, creators risk sacrificing their solidarity and their power—at the very moment when rising platform precarity makes the stakes of solidarity higher than ever.

9

#RWAShitShow

CARE'S FAILURE AND REPAIR

ON DECEMBER 23, 2019, I stared at my phone in disbelief. A Tweet from bestselling African American historical author Alyssa Cole was blowing up on Twitter. But at first, it didn't make any sense to me. Cole wrote:

> One of the reasons I believed in RWA was because I saw how hard my friend, Courtney Milan, worked to push the organization's inclusiveness. Today, the day before Christmas Eve, RWA notified her they'd agreed with ethics complaints filed against her for calling out racism.[1]

As a result of the decision, Milan had been expelled from RWA for a year and banned from all future leadership positions.

Wait ... what??

For at least five years, Milan, who is Chinese American, had championed RWA's push for inclusion. Many of the reforms I described in chapter 6 rose directly or indirectly from her presence on the RWA board from 2014 to 2018. As a pioneer of digital self-publishing, she'd also given a voice to indie authors in the organization. She'd recently won an RWA service award for her work on diversity issues.

The board's decision seemed inexplicable to me. How could Milan be thrown out after all the important work she'd done? But to many, the reasons behind the decision seemed all too obvious: RWA's promises to change had been lip service, they concluded. This was retaliation for Milan's advocacy.

Within twenty-four hours of Cole's tweet, Romancelandia responded with a collective "*WTF?!?!*"

A hashtag, #IStandwithCourtney, swept through Twitter like wildfire. The RWA board backpedaled, rescinding the penalty on December 24, but the damage was done. Thanks in part to Milan's diversity efforts, nearly half the board members were now authors of color. All eight of them resigned in protest. Like dominos, the RWA president, president-elect, and new executive director resigned. Over the next few weeks, the 2020 RITA Awards were canceled. Publishers and sponsors dropped their RWA sponsorships. Chapters disaffiliated. Thousands of members resigned. Within weeks, this longstanding central pillar of Romancelandia had crumbled.

Unlike so many other RWA conflicts over the years, this one caught fire in the national media. The *New York Times*, the *Washington Post*, and many other outlets reported on the scandal. In many ways, they noted, the meltdown reflected a much larger story—the escalation of America's simmering racial tensions, political polarization, and culture wars that had escalated since Donald Trump took office in 2016. As Black contemporary author LaQuette Holmes put it to me, "RWA is a microcosm of this country."

That never seemed clearer than during the #RWAShitShow of 2019–2020.

A Crisis of Care

In the introduction to this book, I argued that if you want corporations to treat you fairly, you need a united community. But if you want a united community, that community, in turn, needs to treat all its members fairly. So far, much of this book has supported the first part of that argument. I've tried to show how historically specific social, political, and economic forces created conditions that shaped Romancelandia into a unique female-dominated business enclave, stressing an ethic of care and mutual aid. I've shown how that ethic gave rise to an open-elite network, a structure historically associated with innovation. It encouraged well-established authors and newcomers to share advice, quickly spreading information about digital self-publishing. Along the way, the network, formalized in RWA, lobbied successfully to improve romance authors' rights, even though not all authors benefited uniformly from its victories.

The second part of my argument has surfaced time and time again throughout this book: If you want a united community, you need to treat everyone equitably. This final chapter shows what's at stake when that doesn't happen—not just in Romancelandia, but in many other organizations, associations, professions, and even the United States in general. Without an ethic of care that tries to recognize and meet the needs of its entire community, not just those of the dominant group, collective action and mutual aid become increasingly out of reach, often at times when unity is needed most.

For romance authors working in platformized publishing, the meltdown couldn't have come at a worse time. As technology platforms gain unprecedented power over communication and cultural production, solidarity among solo creators is more important now than ever.

This chapter starts by summarizing the #RWAShitShow. It calls out how a color-blind ethic of care hurt marginalized authors while also undermining white authors' trust in the organization. It follows romance writers' attempts, especially by authors of color, to build a new and improved RWA 2.0, and concludes with a reminder of the high stakes of solidarity in the platform era.

The #RWAShitShow

For forty years, Romancelandia has reflected major shifts in US society, interpreting and adapting to technological, social, and economic changes. As we saw in chapter 6, this country's long-overdue reckoning with abiding social injustices, and expanding divides between groups, reached deep into RWA. In the 2010s, across the country, trust in institutions like government and the media reached an all-time low.[2] After Trump's 2016 election, hate crimes increased.[3] So did protests against police violence and other forms of social injustice.[4] A 2019 Pew poll revealed deepening divides in racial attitudes—a majority of white people (62 percent) thought the country had already done enough to advance racial equality. Only a small minority of Black people (22 percent) agreed.[5]

As we saw in chapter 6, in the mid-2010s, creators in many media industries, including film, children's fiction, and romance, increasingly called attention to bias and exclusion, with hashtags like #OscarsSoWhite and #WeNeedDiverseBooks. In romance, marginalized authors and their allies called attention to bias in the RITA Awards and lobbied publishers for more inclusive stories. Marginalized authors formed their own networks within and outside of RWA. On Twitter, on romance blogs and podcasts, on Discord servers and group chats, Romancelandians engaged in extensive examinations of issues like institutional racism in the publishing industry.

In the summer of 2019, this long-running conversation focused on a start-up publisher called Glenfinnan.[6] One of Glenfinnan's editors, Sue Grimshaw, had spent a decade as the romance buyer for Borders. Some authors noted the chain had a reputation for relegating Black romance to African American shelves, not romance.[7] They also noted that on Twitter, Grimshaw had liked right-wing and racist Twitter posts, including one that called white supremacy a liberal hoax.

"There was a consistent pattern to the tweets Grimshaw liked," wrote romance scholar Laura Vivanco on the *Teach Me Tonight* romance blog.[8] Carolyn Jewel, then president of RWA, shared that she'd blocked Grimshaw's Twitter feed because she found it full of "likes of hateful, racist tweets."[9]

After tweets called attention to the pattern, Grimshaw lost her job at a publishing house and moved to Glenfinnan. Contributing to the Twitter conversation, Courtney Milan took a closer look at the start-up and raised concerns about another editor, Kathryn Lynn Davis. Davis had written a book in 1999, which had recently been reissued, called *Somewhere Lies the Moon*. Milan tweeted that the book was a "fucking racist mess" rife with "standard racist tropes" and stereotypes about Chinese women—the kinds of stereotypes that "get women like me assaulted and harassed," she wrote.[10] Her concern, she told me later, was less about Davis's book than about institutional bias that occurs when stereotypes embed themselves in organizations like Glenfinnan.

In August 2019—just a month after Milan received the RWA service award—Davis accused Milan of cyberbullying and filed four ethics complaints against Milan, including harassment and engaging in conduct "injurious to RWA." In a long letter, Davis claimed she had lost a three-book contract as a result of Milan's posts. Suzan Tisdale, owner of Glenfinnan, filed similar complaints.

For the next several months, the case moved forward. An ethics panel was formed to investigate; it presented a summary of the case to the board of directors in December. Most of the claims were rejected: RWA's code of ethics clearly stated that social media disagreements and harsh book reviews did *not* violate the ethics policy. But the panel recommended Milan be censured for conduct injurious to RWA.

Board members later called the panel's report "nebulous," lacking examples and evidence. Several said they felt pressured to vote on faith, without a full understanding of the case. Nevertheless, in a 10–5 decision with one abstention, the board sided against Milan.[11]

In January, an independent audit would vindicate Milan, ruling the outcome "unjustified."[12] But for now, the board suspended Milan's membership and banned her from future leadership positions.

The decision and the subsequent Twitter storm left everyone astonished, confused, and angry. Many members believed the decision resulted from personal rancor toward Milan, in retaliation for her constant prodding for greater diversity within RWA. Davis walked back her claim that she'd lost a book contract and said she felt RWA had used her to penalize Milan.[13] RWA hired law firm Pillsbury Winthrop Shaw Pittman to conduct an audit of the case.

After reviewing all related documents and interviewing twenty-one people, including Tisdale, Davis, Milan, ethics committee members, and board members, the firm issued a fifty-eight-page audit, finding the board's decision "an unjustified outcome" based on "deficiencies in RWA's policies and procedures" and "inadequate understanding by Board members of their role and obligations under RWA's governance structure."[14] In other words, RWA's ethics code was a patched-together hodgepodge of unenforceable strictures. While informal networking and family feeling had glued the group together, too much informality resulted in slipshod governance.

Nevertheless, many members considered the Milan affair as the last straw, the ultimate proof that RWA could never change. While the law firm audit specifically said that personal rancor wasn't a factor in the decision, and that the implosion resulted from bungled procedures, poorly written policies, and a lack of legal consultation, that explanation seemed superficial to critics. It was unlikely, they noted, that thousands of members would have resigned had RWA, and the publishing industry more generally, addressed the shortcomings of color-blind care earlier and more deeply.

Color-Blind vs. Identity-Aware Care

When I shared the story of the RWA meltdown with friends and colleagues, several of them visibly shuddered. RWA could easily be their own professional organization or employer, they confided. Associations around the country were grappling with diversity and inclusion, but one study of eight hundred US companies concluded that most organizations were just "going through the motions," making requisite nods to diversity without real change.[15] Corporations and organizations run by white people would be unlikely to invest in deep change, after all, since, as we saw above, most white people believe enough progress has been made on racism, while most Black people do not.[16]

This divide led RWA members on both sides of the issue to resign en masse. Membership dropped from around nine thousand people in 2019 to 3,300 in 2022. Some members quit because they didn't believe RWA could change. Others, because they didn't *want* RWA to change. As journalist Lois Beckett noted in a deeply reported *Guardian* story in 2019, some authors thought RWA should be a no-man's land, free of politics. "If we're all divisive, divisive, divisive, we're screwed," one white member said. Black contemporary romance author Kianna Alexander responded that in the era of Donald Trump, "there was no space where she could avoid politics."[17] This exchange exemplifies the way color-blind care undermines unity: some white authors tried to deemphasize division and conflicts between groups, smoothing over problems that didn't seem to affect them deeply and that they didn't really see.

In their book #*Hashtag Activism: Networks of Race and Gender Justice*, media scholars Sarah Jackson, Moya Bailey, and Brooke Foucault Welles summarize the problem with such "color-blind narratives." When "I don't see color" is stated as a positive affirmation, they argue, there's an underlying assumption that the goals of inclusion and diversity have already been achieved.[18] This view dovetails with neoliberal feminism, discussed in chapter 7, which presumes that gender inequality has disappeared. Neoliberal feminism's emphasis on individual choice and happiness over collective action also permeates color-blind racism. Eduardo Bonilla-Silva notes that color-blind racism places the onus on the individual, rather than society, to overcome barriers.[19] Both these trends assume that if equality hasn't fully been achieved yet, it's just a matter of time. As contemporary Black romance author C. Chilove explained this misconception to me, "It's like Martin Luther King Jr. held a march and then we could all sit at the counter."

At first blush, color-blind narratives seem well-meaning because they acknowledge that all people are created equal. However, "color-blind" usually ends up meaning a default to the white experience: This view fails to recognize how barriers, challenges, and responsibilities are *not* distributed equally. A color-blind mindset "perpetuate[s] the invisibility of members of counter publics"[20]—that is, underrepresented, misrepresented groups outside white, straight, cisgender culture. It is literally blind to the needs of people outside the dominant group.

Adding insult to injury, the cover of the January 2020 *Romance Writers Report*—just one month after the #RWAShitShow began—literally illustrated how color-blind care misrepresents racial dynamics. In a cartoon graphic, a white woman climbs a mountain slope, while reaching down to help a Black woman toward the peak. In a color-blind view, it's a picture of two people helping each other climb a mountain. In an approach that acknowledges racial dynamics, however, it implies that Black writers must depend on white benevolence to achieve equality—the classic "white savior" trope.

One alternative to color-blind care is what journalism scholar Sue Robinson calls "identity-aware care." This kind of care recognizes that important aspects of people's identities—including race, ethnicity, language, sexual orientation, profession—powerfully influence their life experiences, their interpretations of the world, their opportunities, and their values. Drawing on intersectionality theory, which examines how intersecting aspects of identity create unique experiences of oppression,[21] identity-aware care proactively acknowledges that different community members need different kinds of support to reach the same goals. As RWA and greater Romancelandia discovered, collective action and mutual aid are only possible when everyone gets what they need to achieve a shared outcome.

Not surprisingly, this process of instilling identity-aware values struck some (white) members as excessive and potentially divisive. They feared it undermined solidarity in Romancelandia. Those who mentioned such views publicly were quickly called out on social media. Trust and goodwill eroded as the organization continued to blunder and as social media cast national attention on every misstep.

After the RWA implosion, it was clear that the organization and its traditions simply couldn't continue without the development of robust identity-aware care. Many members felt it was already too late. Over the next several months, as the nation suddenly entered the COVID-19 lockdown, thousands of RWA members would resign and dozens of chapters would disaffiliate. The future of RWA hung in the balance.

Rebooting the Network

In December 2019, LaQuette Holmes, author of contemporary Black romance, was ready to put her feet up. She was days away from ending her term as president of RWA's New York City chapter. As chapter president, she'd spent two years pushing hard for diversity in romance. She'd organized a summit in Manhattan for Black authors and major publishers. In July, she'd delivered a showstopping speech on inclusion at RWA's landmark 2019 annual awards ceremony. She'd taken part in the standing ovation as three authors of color finally won RITAs.

So, as Christmas approached in 2019, LaQuette felt she'd done her part. She was ready to turn her attention back to her family and her new contracts with Harlequin and St. Martin's Press. Even better, her good friend C. Chilove was also wrapping up her term as president of RWA's Cultural, Interracial and Multicultural Special Interest Chapter. "We were planning on riding off into the sunset," LaQuette told me.

Then came the #RWAShitShow, undermining literally years of work that LaQuette, C. Chilove, Adriana Herrera, Patricia Oliveras, Farrah Rochon, and many authors of color had put into making RWA more inclusive.

Throughout January, romance writers of color conferred over email, text, Twitter, and phone calls, deliberating over next steps.

"We were actually thinking about starting our own thing," C. Chilove told me. "But we also knew how much RWA had benefited us. It helped me get those deals. Thinking of the people coming behind us, we knew we had to do something."

By February 2020, the lingering remnants of the former board had resigned to make way for a new special election. LaQuette and C. Chilove joined the board. Alyssa Day, a former attorney and RWA board member, who is white, agreed to serve as interim president until regular elections could be held. "If it had not been for Alyssa, I don't think much would have been accomplished," Chilove told me. "She had been on the board, so she understood protocol and procedure. She was able to steer that ship, as tumultuous as the storm was, because she had had that previous experience."

In March 2020, the new board took office. One third of new board members were women of color. On RWA's professional staff, a new executive director, Leslie Scantlebury, who is Black, took the helm, calling for "an RWA 2.0 that is equitable and inclusive, where our members from marginalized communities feel like they belong."[22]

By now, though, much of Romancelandia had lost faith in the change-from-within approach. Thousands of members resigned. By 2022, membership had plunged by more than half to 3,316. By this point, many members simply didn't think RWA could be fixed.

"The conclusion I came to in January of last year was that I don't care about RWA anymore because they can't possibly get rid of all the racists," Courtney Milan told me a year after the meltdown.

Who Needs RWA Anyway?

Other authors wondered if RWA should even exist anymore. Times had changed from the days of letters and phone calls. A new crop of authors had never even considered joining RWA, not with so many blogs and podcasts and Discord servers bringing them together. Journalist Chloe Angyal, for instance, joined two romance Discord servers while she was shopping her debut ballet-world romance, which came out in 2023. She'd relied on romance reader friends to critique her novel and reached out privately on Twitter to authors Olivia Dade and Cat Sebastian, who shared marketing advice with her.

Similarly, Erin Wright, a bubbly librarian in Boise, Idaho, stumbled into an online writing community one day. "I thought, this is so cool, people who make a living writing. I didn't know you could do this," she told me. She started proofreading and ghostwriting, then self-published her own romances. She'd heard about RWA, but never saw a reason to join. Instead, she headed to Romance Author Mastermind, an event for intermediate and advanced authors. Later, she started a consulting service for authors interested in "going wide," a writers' strategy for resisting Amazon's monopolistic tendencies. Writers who go wide refuse to participate in any of Amazon's exclusivity programs, selling books through all possible platforms, including their own websites.

Angyal, Wright, and many other authors could now build romance careers without RWA. Authors who had been RWA members began to wonder why they still belonged. Many decided it just wasn't worth it anymore, especially if it put them on the wrong side of an inclusion debate. Who really needed RWA anyway?

For many authors, especially writers of color, fighting to right the sinking ship of RWA seemed pointless. So, when Chilove and other authors of color joined the new board, "friends were upset with us," Chilove told me. "People said, 'How could y'all do this?' Our argument was, 'If we don't, who will?'"

LaQuette and Chilove saw two reasons to try to repair RWA. For one, RWA could provide a bulkhead against Amazon's overwhelming platform power (which we looked at in chapter 7). The platform had devalued books through Kindle Unlimited; arbitrarily changed compensation rates on Kindle Unlimited; been slow to crack down on plagiarists and book stuffers; and essentially locked most authors into permanent dependency. It had also gutted parts of traditional publishing. Just a few years earlier, Carolyn Reidy, the CEO of Simon & Schuster, had more or less announced the death of traditional romance publishing in a 2017 speech at the Frankfurt Book Fair. "The romance market, which used to be huge in mass market, has pretty much dried up and gone to digital originals. It has put pressure on pricing of all e-books . . . those are customers who, if they wanted a book, used to come to us and now they go elsewhere."[23]

"It's as if people can't look beyond the now to see what could actually happen in the industry if there is no RWA," LaQuette told me. "Without RWA, there's no one to advocate for us. What happens if Amazon goes awry? Who's going to call them up and say, 'Don't do that.' You can't get a person on the phone at Amazon. You can't. But RWA can."

The second reason to maintain RWA was, ironically, to improve and enforce diversity. Chilove had worked in diversity and inclusion for fifteen years and headed RWA's diversity task force. She believed that lasting change depended heavily on behind-the-scenes infrastructure and policy—in other words, in good bureaucracy.

Sociologist Max Weber, writing in the early twentieth century, noted that while bureaucracies can trap individuals in an "iron cage" of rigid efficiency and control, they can also ensure fairness and uphold codes. Formal organizations, policies, and rules "transcend and constrain the actions of individuals," according to communication scholars Daniel Kreiss, Megan Finn, and Fred Turner.[24] They keep "the whims of individual members in check" by mitigating tendencies of in-groups to exclude and marginalize others, and provide recourse for those injured along the way. If RWA's policies and procedures could be designed to be inclusive and enforce equity, romance authors might find more protection against platforms, but also against institutional racism.

"One of the most significant things I personally feel that happened was we codified the diversity language and tried to embed that within the fabric of RWA," Chilove said. That included restructuring and organizing the new code of ethics, "to make sure that what happened with Courtney Milan didn't happen again."

The Atomization of Mutual Aid

As we'll see in the conclusion, a rebooted RWA wasn't the only imaginable way to create solidarity against platforms and advance diversity. It would be possible to create a new organization. But that seemed unlikely. "Who's going to do that?" LaQuette asked me. "Getting people to step up and take on leadership roles or committees to do work, it's difficult to get people to commit. Who's going to start that from scratch and build it?"

At the moment when RWA was falling apart, social forces—including the pandemic—were making it more work for fewer volunteers to organize authors for mutual protection against Amazon. In chapter 7, we saw how the 1990s and early 2000s intensified the discourse of American individuality, glorifying entrepreneurship, and romanticized the solo worker in the gig economy. This corresponded with a decline in collective and community activities, and the traditions of volunteering and civic participation. All this makes it more unlikely and difficult to organize for collective action.

As political scientist Robert Putnam documented in his book *Bowling Alone*, community involvement declined profoundly over the decades, as part of a much larger trend of disconnection.[25] Putnam attributes this decline to social forces including suburban sprawl and commuting, increasing work pressures, and TV and other home-based, individual media forms. Meanwhile, American women now had far more demands on their time than ever. Although full-time careers became the norm for white, middle-class American women by the 1980s (and much earlier than that for women of color), family and social responsibilities were never adequately redistributed. Time-use studies show that even in two-income families, women continue to do the majority of housework and child-raising. Something had to give: for many, it was civic engagement and the relational labor it entails. Putnam notes that this decline in engagement went hand in hand with a decline of trust across America.

RWA had long depended on extraordinary effort from volunteers, as well as mutual trust among members. So, as members lost trust in the organization and each other, those volunteers who stayed had to put in more and more work. If those volunteers were from historically marginalized groups, the additional workload was ironic, given that marginalized members *already* had to work harder to get published.

"Getting volunteers to help with anything was like pulling teeth," said Caraway Carter, an author of male-male romance who served as president of the Orange County, California RWA chapter in 2019 and 2020. "Everybody wanted to come to meetings, but nobody wanted to help." The scandal and pandemic made things much worse. Few members were willing to invest their dwindling energy and volunteer time into an organization tainted by a race-related scandal.

Two Steps Forward . . .

During the next six months, while the world went into lockdown, the new RWA board wrestled with financial challenges (dues were way down, publishers' sponsorships were gone, and RWA was tied into expensive hotel contracts for the next few conferences). They created a new mentoring program, a class for first-time authors of color, and a new series of "deep dive" workshops to help address the specific needs of subgroups of authors, from newbies to indies to traditionally published experts.

Controversies continued to rage through Romancelandia. Progressives and conservatives seemed equally unhappy. "We got the nastiest emails from people on both sides. Some people who think they're progressive would tell us how terrible we were, as if we weren't human beings," said LaQuette, who was elected president in November 2020. "Then we got *exactly* the same kind of emails from the conservative people. There are people on both sides who just want to see RWA burn down."

Still, the organization continued to advocate for authors' rights in a threatening digital landscape. RWA joined forces with other writers' organizations to protest Amazon's return policy for audiobooks, which let listeners return audiobook downloads within a year for a full refund, no questions asked. It escalated its complaints against Dreamspinner Press for failing to pay royalties it owed authors, many of whom wrote LGBTQ+ romance. Previously, members had faulted RWA for dragging its feet on the issue. When the company failed to respond, RWA banned the publisher from its list of Qualifying Markets, essentially excommunicating it from Romancelandia. In 2020, RWA joined with the Authors Guild in an open letter to the Internet Archive, requesting it shut down a pandemic related "national emergency library," which was publishing books to which it had no rights. In 2023, it joined with other creator organizations to advocate for legislation protecting creators from AI infringement on creators' rights.

. . . Three Steps Back

While all this went on behind the scenes, the new board and RWA's remaining members pinned high hopes on the new VIVIAN awards. Entries would be judged by a detailed rubric and judges would receive mandatory diversity and inclusion training. Librarians, editors, and other members of greater Romancelandia would judge the final rounds, rather than former winners, who might be biased by their own subgenre's norms. Judges were instructed to alert RWA staff of objectionable or harmful content in storylines; flagged books would be disqualified. To encourage entries, the board dropped the entry fees—a blow to the dwindling coffers, but well worth it for its success in attracting marginalized authors to enter. As a result, the 2021 finalists were the most diverse awards group in the history of the organization; 17 percent of VIVIAN finalists were marginalized authors, compared to 4 percent in the previous RITAs.

Things were looking up. Then in July 2021, the board received advanced notification of the winners.

At Love's Command, a Christian-themed romance, had been selected as top romance with Religious or Spiritual Elements. The hero had taken part in the massacre at Wounded Knee and seeks divine forgiveness for his participation in the slaughter of more than 250 Lakota men, women, and children. Many in Romancelandia felt that a character who took part in genocide, no matter how repentant they might be, crossed the line "beyond which no happy ending is possible," as Sarah Wendell and Candy Tam had described the rape trope (see chapter 2). The new VIVIANs brought back reminders of the 2015 RITAs, when a finalist featured a Jewish prisoner and a high-ranking Nazi during the Holocaust. Sarah Wendell of *Smart Bitches* had written in protest to the RWA board, calling the book "deeply offensive."[26] Now, *At Love's Command* seemed equally insensitive.

Author Jenny Hartwell sent a letter to the RWA board, which she later posted on Twitter. "Aren't there some people who shouldn't be redeemed? Nazis. Slave owners. Soldiers who committed genocide?" she wrote. "Can this author write this story? Absolutely. Free speech is important. But should our organization give this story its highest award? Absolutely not."[27]

The Twittersphere lit up.

"So, RWA has confirmed that 'inspirational romance' is white supremacist fantasies," tweeted one author. "Nothing's really changed at RWA," tweeted another.[28] To many, this was just one more sign that the organization was beyond help.

While the situation seemed similar to 2015, the board responded in a very different way. Rather than ignoring the issue, the board convened an emergency meeting and rescinded the award.

"We cannot in good conscience uphold the decision of the judges in voting to celebrate a book that depicts the inhumane treatment of indigenous people and romanticizes real world tragedies that still affect people to this day," they wrote.[29] The board appointed a task force to prevent similar offenses and cancelled the following year's awards to leave time for an overhaul.

Still, for many members who'd hung on through the implosion, the award was the final proof that even the best of intentions couldn't change the organization.

Social Media's Double-Edged Sword

For LaQuette, the situation held a different lesson. Social media, she concluded, was a great way to call attention to social injustice. But it was a terrible way to fix it.

"You can't repair anything under a spotlight," she told me. The spread of misinformation and speculation disheartened her, especially when she had to step down as president in late 2021 due to a family health issue.

"People on social media concluded it was me giving up on the organization, but it had absolutely nothing to do with that," she said in frustration. "My son needed me." Chilove also stepped down because of family demands. On Twitter, she said, it looked like "all the Black women are leaving. But it was just what I needed to do for myself."

For RWA, and for much of the rest of American society in the past fifteen years, social media was proving to be a double-edged sword. Social media had helped LaQuette, C. Chilove and other authors of color gain visibility and power in Romancelandia by calling attention to industry racism and exclusion long ignored by RWA. In the book *#Hashtag Activism*, Sarah Jackson, Moya Bailey, and Brooke Foucault Welles argue that hashtags, like #OscarsSoWhite, are hugely effective in highlighting issues previously swept under the carpet. They create "a shorthand story that is easily recognizable and speaks to much broader concerns."[30] For instance, the #RitasSoWhite hashtag echoed #OscarsSoWhite, highlighting a broader pattern of social injustice spanning multiple realms.

Ever since RWA's second conference, on the Queen Mary, bitter controversy, infighting, and resignations had been part of RWA's history. As early as 2002, board minute meetings included comments like, "We need to take a hard look at the ways in which we choose to disagree."[31] These controversies were often a manifestation of care, as authors battled to make sure everyone's competing needs were met. As I mentioned in earlier chapters, some issues of *Romance Writers Report* in the 1980s and 1990s devoted up to a dozen pages to debates and controversies. But even though these debates often became acrimonious, they stayed within the confines of *PANdora's Box, Romance Writers Report*, and board meetings. This tacit agreement not to air dirty laundry allowed many members to continue to ignore important issues. But those that were not ignored could be addressed outside of the spotlight.

Social media, however, made these battles for resources—characteristic of communities of care—very public. The upside is that it brought attention and calls for change from a much larger community. The downside is that social media is often a terrible forum to communicate subtleties and nuances, or to explain how technical minutiae like a poorly written and unenforceable ethics policy, and lack of governance experience among volunteer board members, contributed to the meltdown. At the end of the day, this larger social media community lacked the context of long-established, in-person, trusting bonds and interconnected relationships that had long characterized Romancelandia in general, and RWA in particular through its open-elite network structure.

Without a basis of trust, change becomes difficult, as Barack Obama pointed out in a 2019 talk. "If I tweet or hashtag about how you didn't do something right, or used the wrong verb . . . that's not activism. That's not bringing about change. If all you're doing is casting stones, you're probably not going to get that far,"[32] he said. As Alicia Garza, co-founder of Black Lives Matter, put it, "You cannot start a movement from a hashtag . . . what people are willing to do on social media doesn't always translate into what they're willing to do in their everyday lives. Movement building and participation require ongoing engagement and the levels of engagement must continually shift and increase."[33]

My point here isn't to argue that social media and Twitter are either good or bad for social activism. Both were true in the case of RWA in different ways at different times. Rather, I want to highlight how particular modes of communication generate particular kinds of interactions that affect the structure and operation of networks and organizations. For RWA, Twitter offered an important, effective platform to call for change. Social media brought national attention to issues that had long remained within the pages of *Romance Writers Report* or on RWA email loops and forums. But, according to LaQuette, social media *also* made internal cooperation, reform, and repair more difficult, bringing national attention to every awkward step toward change. And change was desperately needed for reasons of inclusion and equity, and in order to stand up to the growing threat of platformized publishing.

When Care Fails

Throughout the book, I've argued that Romancelandia's unique open-elite network structure, fostered by a feminist ethic of care, helped make romance writers the most innovative and successful authors in digital publishing. This chapter warns how quickly supportive structures and culture can collapse when they fail to address their own internal contradictions. In this case, RWA failed to institute identity-aware care to effectively promote diversity, inclusion, and equity, and to find ways to maintain trust. Maybe RWA collapsed simply because structural and institutional racism are insidiously, notoriously, perhaps impossibly, difficult to combat. "You can't get rid of all the racists," as Courtney Milan put it.

It's also possible that much-needed repair might have played out differently in a broader social context of trust and goodwill. Instead, it took place in a culture plagued by four years of a divisive US president with a long, well-documented record of deceit, dishonesty, and racist, sexist behavior. It occurred in a context of plunging levels of public trust in institutions and organizations and amid the mixed blessings of new communication modes like Twitter, which amplified both calls for equity *and* the swift cancellation of dissenting views.

If, as LaQuette told me, RWA is a microcosm of American society, its fate has lessons and warnings for much larger groups of workers and communities. Finding ways to swiftly adopt identity-aware care, to address long-standing exclusions that remain invisible to dominant culture, and to build trusting relationships is critical. The consequences of failure and collapse may leave already fragmented and isolated workers with fewer protections in many fields, not just cultural production. In a culture of distrust, public shaming, division, and social isolation, the failure of care harms everyone who would benefit from solidarity and mutual aid in the face of an increasingly platformized society.

In the two years after RWA's implosion, two-thirds of its members left. But thousands stayed to rebuild. LaQuette's most meaningful moment as president came at the group's 2021 retreat, its first in-person conference since the meltdown and the pandemic. The event, at a hotel in Tennessee, was barely a tenth of the size of past RWA conferences, with dozens, not hundreds, attending; most were aspiring authors. "It was clear that these writers needed to be together," LaQuette said. "I had this moment where I suddenly realized that my role was to be a tether. To bring them together and keep them together. They needed that feeling of community."

Romancelandia Reboot

THE FUTURE OF CARE

"WHERE DO I FIND THE ROMANCE WRITERS?" I ask at the front desk of a resort in northern Virginia in July 2022. Of the half-dozen or so romance events I'd attended over the years, this year's RWA conference is the only time I've ever had to ask. In years past, hundreds, sometimes thousands, of attendees swarmed the lobbies, hallways, conference rooms, elevators, bars, lounges, and cafes of any space they occupied. This time, when I arrived in the resort's white marble lobby, I couldn't spot any of them. No gargantuan romance cover posts. No big sponsor banners. No name tags with colorful ribbons reading "erotic" or "inspirational" or "first time attendee." No swag room bursting with freebies. No parties with burlesque dance instruction and swag like red tasseled pasties (still my all-time favorite RWA party favor).

Eventually, a concierge directed me up two escalators to an oddly hushed space. There, I found two ballrooms, one empty except for hotel staff setting up the lunch buffet, and the other filled with the conference's two hundred attendees listening intently to a talk about evoking emotional reactions from readers. Past events had boasted three conference tracks with multiple simultaneous sessions, and so much hallway conversation that I once nearly fell over three writers who'd plunked down on the floor to chat.

But small as it was, in the newly post-pandemic world, there was something energizing about being in a huge room filled with people, all intently focused on a panel about story craft. The attendees seemed to feel the same. After the session, the lunchtime din was as deafening as any I'd heard at other romance conferences. It was clear that the spirit of community was alive and well in Romancelandia.

But would it continue to thrive within RWA, or find new outlets? That wasn't so clear.

"I actually don't think we need RWA," Courtney Milan told me when we spoke in December 2020. "The question then is, what do we do as a community to make up for the loss of institutional work? What can we do as a community to lift each other up?"

So far, no one knows what this emerging community might look like. Maybe RWA will regrow, renewed and repaired, as a central pillar in Romancelandia. But maybe not. I see at least three possible visions of Romancelandia's future emerging, models that raise broad questions for other organizations, movements, and any group of outsiders struggling to become insiders in an age of platformization.

Future One: RWA 2.0

In one version, the future of Romancelandia might look a lot like the early RWA back in the 1980s—smaller, more intimate, driven by personal, trusting relationships, but now with a strong awareness of identity.

That's what I saw at the 2022 annual convention, once I finally found the authors. During a break between sessions, I ran into Shirley Hailstock, who had been RWA's first Black president back in 2002. In a pink plaid shirt, she was as exuberant as ever, chatting in the registration room with Leslie Scantlebury, the executive director, who is also Black. After the conference, she posted an enthusiastic note back to her home chapter in New Jersey, which had seceded from RWA. "It was great!" she wrote. "The conference was smaller than usual, but it allowed me to talk to everyone and get to know them. The Seattle chapter had a party in their suite and the food and conversations were outstanding."

That party reminded me of that other hotel room gathering I described in chapter 3, when Rita Clay Estrada, Vivian Stephens, and a crowd of aspiring authors bonded over drinks served out of Estrada's bathtub at a 1978 Houston conference. Founding member Kit O'Brien Jones had said, "I believe Romance Writers of America was founded there in that crowded hotel room, that night."

I sensed that same spirit of bonding, of joyful "us against the world" at the 2022 conference. LaQuette felt it too, she told me over dinner that night. She'd also felt it a year before, at the even-smaller RWA conference in Tennessee.

"One thing I really valued was that everyone talked to everyone," she said. "Aspiring writers who would have had a hard time meeting up with the president of RWA at a past conference, they could sit down and chat now."

For weeks after the DC conference, I saw attendees connecting on the post-conference thread, discussing ways to continue that sense of connection and renew the organization. These fledgling conversations reminded me of something Alicia Garza, cofounder of Black Lives Matter, wrote in her book *The Purpose of Power*:

> Only organizing sustains movements. They become the places where people can find community and learn about what's happening around them, why it's happening, who it benefits and who it harms. Organizations are the places where we learn skills to take action, to organize to change the laws and change our culture. Organizations are where we come together to determine what we can do about the problems facing our communities.[1]

That said, as we saw in chapter 9, RWA is still working against its own long history of exclusion, as well as a collapse of trust and prestige, volunteer burnout, and severe financial challenges. Plus, we live in a very different socio-technical environment than Vivian and Rita did when the group was founded. As I've noted throughout the book, in those days, telephone wires, stamped letters, a print magazine, and an annual conference held the network together by providing rare resources for learning the craft. Today, you can learn just about anything on YouTube—including how to write romance. It's much easier for writers to connect and teach each other now, and with the dissolution of trust across American institutions, the era of huge, in-person organizations may be fading, leaving writers and others less connected in important ways. So RWA may rise once more, but it might be just one node in an expanding network of romance writer groups getting bigger each day.

Future Two: A Network of Networks

In the wake of RWA implosion, chapters in Las Vegas, New Jersey, Southern California, and dozens of other cities disaffiliated from RWA and became their own independent organizations. These groups joined a thriving ecosystem of existing romance writing groups, networks, and events, including the Romance Authors Mastermind conference, GayRomLit, Romance Slam Jam, and many more. Given the proliferation of romance groups online and off, another possible future for Romancelandia would be a looser affiliation of author groups, no longer dominated by a single, central association. Smaller, more flexible networks might prove to be more inclusive and innovative.

Take, for instance, Regency Fiction Writers, the new name for the former Beau Monde online chapter of RWA, which broke ties seven months after RWA's meltdown. Along with dozens of other RWA chapters also disaffiliating in the wake of the meltdown, Regency Fiction Writers represents one node in a growing network of romance writing groups, formal and informal.

Before the meltdown, Beau Monde had some 350 members, which dropped to about two hundred by the time the chapter disaffiliated. Almost immediately after it became Regency Fiction Writers, the numbers rebounded, nearing four hundred in August 2022. Some of those new members weren't romance writers at all. "If we were going to break away, it was important we be welcoming to all genres," the group's president, Janna MacGregor, told me. In a time of change and innovation, she said, "this was an opportunity to expand our borders, to get more inclusive and let in people with different types of expertise."

Given the infinite ways that romance writers constantly connect with each other through Twitter and Mastodon and Discord, through podcasts and blogs and group chats, it's possible that these smaller, independent groups might connect loosely together, forming a network of networks. A coalition might even take on some of the functions that RWA once served. In this future, an identity-aware ethic of care could show up in a series of regional, interest-based, and/or identity-based subnetworks. These smaller organizations may be able to come together for industry advocacy efforts or other joint ventures. They offer the advantage of smaller, more focused groups that might build trust more easily than a massive organization.

On the other hand, RWA didn't collapse just because it lacked effective policies to handle one complicated ethical dispute, but because underneath, it was struggling to cope with differences between dominant and marginalized groups, just as the country as a whole was. So, the fragmentation of small groups might make it harder to come together for collective action without well-funded, centralized coordination. And smaller groups might easily be more exclusionary than RWA. As we saw in chapters 7 and 9, racism and exclusion can be hard to regulate in informal settings, or without clear, well-crafted infrastructure.

Smaller groups with a loose affiliation might have a harder time meeting the needs of members with a wide array of backgrounds and experience. "How do you meet everyone's needs? RWA was very good at offering craft classes for beginners, but also continuing education for more experienced authors, and you need that," MacGregor told me. The in-person energy of a massive conference would also be missing from this network-of-networks model, unless groups connect to create larger events. "Most business was done at the bar," MacGregor said fondly of RWA conferences. Smaller groups would miss out the serendipitous magic of bumping into Nora Roberts over cocktails or having a smoke outside with Beverly Jenkins.

Future Three: Writers Unite

A year after the RWA implosion unfolded, membership in the Authors Guild, an advocacy organization for writers, grew 20 percent. Many new authors were romance writers looking for a new institutional home. So, a third option for Romancelandia's future is that romance writers join up with larger writing associations, or even unionize (although the latter would require substantial changes in labor law, as we saw in chapter 3). Once literary outcasts, romance writers now hold a powerful voice in publishing. As I write, several of twenty-nine members of the Authors Guild Council, its governing body, are prominent romance writers, including Sylvia Day and Eloisa James, current vice president of the council. In 2021, the Guild offered its first online forums for romance writers, who quickly began spreading their collaborative ethic. "The Romance Writers even decided to set up monthly review sessions in which interested members provide feedback on each other's manuscripts," according to the Authors Guild annual report in 2021.[2] At the same time, the Authors Guild has started to stress community building more than in the past, by adding regional chapters, much as RWA did decades ago.

In this future, the Authors Guild would become romance writers' go-to advocacy group. The group has already worked closely with RWA and other writers' associations, so it's well equipped to advocate for writers. What's lost in this model would be the uniquely close community sense of Romancelandia (surely no tasseled pasties at Authors Guild events?), particularly its sense of sisterhood in an almost entirely female industry. They would also almost certainly lose the open-elite network structure, where aspiring authors have ready, everyday access to established authors. Full membership in the Authors Guild is only open to authors who have published a book traditionally or made at least $5,000 from a self-published book. While lower membership tiers are open to "emerging writers," the group historically has not been designed to foster the kind of easy fellowship and solidarity among a wide range of authors that RWA promoted. Still, the organization commands the attention of the publishing industry, including Amazon, and could serve a central advocacy role in the emerging network-of-networks model.

The Future of Care

So, what will Romancelandia look like in the future? A renewed, identity-aware central organization? A loose network of networks, befitting the digital and social media era? A merged network where the rest of the literary world embraces romance authors as equals, and all writers advocate collectively for their interests? It's much too early to tell. But the seeds of each of these possible futures already demonstrate an ethic of care and practices of relational labor.

Throughout this book, I've argued that, over forty years, romance writers created a powerful model of female solidarity, which, while flawed, helped them become the most innovative authors of the digital age. Deeply rooted in an ethic of care, which prioritizes meeting the needs of everyone in the community over individual advancement, the romance network helped a disparaged group of literary outsiders reinvent an industry and improve their position in the new, digital, political economy of publishing. The group did not benefit all writers equally. But it did demonstrate what an ethic of care can do for a community, even when imperfectly implemented. Care can lower the cost of relational labor, making it easier to connect and seek advice across differences of experience, and foster innovation and well-being.

This message has never been more important than right now. As I write this in the summer of 2023, both cultural producers and a broader set of workers are already testing new forms of self-organization and collective action on a scale not seen since the mid-twentieth century. Screenwriters and TV and movie actors are striking simultaneously for the first time in sixty years, because streaming platforms and other digital innovations have drastically decreased their pay.[3] Tens of thousands of Uber drivers, DoorDash couriers, and even take-out diners have been locked in arbitration and lawsuits against the platforms they work for, over pay and working conditions and whether or not they're misclassified as independent contractors.[4] As workers at Starbucks, Amazon warehouses, and Apple stores have voted to unionize, American public approval of unions climbed to 71 percent, its highest peak since 1965.

As both cultural producers and other workers seek more power in the face of platforms and corporations, the forty-year history of romance writers should stand as both a lesson and a cautionary tale about the impact of open networks and an inclusive ethic of care.

It's not just romance writers who've incorporated these tactics successfully. We see this kind of self-organized, open-elite network succeeding in very different types of organizations, formal and otherwise.

- The **Olori Sisterhood,** an informal network of Black women in politics, is now "a political force" making change on "the biggest stages."[5] After meeting at a conference in 2010, a core group from Brooklyn bonded, stayed in touch, and committed to supporting each other's success (their name means "leader" in Yoruba). The group expanded over the years, and now lifts up Black women candidates at every level, from local politicians to Kamala Harris.

- The **Journalism and Women's Symposium (JAWS)** started with a handful of women reporters meeting in 1984, seeking solidarity in a male-dominated field. For nearly four decades, the group has created an open-elite network of junior and senior women journalists. The group has lobbied successfully for more diversity in newsrooms and inspired innovative initiatives.

- **The OpEd Project** intentionally created an open-elite network to diversify white, male-dominated opinion media. By matching seasoned journalist-mentors with underrepresented experts inexperienced in public writing, the group has helped more than 22,000 people, mostly from marginalized groups, publish tens of thousands of opinion pieces in influential media outlets. (Proud disclosure: I've been part of The OpEd Project since 2012.)

- At IBM, the company's many affinity groups for historically disadvantaged groups (including women, Latinx, Black, LGBTA+, Asian, and disabled employees) are led by nonhierarchical **"catalyst teams."** These groups create open-elite networks by design, bringing together every level of worker, from entry level programmers to senior executives. Their leadership teams of twenty or so foster ties across departments and levels of experience and seniority. Internal research shows that catalyst teams helped participants build broad, multi-level corporate networks—which usually take years to build.

Care Means Conflict

I guarantee that each and every one of these groups has discovered along the way that neither a community of care nor an open-elite network is synonymous with peace, love, and joy. To the contrary. Joan Tronto points out that care is contentious and political, as members constantly debate how to balance competing interests, recognize unmet needs, or deal with those who heedlessly trample on cultural sore spots. Communities across the United States, from academic departments and universities, to professional associations, to foundations, to employers, are trying with mixed success to address inequalities in a social environment of division and distrust—sometimes aided and sometimes undermined by new forms of media. In the last chapter, we saw what can happen when care fails. When groups move too slowly, fail to maintain trust, and make blunders in the unwinking public eye of social media, their power to help their members can evaporate overnight. Such failures, in the age of rising platform power, have serious consequences for individual producers and workers who need solidarity now more than ever.

If this all sounds much bigger than Romancelandia, that's because, of course, it is.

As LaQuette and other authors told me over and over, "romance is a microcosm of society." This book offers important lessons and warnings for that society, and questions for anyone trying to create more cohesive communities and greater solidarity in the face of fragmenting social forces. Some of those lessons, and the questions they might raise in other communities, include:

1. Open-elite communities, where experts and newbies mingle, can foster information sharing, innovation, and solidarity. (Is your community more of one or the other? What would make it valuable for people with different levels of experience?)
2. Failures of care and inclusion leave every community member—even those historically privileged or dominant—more vulnerable and precarious. (What external threats does your community face? Who would benefit if your community/group/organization falls apart?)
3. Failures of care need to be addressed swiftly and effectively, or community may dissolve at the very moment solidarity is needed most. (Are there unmet needs, longtime complaints, in your professional world, problems everyone has long known about but not addressed? Could issues that might seem to affect just a few members of your community end up harming everyone? What would be lost?)
4. To thrive as they grow, informal communities and networks need formal structures, procedures, and experienced management. Institutional practices—from codified procedures for diversity and exclusion, to legally sound ethics policies, to the selection of experienced, well-trained managers—can help foster the trust necessary to survive. (Does your organization or community rely on conventions that aren't codified or enforceable? How do we draw on the good parts of bureaucracy to make networks stronger and more inclusive?)
5. "Care" is contentious. Debate—sometimes painful debate—is a necessary part of that care, and communities need to invest relational labor to build the trust necessary to survive those contentious, nuanced,

sometimes intractable debates. (How can we disagree productively with each other? How can we feel less threatened by conflict?)

I write this at a time when many members of American society are feeling discouraged, disillusioned, isolated, and economically precarious. But if there's one thing that Romancelandia always has—and always will do better than anyone—it's finding hope and community. I hear it in every conversation I have with authors. And I saw it come to life in November 2021, in a spontaneous online upsurge called Romancing the Runoff.

Romancing the Runoff

In November 2020, during the high anxiety presidential and congressional elections, an author named Bree Bridges, who writes with Donna Herren as Kit Rocha, was feeling helpless. She texted her coauthor, and her friends Alyssa Cole and Courtney Milan. "I'm thinking of an auction," she said, to raise funds to support Democratic groups in the crucial runoff for a Senate seat in Georgia. Fellow romance author, lawyer, and voting rights activist Stacey Abrams (who wrote romance as Selena Montgomery and now publishes under her own name) had launched a successful registration drive for Black and Democratic voters in Georgia. The auction, organized by and for Romancelandia, would support that work.

Within a day, the four authors had set up an auction website, and gathered romance-related contributions—signed books, manuscript critiques by agents and editors, TV pilot consulting, and much more. They set what they thought was an ambitious goal—$25,000. When the auction opened, they met the goal in seven minutes flat. In the end, they raised nearly $500,000.

"It showed the power of networks of people who want to do good and be around each other," Courtney Milan told me. Everyone I spoke with who was involved in any way—those who'd been hurt by the meltdown, those who had resigned RWA, those who had stayed and tried to renew the organization—told me they felt a sense of healing and renewal. I felt it too.

To be sure, Romancing the Runoff and its organizers represent only one node in the sprawling network of Romancelandia—a node actively committed to progressive causes, which certainly doesn't represent all romance writers or readers. Then again, virtually all romance writers are social disruptors in some way, unsettling gender roles and ideas of happiness, and forming powerful communities. In that way, Romancing the Runoff reveals the power of romance authors united for change.

Happily Ever After?

I told you at the start that I'm a sucker for a happy ending. In a way, this book reads like romance itself, following a classic arc. The meet-cutes in early Romancelandia, including the founding of RWA and *Romantic Times*; the hardships of what Pamela Regis calls "corrupt society," like sexism, racism, and exploitation of writers;[6] the growth and thriving of solidarity and unity, despite conflict, like Romancelandia's gains in the publishing world; and the point of "ritual death" when all hope of a happy ending seems lost (RWA's implosion). Will Romancelandia get its optimistic, emotionally satisfying ending? Will other workers in a precarious economy?

I hope so.

After all that Romancelandia has been through, especially since the 2020 implosion, it may seem naive that I still believe in the transformative power of relational labor, inclusion, and the ethic of care—not just for Romancelandia, but for a larger, divided, distrustful society. But romance authors and readers have *always* been ridiculed for their rose-colored glasses. They've been derided for complicity with the status quo while also scolded for pushing the boundaries of propriety. And yet, through it all, romance authors continue to use romance as a space to imagine a world where love and community and caring can reshape the world. In Romancelandia, in its longtime ethic of care, and in its many efforts to reshape that care to fit an era of renewed social awareness, I see the ingredients of an optimistic ending. We may not see a happily ever after—even romances rarely end that way anymore—but my money's on a "happily for now." Or maybe a "happily even though."

And, to me, those endings seem like a pretty good place to start.

ACKNOWLEDGEMENTS

Dear reader, will you ever forgive me if I start by saying this book was a labor of love?

I hope you will. Because this labor would not have been possible without the love and care lavished on me, my boys, and this project through personally turbulent times. For all of you, and many more who helped along the way, I wish you the happiest of ever-afters.

First: I am indebted to Janice Radway, who graciously weighed in at key moments of this process, dramatically improving the book each time. Like countless students and scholars before me, I feel lucky to have her mentorship.

Second, my friend and advisor Fred Turner. I can't thank Fred and his wife Annie Fischer enough for all their support at a difficult time, and especially for their extraordinary New Years' millinery skills. Thanks, too, to Jay Hamilton, for lending me not only his brilliance but also his teenage son to babysit my kids. Enduring gratitude to Woody Powell and Theodore Glasser, who spent years honing my thinking on this project. I was also lucky to benefit from the wisdom and friendship of Stanford friends and colleagues Angèle Christin, Dawn Garcia, Cheryl Phillips and her fabulous wife Catherine, and many others.

Beyond Stanford, Gina Neff served as this project's fairy godmother right from the start, swooping in from Seattle or Budapest or Oxford at exactly the right instant, with exactly the right advice. A special thanks to the ever-expanding sisterhood of the pomodoro: Morgan Ames, Anita Varma, Jakki Bailey, Andrea Won, Angie Chuang, Katherine Isbister, Sue Robinson—you don't all know each other, but you're united by the tomato timer.

As you'll see in the pages ahead, Professor (and pomodoran) Sue Robinson had a profound impact on this book, teaching me how to deepen and refine its theory without killing *all* my darlings. Just some of them. Intellectual and personal inspiration came from C. W. Anderson, Seth Lewis, and every single Badass Women of Communication, especially two of its instigators, Brooke Duffy and Nikki Usher. Special thanks to Sarah Banet-Weiser, Catherine Rottenberg,

Shani Orgad, Rosalind Gill, and Jo Littler for bringing together a superstar group of feminist thinkers in Paris in 2022.

My extraordinary band of colleagues at the University of Colorado, Boulder, makes it a joy to come to work every day: Karen Ashcraft, Angie Chuang, Jennifer Ho, Pat Ferrucci, Jolene Fisher, Lisa Guinther, Marina Dmukhovskaya, Dave Martinez, Malinda Miller, Sandra Ristovska, Erin Schauster, Nathan Schneider, Elizabeth Skewes, Ross Taylor, Kay Weaver, and Erin Willis, to name just a few. Special thanks to Andrew Calabrese for telling me about the Love Train! I'm also grateful to my OpEd Project colleagues, especially Chloe Angyal, the Baxter Sisters, Chelsea Carmona, Mary Curtis, Deborah Douglas, Zeba Khan, Katie Orenstein, Teresa Puente, Lauren Sandler, Princella Talley, Michele Weldon, Katarina Wong, Angela Wright, Neil Young, and Ashley Zwick. These women-and-Neil taught me all I know about teaching and commitment to social justice. You inspire me.

It took several skilled midwives to birth this book. Exquisite wordsmith Kate Washington polished my early efforts. The brilliant Carole V. Bell served as a kind, rigorous, and encouraging sensitivity reader, gently and cheerfully correcting my blind spots. If you're a white researcher studying race, you should call her. Over the years, my research assistants Wen Lei, Shannon Mullane, and Lexi Reich kept me organized and on track (*not* an easy task). Graduate student Ashley Carter brought great insight and invaluable energy to our collaboration on LGBTQ+ romance, and Rania Al Namara, Nihal Alaqabawy, and Shreyoshi Ghosh lightened my load in wonderful ways.

This book is only possible because so many Romancelandians generously shared their time with me. See their names in appendix 1: Thank you for lifting my spirits with your writing and your wisdom! Steve Ammidown, former archivist at the Browne Popular Culture Library, knows everything about romance history. Michael Capobianco, former president of the Science Fiction and Fantasy Writers of America, knows everything about SFWA history. Bella Andre, LaQuette Holmes, Beverly Jenkins, Brenda Jackson, Courtney Milan, Shirley Hailstock, Vivian Stephens, and Rita Clay Estrada all spoke with my several times over the past eight years and shaped the book in critical ways. I especially appreciate last-minute help from Olivia Waite and Carole Bell in crafting the Romancelandia map.

None of this, *none of this*, would have been possible without Erika Acosta, Mary Huang, Jasmine Jordan, and Ha Pham, the wonderful women who helped care for my twin toddlers as they grew into fine young men. Without them, I'd still be in grad school, my children would be feral, and there would be no book.

There would also be no book without a year-long fellowship from the American Center for Learned Societies, supplemented with additional dean's office funding from the College of Media, Communication and Information (CMCI) at University of Colorado, Boulder: thank you, Lori Bergen, for making that happen. Two De Castro Research Grants from CMCI and a THRIVE grant sponsored by the Office of Faculty Affairs, the Boulder Faculty Assembly, and the Research and Innovation Office sent me traveling to the RWA archives and paid for other vital research tasks. And let me note this: the THRIVE grant and the ACLS fellowship both specifically sought to help junior faculty heavily impacted by the pandemic, including single moms. These grants made a life-changing difference for me and other grant recipients. Thank you for recognizing the disproportionate burdens of caregiving.

And, *of course*, this book wouldn't be here without editor extraordinaire Meagan Levinson of Princeton University Press and the whole PUP team, including Eric Crahan, Erik Beranek, Lachlan Brooks, and Mark Bellis. Encouraging! Supportive! Patient! Enthusiastic! You folks are exactly what all the authors in this book dream about. Thank you for believing in the project and making it better.

By the way, you might have noticed I dedicated this book to men I love most. So, I'll end by thanking some of the most important women in my life: Clary, Mary Claire, Karyn, Katherine, Kendra, Aunt Pat & Aunt Carolyn, Sarah, and all my mom pals in Sacramento, Stockton, Palo Alto, Longmont, and Niwot.

Most important of all, my mother, Peggi Berge, who exemplifies the ethic of care in every single thing she does.

Finally, dear reader, in the spirit of open networks and an ethic of care, I thank you. If you're taking the time to read this, that means we share some interests: in romance, in women's writing, in cultural production, or social equity. You might agree with some things I've said, and probably not with others—that's how opinions work, as Nora Roberts once wrote in her blog—but either way, I'd love to hear your thoughts. I'm easy to find: reach out any time. In any case, thank you.

Interview Participants

This book would not exist without the generosity of my interview subjects. Thank you.

I conducted a total of eighty on-the-record interviews from 2014 to 2023, and countless informal and off-the-record discussions. On-the-record interviews were either in person, on the phone, or done via Zoom. Of the sources below, I spoke with 25 percent of them multiple times over the years as my research evolved.

Authors are listed under their best-known pen names, unless they write under their real names.

Romance Authors

Jeff Adams	Laura Drake	Beverley Kendall
Bella Andre	Pintip Dunn	Jeffe Kennedy
Chloe Angyal	Kim Fielding	Jayne Ann Krentz
Brent Archer	Tina Folsom	Rachel Lacey
Brenna Aubrey	Shana Galen	Kathryn Le Veque
Angeline Bishop	Shirley Hailstock	Hudson Lin
Clair Brett	Lorraine Heath	Janna MacGregor
Terri Brisbin	LaQuette Holmes	Donna MacMeans
Grace Burrowes	Desiree Holt	Courtney Milan
Collette Cameron	Linda Howard	Julie Miller
Caraway Carter	Piper Huguley	Priscilla Oliveras
K. J. Charles	Brenda Jackson	Theresa Ragan
C. Chilove	Eloisa James	Aleatha Romig
Rita Clay Estrada	Beverly Jenkins	Jeff Salter
Sonali Dev	Komal Kant	Roxanne St. Claire

Karelia Stetz-Waters   Olivia Waite   Beth Yarnall
Damon Suede   Erin Wright   Maisey Yates

Other Authors

Michael Capobianco, author, SFWA past president
J.A. Hennrikus, author, Sisters in Crime member
Hugh Howey, sci-fi author
Cat Rambo, author, SFWA past president
Jeff Rivera, young adult author
Shanna Swendson, fantasy and mystery author

Editors, Agents, Publishers, Industry Observers and Others

(with titles at time of interview)
Mary Altman, editor, Sourcebooks
Steven Axelrod, literary agent
Kate Baker, staff, Science Fiction Fantasy Writers of America
Len Barot, editor, publisher, author, Bold Strokes Books
Michael Cader, editor, *Publishers' Lunch* (book industry newsletter)
Jane Friedman, editor, *The Hot Sheet* (book industry newsletter)
Joanne Grant, editor, Harlequin
Leah Hultenschmidt, publisher, Forever (Grand Central)
John Jacobson, editor, Harlequin Desire
Angela James, founding editor, Carina Press (Harlequin)
Jo Carol Jones, RT conference director; BookLovers con director
Allison Kelley, RWA executive director
Ted Kitzmiller, author's husband
Gina Kitzmiller Christopher, author's daughter
Dianne Moggy, editor
Kristin Nelson, agent
Dominique Raccah, publisher
Leslie Scantlebury, RWA executive director
LaToya Smith, literary agent
Vivian Stephens, literary agent and editor, Candlelight, Harlequin
Jess Verdi, editor, Crimson Romance (Simon & Schuster)
Sarah Wendell, author, blogger, podcaster, *Smart Bitches, Trashy Books*
Deb Werksman, editor, Sourcebooks Casablanca

APPENDIX 2

Methodology

Much of the research here, including all quantitative analyses, has been published in peer-reviewed academic journals. This appendix provides greater detail on methodology summarized in preceding chapters. For more methodological detail, please see Larson 2019, Larson 2022, and Larson and Ready 2022.

Network Ethnography

Overall, this book takes an approach known as "network ethnography." This approach combines social network analysis (SNA) with traditional ethnography to describe relationships between individuals, organizations, and the media ecosystem.[1] Network ethnography tries to correct for weaknesses in social network analysis (SNA). Although SNA excels at showing overall relationship patterns, it suffers from several limitations: it lacks deep cultural context and it often provides a snapshot of relationships only at one moment in time. Conversely, traditional ethnography excels at deep cultural explanations through "thick description" based primarily on observation and interviews. However, dispersed communities provide a challenge to traditional ethnography: it is difficult to capture large-scale relationship patterns when people are distributed across time and space. This has been a particular challenge for ethnographers of cultural production because much creative work doesn't happen on a factory floor, where a scholar can easily watch it, but rather takes place in the nebulous, shifting spaces of writing, composing, and posting on social media. The authors I wanted to study did most of their work alone at home or in coffee shops, intentionally shutting out the outside world. Another limitation of traditional ethnography is that researchers' identities inevitably shape that interpretation.[2] (This also happens with quantitative methods as well, as many fine scholars of science, technology, and society have observed.[3] But that's a subject for another book.)

Network ethnography helps overcome these problems by combining the systematized analysis of relationship patterns and the cultural context shaping those patterns. The approach had already led to important contributions in communication research, in studies of dot-com workers in the 1990s by Gina Neff,[4] news outlets in Philadelphia by C. W. Anderson,[5] and of media coverage in Madison, Wisconsin by Sue Robinson.[6] Following, and often generously advised by, these and other scholars, I adopted a combination of interviews, participant-observation, archival research, and social network analysis for this study.

Interviews

From 2015 to 2023, I conducted on-the-record interviews with eighty people. Interviewees include fifty-one romance authors; six writers from other genres; fourteen agents, editors, and publishers; and nine industry observers. Average interview time was forty-five minutes, but some were much longer. I reinterviewed twenty-two of these generous participants at least once, and several became long-term advisors on the project. I also interacted informally on multiple occasions with many of these participants at conferences. Because this study focuses on cultural *production*, with reception as an overlapping concern, my formal methods concentrated on authors, editors, and publishers. This does not mean I neglected readers: virtually all romance authors and romance editors are dedicated fans of the genre. In addition, I conducted dozens of informal interviews with romance readers at RT and at RWA reader events.

For interviews, I purposefully oversampled underrepresented authors, including authors of color, men, and non-RWA members (note that more than half my interviews occurred before the RWA meltdown, so some authors who were members at the time subsequently left RWA).

To find participants, I started with key informants,[7] selected by combing through self-published bestseller lists and asking industry insiders for the names of influential authors in traditional and indie publishing. When my survey was complete, I interviewed fifteen of the twenty authors most commonly named as advice-givers. Through snowball sampling, these interviews led to a total of eighty non-anonymous interviews.[8] About half my interviews happened between 2014 and 2017, with the remainder between 2018 and 2023. Interviews took place by phone, on Zoom, or in person. My average interview lasted forty-five minutes, although some went much longer. (My

TABLE A.1. Interview Subjects, by Category: Self-Reported Gender and Race

	Romance Writers (n = 51)	Non-Romance Writers (n = 6)	Editors, Publishers, Agents (n = 14)	Industry Observers / Others (n = 9)
Female	*90%*	*50%*	*86%*	*88%*
Male	*10%*	*50%*	*14%*	*22%*
Black	*16%*	*17%*	*14%*	*11%*
Asian	*8%*	*0%*	*0%*	*0%*
Latinx	*2%*	*0%*	*0%*	*0%*
Other	*2%*	*0%*	*0%*	*0%*
White	*72%*	*83%*	*86%*	*89%*
RWA member at time of interview	*67%*	*n/a*	*n/a*	*n/a*

two interviews with the lovely and brilliant Vivian Stephens lasted nearly two hours each, with follow-up by email and mail.) All interviews were recorded, transcribed, and analyzed using the qualitative software NVivo.

To improve the credibility and accuracy of my qualitative data, I implemented a practice called "member checking" or "respondent validation," where results and interpretations are shared with interview subjects, who offer input.[9] I shared text excerpts of relevant book sections with the twelve most quoted participants in this book, including six authors of color and two authors who write lesbian or male-male romance. These authors responded with observations and corrections, which I incorporated into the narrative.

To help amend my blind spots as a white, cisgender, heterosexual woman, I contracted two sensitivity readers: one, a Black romance author, and the second, a communication scholar of African descent with expertise in race, gender, and media (see the acknowledgements). Their insights and additions resulted in important improvements to the book. All errors and omissions are entirely my own.

Participant-Observation

Between 2016 and 2022, I spent eighty hours at six different romance events (four national RWA conferences, one RT conference, and a romance conference at the National Archives). At these events, I attended panels, sat down at lunch buffet tables, and crashed awards ceremonies and parties hosted by local and online RWA chapters. I conducted informal interviews, and I observed how authors interacted with each other. I also met other researchers, including Jennifer Lois and Joanna Gregson, who had long been examining the romance community and who were as helpful and welcoming as the rest of Romancelandia. During observations, I took extensive notes at the events themselves, then went home and recorded my impressions and conversations. I taped interviews and took pictures for my own reference of my interview subjects and the venues. I later coded these notes in NVivo to identify for patterns and themes.

Archival Research

In 2020, I received a de Castro Research Award from the College of Media, Communication and Information at University of Colorado Boulder to support a deep dive into the archives of Romance Writers of America. Although the archives were closed to the public during COVID, the archivists at the Browne Popular Culture Library at Bowling Green State University in Ohio generously digitized thirty-two recordings of RWA panels dating back to 1983, which I then had transcribed. The archivists also scanned ninety-four articles from the *Romance Writers Report* magazine for me, from 2000 to 2015. In the summer of 2022, I received a THRIVE grant from the University of Colorado, Boulder, which let me travel to Bowling Green and spend a week poring over all issues of the *PANdora's Box* newsletter for PAN members, as well as most issues of *RWR* from the 1980s to the present. There, I digitized another 116 articles. I selected these documents based on major themes emerging in interviews, including, but not limited to, feminism, balancing work and family, professional practices, marginalized authors, industry statistics, and internal surveys. With the help of my outstanding research assistant Lexi Reich, I coded these documents in NVivo according to the book's major themes and pulled quotes and examples from these texts to support arguments throughout the book. This work was supplemented with extensive background research in contemporary media accounts of romance writers from 1980 to the present. For the sake of comparison, and with the help of another phenomenal research assistant, Shannon Mullane, I contacted the archives of the Science Fiction Fantasy Writers of America and the Mystery Writers of America, looked at several decades of newsletters, and had relevant articles digitized, coded, and analyzed in NVivo.

Survey Research and Analysis

In 2015, as part of my doctoral dissertation, I sent a survey to RWA's entire membership (n = 10,240), asking forty-nine questions about professional practices and income. I asked authors to recall all book-related gross earnings from romance, including self-publishing and traditional publishing. I also asked about attitudes toward the industry, frequency and type of advice-seeking and networking, their use of technology, and common sources of advice. I also included a name-generator question, asking participants to name the three people they turned to most frequently for advice.

Initially, I asked RWA, Mystery Writers of America, and Science Fiction and Fantasy Writers of America to participate in the survey. However, only RWA agreed, and provided me access to their entire membership list. Survey participants were entered in a drawing for five $20 Amazon gift cards, and one entry to the 2016 RWA convention, provided by RWA. In all, 4,270 (41.7 percent) responded, though not all respondents answered every question.

Respondents' average age was fifty-one and most were middle-income, with median income ranging from $75,000 to $100,000. Compared to the US population in 2015, survey respondents were more likely to be female or other (98 percent vs. 50.4 percent of Americans), college educated (80 percent vs. 33 percent of Americans),[10] and white (89 percent vs. 73 percent of Americans).[11] See table A.2.

Representativeness. Restricting the survey to RWA members ensured the response population would be career-focused romance writers. However, RWA does not represent all romance writers. RWA provided benchmark statistics for total membership, which I compared to the survey respondent population. The groups had a similar mean length of membership, but survey respondents had more publishing experience than the general membership.

Because I wanted to look at actively publishing authors who considered romance writing a career (even if it wasn't always a lucrative or full-time endeavor), I filtered my survey results for authors who reported nonzero income for 2009 and any income, even zero, for 2014 (n = 668, including twenty-three zero income earners in 2014).

This ensured a population that was actively publishing before and after 2010, when both e-books and digital self-publishing grew sharply, and it captured data from authors who began, or ceased, to earn income during these years. I excluded respondents who reported zero income for *both* 2009 and 2014 (n = 63), because they were not active in income-generating publishing during this period. Some analyses applied additional filters and have smaller samples, indicated in the tables.

TABLE A.2. Survey Respondents Descriptive Statistics

Total respondents = 4,270	
Age (average)	51
Education level (average) (n = 4,125)	College graduate
Household Income (median) (n = 2,345)	$75,000–$100,000
Gender	
Female (n = 4,040)	98%
Male (n = 79)	2%
Other gender (n = 8)	0.2%
Race/Ethnicity	
White (n = 3,650)	89%
Black (n = 158)	4%
Multiracial (n = 105)	3%
Latinx (n = 75)	2%
Asian/Pacific Islander (n = 58)	1.4%
Native American (n = 19)	0.5%
Other (n = 23)	0.6%

Not all respondents answered every question. Total percentages within categories may not add up to 100 percent due to rounding.

Income Analysis. I asked about income in three categories: traditional romance publishing, romance self-publishing, and "other" forms of romance income, such as short stories or auxiliary rights. Income figures are reported in 2014 dollars. In my analysis of the percentage of authors earning more than the median income, I used women's median income in the United States as my benchmark, given the predominantly female response set. For this analysis only, I excluded the ten men who responded to the income analysis. I also analyzed income by race, excluding twenty-three authors who did not report race.

Tests of significance comparing median income used the Wilcoxon signed rank test for paired nonparametric data. Tests of significance comparing increase in percentage of authors earning benchmark amounts or holding day jobs used two-sample tests of proportion. Relevant tables are included in chapter 8 (tables 8.1, 8.2, and 8.3).

Advice Network Analysis

With Dr. Elspeth Ready, I conducted a social network analysis of romance writer advice networks. The survey asked respondents to name three people they turned to most frequently for advice. In all, 749 people answered this question, providing 4,615 advisor names, of whom 1,227 also responded to the survey. Using the software package Igraph in R, we constructed a network of 7,652 unique names, including all survey respondents and named advisors. Because we lack data on individuals not responding to the survey, a subset of this total network, consisting of the advice relationships between the 4,264 non-anonymous survey responders is used for some analyses. (It's important to note that the SNA subsample is more expansive than the income subsample I used for the income analyses above, which only included those who answered the income questions for 2009 and 2014.)

Using this network construct, we first analyzed the network to see if race, income, geography, publishing experience and category, and RWA national conference attendance correlated with advice-seeking cliques. To do so, we calculated assortativity coefficients, where 1 = an entirely exclusive group, never seeking advice from people who did not share a mixing factor (race, income, etc.) and 0 = an entirely open group, no more likely to seek advice from people who shared the factor (see table A.3 below). All analyzed factors were closer to zero than one, indicating that none of the analyzed factors played a strong role in creating cliques.

TABLE A.3. Categories of Romance Writers:
Traditionally Published vs. Innovators

Category	n
Established Innovators	648
Established Traditionals	369
Aspiring Innovators	1,160
Aspiring Traditionals	603
Unpublished	1,338
Total	4,118

Note: Total survey respondents = 4,276, but we removed twelve anonymous respondents from the network and had insufficient information on the publication record of 146 respondents to assign them to the categories above.

TABLE A.4. Cliquing Factors: Assortativity Coefficients

Factor	r
Membership in local chapter	0.27
Type of publication (indie, traditional, hybrid)	0.15
Published Author Network membership	0.15
Race* (white author/author of color)	0.11
Writing Income <= $500,000/year**	0.08

*Race assortativity calculated excluding 181 individuals of unknown race.

** Income calculated assuming all unpublished authors had zero writing income. Published authors who did not report their income are excluded. Assortativity on this variable increases to 0.16 if we assume none of the latter had incomes of more than $500,000.

TABLE A.5. Proportion of Group Asked/Not Asked for Advice, Sought/ Did not Seek Advice

	Not asked for advice	Were asked for advice	Did not seek advice	Did seek advice
Established Innovators ($n = 593$)	52%	48%*	33%	67%**
Established Traditional ($n = 424$)	64%	36%	31%	69%
Aspiring Innovators ($n = 1,097$)	66%	34%	32%	68%
Aspiring Traditional ($n = 635$)	67%	33%	27%	73%
Unpublished ($n = 1,515$)	87%	13%	38%	62%

* Established innovators were more likely to have been asked for advice than any other group of authors (adjusted p-values all < 0.001).

** No significant differences in the proportion of any type of published authors who sought advice. Unpublished authors sought advice less than aspiring authors who had published at least one book (self-published or traditional, adjusted p < 0.05).

Next, to study advice patterns, we sorted groups into a mixing matrix. Authors were classified as "established" or "aspiring," based on whether or not they'd published before the indie boom in 2010. We cross-tabulated these categories with publication format (indie, traditional, or unpublished). Authors were characterized as indie if they'd self-published at least one book, even if they'd also published traditionally (see table A.5). Our matrix showed the number of ties between types of authors, divided by the total number of advice

TABLE A.6. Proportion of Outbound Ties in Each Group Distributed to Other Groups

Established Innovators		Established Traditionals	Aspiring Innovators	Aspiring Traditionals	Unpublished
Established Innovators (n = 648, 492 edges)	54%	16%	22%*	5%	2%
Established Traditional (n = 369, 268 edges)	49%	24%	12%	10%	3%
Aspiring Innovators (n = 1,160, 829 edges)	27%	7%	45%	14%	5%
Aspiring Traditionals (n = 603, 478 edges)	22%	12%	28%	28%	8%
Unpublished (n = 1,338, 776 edges)	24%	10%	29%	17%	18%

*Compared with established authors who only published traditionally, established innovators form significantly more advice ties with aspiring innovators, adjusted p < 0.05; in fact, established traditionals interacted with aspiring innovators less often than any other group of authors.

ties coming from each group, creating a proportion of ties across group types adding to 100 percent. We looked at who asked for advice or didn't (table A.5) and whom they were most likely to ask advice from (table A.6). To determine significance levels, we performed proportion tests, with Holm adjustments for multiple pairwise comparisons where appropriate.

Limitations. For both the income and social network analyses, the sample included only RWA members, so the data are silent on authors who were not RWA members in early 2015. Due to the length of the survey, we asked for only three advisor names—patterns may have been different if we had not limited responses. These analyses do not examine the kinds of writing advice offered, or frequency of advice seeking (for those questions, we relied on other survey questions and interviews). As explored in chapter 6, survivorship bias is of particular concern given reports of racial discrimination within RWA: authors who did not find RWA welcoming or useful may have been less likely to join and thus be included in the survey. It is also important to note that respondents in 2015 overwhelmingly identified as women, but the genre's characters and authors may be changing as definitions of romance expands. Our network analysis shows relationships only at one moment in time and sheds no light on networking patterns before or after 2015. These patterns may have changed substantially as digital publishing continued to grow, and after RWA imploded.

All these limitations should be taken seriously. At the same time, these findings have been rigorously peer-reviewed and published in top journals within the communication field and provide the best and most extensive income and networking data available to date on romance writers.

For more detailed methodology, refer to Larson 2019, Larson and Ready 2022, and Larson 2022.

NOTES

Introduction

1. Mas & Pallais, 2020: 631.

2. Dua et al. 2022.

3. Freelancers Union 2018.

4. Bowers et al. 2022.

5. Beck 2000: 73.

6. de Peuter 2011.

7. Moreno and Boudette 2023.

8. McRobbie 2015: 4.

9. O'Meara 2019; Hund 2023; Petre, Duffy, and Hund 2019; Cohen and de Peuter 2020.

Chapter 1: Brenna's Choice

1. As I mention the intro, in this book, I use the term "women" to refer to any person who self-identifies as such.

2. Before digital publishing, only a few originally self-published print books had become bestsellers. Those rare exceptions included *The Celestine Prophecy*, which author James Redfield sold out of the trunk of his car until Warner Books picked it up in 1993, and *Rich Dad, Poor Dad* by Robert Kiyosaki and Sharon Lechter, in 1997.

3. Waldfogel and Reimers 2015: 52.

4. Larson 2019.

5. Flood 2016.

6. Holson 2016.

7. Milliot 2023.

8. Bonilla-Silva 2022; Golash-Boza 2017; Lipsitz 2006; Jackson, Bailey, and Welles 2020.

9. Circana BookScan and Circana PubTrack Digital, 2023, "2023," Circana report, in the author's possession. Grateful thanks to Circana's Kristen McLean, executive director, books and entertainment, for sharing these reports.

10. Snitow 2003: 143.

11. Radway 1991: 12.

12. Roach 2018: 13.

13. Frederick 1975, 231.

14. Nightline 1983.

15. Gottlieb 2017.

16. Soloski 2020.

17. For a deep dive on feminized labor and its implications, a good place to start is Arlie Hochschild's canonical works *The Second Shift* (1979), *The Managed Heart* (1989), and *The Time Bind* (1997). Within cultural production, start with the work of Angela McRobbie, Rosalind Gill, and Brooke Erin Duffy.

18. Hesmondhalgh 2018: 14.

19. Dua et al. 2022.

20. Banks 2007: 4.

21. Former *New Yorker* editor Tina Brown originally coined the phrase to describe how her friends all seemed to be taking on "free-floating projects, consultancies, and part-time bits and pieces" (Brown 2009, *The Daily Beast*). Today, the term is sometimes used to describe a narrower group of people whose work is controlled by algorithms, such as rideshare drivers. I use it more broadly, to refer to the normalization of multiple insecure jobs, freelancing, and self-employment across the economy.

22. Baym 2018.

23. Adkins and Jokinen 2008: 142.

24. Baym 2018.

25. Cohen and de Peuter 2020.

26. O'Meara 2019.

27. Cunningham 2021: 279–85.

28. de Peuter, Cohen, and Saraco 2017; Cohen 2016.

29. Hsu 2023.

30. Bowers et al. 2022.

31. Padgett 2010; Powell and Owen-Smith 2012; Stone and Stone 1986.

32. Padgett and Powell 2012: 55.

33. Collins 1990; Crenshaw 1990.

34. Rottenberg 2020; Banet-Weiser, Gill, and Rottenberg 2020.

35. Gilligan 1982; Held 2006; Tronto 2013; Tronto 1993.

36. Walker and Snarey 2004.

37. Robinson 2023.

38. Poell, Nieborg, and Duffy 2021: 5.

Chapter 2: Mapping Romancelandia

1. Collins 2009; Flood 2020; Cadwalladr 2011. Roberts is one of the few authors in this book I did not interview; I rely on a rich supply of interviews, profiles, and feature stories. Although we met and chatted at two romance conferences, she very graciously declined my request for an interview for the book in 2018. Her assistant, Laura Reeth, explained that Nora was stepping back from romance and focusing more on other genres.

2. Quinn 1998.

3. Flood 2020.

4. Flood 2020.

5. Pedroni 2023.

6. Crusie 2000.

7. Other early small presses featuring lesbian, gay male, or bisexual protagonists included Cleis Press, Alyson Books, Bold Strokes Books, and, later, Ellora's Cave and Dreamspinner.

8. I am indebted to Carole V. Bell for her insights into biased definitions of romance.

9. Romance Writers of America 2023a.

10. Modleski 2008.

11. Radway 1991.

12. Regis 2007: 107.

13. Regis 2007: 14.

14. Roach 2018: 26.

15. Childress 2019.

16. In this way, a book serves as a "boundary object," lying between several fields, recognizable to all, but defined differently by each. Childress notes that, as the book travels across boundaries, from creation to production to reception, it must be reinterpreted and translated from one realm to the other. Often, he notes, things go wrong in translation: his outstanding book *Under the Covers* explains how, why, and what that means for reading culture.

17. Roach 2018: 13.

18. Roach 2018: 21.

19. McLean 2023.

20. Maltese 2020.

21. Waite 2021.

22. Wendell and Tan 2009: 11.

23. Kamblé 2014: 21.

24. Pearce and Stacey 1995: 12.

25. Burton 2000.

26. Radway 1991: 74.

27. Wendell and Tan 2009: 143.

28. Kamblé 2023. These were *Entwined Destinies* by Rosalind Welles (1980); *The Tender Mending* by Lia Sanders (1982); *Toast to Love* by Barbara Stephens (1984); *All Good Things* by Sandra Kitt (1984); and *Adam and Eva* by Sandra Kitt (1985). All were edited by either Vivian Stephens or Veronica Mixon, influential Black editors discussed in chapters 3 and 6.

29. Braverman 1998: 37. See also Cohen 2016: 25–35.

30. Dua et al. 2022. Freelancers Union, 2018.

31. Mulcahy 2019; Giblin and Doctorow 2022.

32. Duffy 2017; x.

33. See Elberse 2013; Hesmondhalgh 2018; Hesmondhalgh and Baker, 2011; Menger 2014.

34. Hesmondhalgh et al. 2021: 18.

35. Jeff Bullas, quoted in Duffy 2017: 16.

36. Rosen 1981.

37. Bucher 2016; Kumar 2019.

38. Neff, Wissinger, and Zukin 2005: 307.

39. Duffy 2017: x.

40. Neff 2012; Kuehn and Corrigan 2013.

41. That said, as we'll see in chapter 8, a subset of authors known as "book stuffers" write romance strictly for money. This group seeks to game Kindle Unlimited's pay-per-page-read algorithm through practices like inserting extra content—meant to be skipped over—into their books.

42. Lois and Gregson 2019: 51.

43. Jenkins 2008: 7.

44. Jarrett 2014; Duffy 2017: 24. Hochschild's (2012) conceptions of emotional labor and Baym's (2018) account of relational labor are also forms of invisible labor.

45. Baym 2018: 19.

46. Jarrett 2014; McRobbie 2010; Hochschild 2012; Hochschild and Machung 1989; Adkins 2001; Duffy 2017; Adkins and Jokinen 2008.

47. Bishop and Duffy 2022; Hund 2023.

48. NPD Books 2017; Larson 2018; Rothschild and Schwartz 2018.

49. Lee & Low Books 2020.

50. NPD Books 2017.

51. Duffy and Pruchniewska 2017.

52. Wight, Bianchi, and Hunt 2013; Glynn 2018. Compared to white families, the gender gap in unpaid household labor is lower for Black families, and higher for Hispanic and Asian families.

53. Cohen et al. 2019.

54. Di Leonardo 1987.

55. Wellman and Wortley 1990: 576.

56. Brenner and Laslett 1991.

57. Like many studies of this time period, this study does not provide a breakdown of race or income.

58. Brenner and Laslett 1991: 321.

59. Murolo 1997.

60. Smith 1974; Collins 1990.

61. Roach 2018: 196.

62. Childress 2015: 45; Childress 2019: 8. See also Childress 2015 for an in-depth analysis of sociology's three competing approaches to field theory—neo-institutionalism, Bourdieu's field theory, and strategic action theory. In addition, actor-network theory usefully clarifies how both human and nonhuman "actors" form connections and shape social action. See Latour 1993 and Callon 1986. Here, I draw on similarities between these theories.

63. These entities, plus Romancelandians themselves, can also be described as "actors," a term from network theory that describes humans or nonhumans who engage in, or structure, relationships and interactions among other actors. In addition to people, Romancelandia's main actors are informal networks, organizations, events, and platforms.

64. Jenkins 2012.

65. Harris 2022; Harris 2021.

66. Grateful thanks to Carole V. Bell, Olivia Waite, and Erik Urdang for helping think through this map.

67. Flood 2020.

68. Roberts 2007.

Chapter 3: The Roots of Romancelandia

1. All information comes from my interviews with Vivian Stephens in 2016 and 2019, cross-checked with other sources. For additional accounts of Stephens's life and impact, see Swartz 2020 and Markert 2016. To hear Stephens's story in her own voice, listen to Julie Moody-Freeman's delightful *Black Romance Podcast* (episodes 5 and 6).

2. In 2019, RWA would call attention to this problem, by introducing a scholarship funding diverse young women to live in New York City while completing internships.

3. Bray 1982.

4. Watkins 1981.

5. Thompson 2012.

6. Coser, Kadushin, and Powell 1982; Thompson 2012.

7. Rosen 1981: 845.

8. Elberse 2013.

9. Hamilton 2004; Elberse 2013.

10. Thompson 2012; Childress 2019. Today, some publishers also take an occasional huge gamble on a promising debut author.

11. Ironically, in the age of big data, having no track record can be better than having a modest one. Thompson, 2012; 2021.

12. Elberse 2013.

13. Today, "surefire" bestsellers by celebrity authors earn far more: consider Barack and Michelle Obama's $65 million advance for two books in 2017 or Bruce Springsteen's $10 million advance for *Born to Run*. Most book industry observers agree that such astronomical advances erode funds available for midlist authors.

14. Thompson 2012.

15. Coser, Kadushin, and Powell 1982.

16. Davis 1984; Thompson 2012.

17. Radway 1991; Davis 1984.

18. Lobato 2019.

19. Markert 2016; Davis 1984; Radway 1991.

20. Markert 2016; Radway 1991; Grescoe 1996: 76. For extensive and insightful explanations, see Radway 1991: chapter 1; Markert 2016: chapter 2.

21. Radway 1991: 40.

22. Markert 2016; Radway 1991.

23. Markert 2016.

24. Radway 1991.

25. Fox 2009.

26. Wendell 2009.

27. Fox 2009.

28. Regis 2007.

29. Markert 2016.

30. Bell, Bryant, and Haddock 2010.

31. Kelley 1984: 138.

32. Kelley 1984.

33. Jenkins 2016.

34. Hund 2023.

35. Coultrap-McQuin 1990.

36. Gallagher 1998.

37. Samuels 1993.

38. Vida 2012.

39. Weiner 2007.

40. Milella, Brooks, and Hudson 1987.

41. National League of American Pen Women 2019.

42. Klein 2019.

43. *New York Times* 1912: 12.

44. Cohen and de Peuter 2020; Hund 2023.

45. Lawrence 2017.

46. Paretsky n.d.

47. See the Sisters in Crime website, www.sistersincrime.org.

48. *Romance Writers Report* 1984.

49. *Romance Writers Report* 1985.

50. Author Earnings 2016.

51. Romance Writers of America 2023b.

52. Giblin and Doctorow 2022: 162.

53. Hiatt 2004.

54. Hiatt 2005.

55. Hiatt 2004.

56. M. Larson 2012: 1.

57. Classic examples include the move to establish medicine as a profession, while excluding midwives and other traditional health practitioners.

58. Larson and Ready 2022.

59. Padgett 2010: 357.

60. Danford 2005.

61. Padgett 2010.

62. Padgett's work on innovation, networks, and Renaissance Florence is so relevant to today's rapid technological change that the National Science Foundation recently granted him some $600,000 to study the relationship of economics, politics, and kinship networks in innovation.

63. Powell and Owen-Smith 2012: 619.

64. Powell and Owen-Smith 2012: 742.

65. Alexander 2019.

66. Baym 2018.

67. Many decades later, Howard would draw criticism for posting on an internal RWA forum that the board's intense focus on diversity was alienating some member and consuming a disproportionate number of resources. She resigned after her comments were met with fury, and noted she was never against diversity, simply the way the board implemented it. "Social media has a lot to answer for," she told reporter Mimi Swartz (2020).

68. Swartz 2020.

69. Hodson 2001.

70. This was a primary concern of Marx, who argued that alienated labor is isolated, rather than collectively organized by a group of creators. Such isolation makes workers easier to control and exploit (Hodson 2001). Similarly, Foucault argues in *Discipline and Punish* (1979) that isolated subjects, constantly believing themselves to be observed, can be more easily controlled.

71. McRobbie 2017: 141.

72. McRobbie 2017: 141.

73. Gilligan 1982; Held 2006.

74. Walker and Snarey 2004.

75. Held 2006: 10.

76. Tronto 2013: 19.

77. Gilligan 1982.

78. Jenkins 2008. By recognizing the porous boundaries between amateur and professional, romance writers anticipated academic discussions of user-generated content and fanfic (Jenkins 2008). Most of these discussions note the breakdown of barriers between professional and amateur creators by noting that amateurs now have production and distribution power, but few address the most important distinction—the intention of, and often success at, earning money for producing content.

79. Everbach 2006: 477.

80. Walters 1981.

81. Walters 1981.

82. Danford 2005.

83. Turner 2006: 132.

Chapter 4: "Women Trying to Annihilate Each Other in the Name of Romance"

1. Huddy 2013.

2. Leviton et al. 2006.

3. Leviton et al. 2006.

4. Alexius and Pemer 2013; O'Neil and Willis 2005.

5. Rita Clay Estrada, letter to Iris Bancroft, February 19, 1982, RWA Archives, Browne Popular Culture Library.

6. Romance Writers of America, "Meeting Minutes: Emergency Board of Directors Meeting," 1982, Browne Popular Culture Library.

7. Swartz 2020.

8. Sue Gross, letter to Rita Clay Estrada, April 28, 1982, General Correspondence, box 13, folder 2, Romance Writers of America Archives, Bowling Green State University Libraries.

9. Tronto 1993: 109.

10. Acker 2006.

11. Gatevackes 2021.

12. Shock 1985: 20–24.

13. Shock 1985: 24.

14. Grescoe 1996.

15. Becker 2008: 35.

16. Becker thinks of "art worlds" as more open and collaborative than Bourdieu's "fields," which Becker characterizes as closed spaces where zero-sum power struggles take place. Both terms, along with other forms of field theory, consider how power flows among various types of actors oriented toward the same issue.

17. Becker 2008: 94.

18. Giblin and Doctorow 2022: 173.

19. Wiessner 2023.

20. Hogan 2023; Testa 2021.

21. Cohen 2016; Cohen and de Peuter 2020; Smith and Duxbury 2019

22. Wiessner 2023.

23. RWA Historical Committee, "RWA Interview with Vivian Stephens," 1986, Browne Popular Culture Library.

24. Swartz 2020.

25. Barbara Keenan, letter to Rita Clay Estrada, March 2, 1982, General Correspondence, box 13, folder 2, Romance Writers of America Archives, Bowling Green Popular Culture Library.

26. Barbara Keenan, letter to Rita Clay Estrada, March 2, 1982, General Correspondence, box 13, folder 2, Romance Writers of America Archives, Bowling Green Popular Culture Library.

27. Sue Gross, letter to Rita Clay Estrada, April 28, 1982, General Correspondence, box 13, folder 2, Romance Writers of America Archives, Bowling Green State University Libraries. Emphasis added.

28. Capobianco, Hartshorn, and Wallace, comps. n.d.

29. Kerstan 1998a: 48.

30. *PANdora's Box* 1990.

31. Abbott 1988.

32. C. Larson 2012.

33. Whitehead 2003; Davies 1996.

34. Winter 2004.

35. Samuels 1993: 10.

36. Bedford 1992: 7.

37. Axelrod 2011: 12.

38. Kerstan 1998b.

39. Laura Taylor, "Becoming a Professional," 1990, RWA Conference Recordings, RWA Archives, Browne Popular Culture Library, Bowling Green State University.

40. Osborne 1985.

41. Grescoe 1996: 220.

42. Huseby 1985.

43. Grescoe 1996: 136.

44. Roux 2021.

45. Carlson 1992: 66.

46. Romance Writers of America 2020a.

47. Swartz 2020.

48. *Romance Writers Report* 1985: 15.

49. *Romance Writers Report* 1985: 15.

50. *Romance Writers Report* 1985.

51. Rothschild and Schwartz 2018.

52. Internal Revenue Service 2023.

53. Padgett and Powell 2012: 55.

54. Waite 2018.

55. Rothschild and Schwartz 2018.

56. Salcedo 2018.

57. Korkki 2016; Skarupski and Foucher 2018.

58. Putnam 2001: 19.

59. Coser, Kadushin, and Powell 1982.

60. *Romance Writers Report* 1985.

61. Hall 1994.

62. Rodgers 1996.

63. Osborne 1985: 2.

64. Walters 1982.

65. Roberts 2019.

66. Maltese 2016.

67. Roberts 2019.

Chapter 5: The Love Train

1. Jenkins 2008; Jenkins 2012; Click and Scott 2017; Hills 2002; Harrington and Bielby 2018.

2. Choyke 2019.

3. Hund 2023; Baym 2000.

4. Jenkins 2012; McCormick 2018.

5. van Dijk 1997; Foucault 1979.

6. Hills 2002; Click and Scott 2017; Jenkins 2008: 200.

7. Click and Scott 2017; Click, Aubrey, and Behm-Morawitz 2010.

8. Special thanks to my colleague Andrew Calabrese for calling my attention to *Where the Heart Roams*, the 1987 documentary about Kitzmiller's train ride.

9. Csicsery, dir. 1987.

10. Grescoe 1996.

11. Kitzmiller 2023.

12. Stewart 1996.

13. Roach 2018; Radway 1991.

14. Jenkins 2008.

15. Beck 2019; Deahl 2022.

16. Choyke 2019: 152.

17. Larsen and Zubernis 2012: 22.

18. Canby 1987.

19. Kamblé, Selinger, and Teo 2020: 269.

20. Krentz 1992: 1.

21. Rodale 2015: 26.

22. Larsen and Zubernis 2012: 1.

23. Lois and Gregson 2015: 465.

24. Flade, Klar, and Imhoff 2019; Kinder and Kam 2010.

25. Harrington and Bielby 2018.

26. NPD Books 2017.

27. Allie Parker, quoted in Pryde 2022: 26.

28. Cohen 2014; Kurtin et al. 2019; Liebers and Schramm 2019; Yuan and Lou 2020.

29. Baym 2018.

30. Lois and Gregson 2019: 51.

31. Radway 1991: 97.

32. Fish 1980: 147.

33. Radway 1991: 7.

34. Radway 1991: 12.

35. Radway 1991.

36. Radway 1991: 15.

37. Radway 1991: 18.

38. Bobo 1988: 43.

39. Kamblé 2014: xiv.

40. Radway 1991: 11.

41. Tronto 2013.

42. Tronto 1993: 108.

43. Baym 2018.

44. Parents Involved in Community Schools v. Seattle School District No. 1, 551 U.S. 701 (2007), 748.

45. Stewart 1996.

46. de Peuter, Cohen, and Saraco 2017; O'Meara 2019.

Chapter 6: Race and Romance

1. Vivanco 2019a.

2. Brockmann 2018.

3. Vivanco 2019a.

4. Vivanco 2019a.

5. Milella, Brooks, and Hudson 1987.

6. Seressia says PREORDER GAME ON 2020.

7. Snyder 2021

8. Beckett 2019.

9. Hurston 1950: 118.

10. Young 2010.

11. Adichie 2009.

12. Hall 1995: 20.

13. Bradley 1995.

14. Hughes 1985: 25.

15. Bray 1982.

16. Macpherson 1999.

17. Beckett 2019.

18. White 2008.

19. Romance Writers of America 2020a.

20. Deseret 1996.

21. Romance Writers of America 2020a.

22. Edmunds-Stills 2020.

23. Romance Writers of America 2020b.

24. Markert 2016; Moody-Freeman 2020.

25. Isaacs 1992.

26. Max 1992.

27. Wheeler 2020.

28. Baym 2018; Radway 1991.

29. Snyder 2023; Beckett 2019.

30. Beckett 2019.

31. Hurston 1950.

32. Bradley 1994.

33. Rosen 2004.

34. White 2008.

35. Reid 2006.

36. Reid 2006: 200.

37. Markert 2016.

38. Romance Writers of America 2020b.

39. Smith 1997: 26.

40. Garcia-Navarro 2018.

41. Nava 2021.

42. Brockmann 2018.

43. Brockmann 2018.

44. See Women of Color in Romance (www.wocinromance.com) and Building Relationships Around Books (www.brabonline.net).

45. Bell 1990.

46. Holder, Jackson, and Ponterotto 2015.

47. Burke and Mattis 2005.

48. Green 2018; Guillaume et al. 2017.

49. McPherson, Smith-Lovin, and Cook 2001.

50. Newman 2002.

51. Sue Gross, letter to Rita Clay Estrada, April 28, 1982, General Correspondence, box 13, folder 2, Romance Writers of America Archives, Bowling Green State University Libraries.

52. Avon Books 2019.

53. Beckett 2019.

54. Beckett 2019.

55. Beckett 2019.

56. Ellis 2021.

57. MacLean 2019.

Chapter 7: Virtual Romancelandia and the Electronic Frontier

1. Rosenwald 2018.

2. Kirschenbaum 2016.

3. Dzieza 2022.

4. Baym 2000.

5. Baym 2000.

6. Fox and Rainie 2014.

7. Papdakis 2000.

8. Uzzi 1996.

9. Rheingold 2000: 59.

10. Duran 1992.

11. O'Meara 2019.

12. Bush 1945.

13. Coser, Kadushin, and Powell 1982.

14. Project Gutenberg 2022.

15. Thompson 2021.

16. Thompson 2012: 277.

17. Grinnan 1998.

18. Baumbach 2007.

19. Hart 1998.

20. Kamblé, Selinger, and Teo 2020.

21. Thompson 2021.

22. Thompson 2021.

23. Ross 2004: 21.

24. Banks 2007: 4.

25. Kerstan 1998b.

26. *PANdora's Box* 1993.

27. Boltanski, Chiapello, and Elliott 2018; Powell 1990.

28. Hacker 2008.

29. Hacker 2019.

30. Harvey 2005: 2.

31. du Gay 1996: 60.

32. Foucault 1979.

33. Smith 2010.

34. Lowe 2018.

35. Hund 2023.

36. Beck 2000: 73.

37. McRobbie 2002.

38. Banks 2007: 65.

39. Deb Stover, "The History of PAN," n.d., in the author's possession. Thank you to RWA executive director Leslie Scantlebury for sharing this internal history document with me.

40. Jenkins 2008; Deuze 2007.

41. Powell and Owen-Smith 2012: 619.

42. Baym 2000: 182.

43. *Romance Writers Report* 1988.

44. Stover, "The History of PAN."

45. Novelists, Inc. n.d.

46. Stover, "The History of PAN," 3.

47. Ellis 2021.

48. Stover, "The History of PAN."

49. Stover, "The History of PAN," 3.

50. Toossi and Morisi 2017: 21.

51. US Bureau of Labor Statistics 2017.

52. Williams and Wittig 1997.

53. Banet-Weiser, Gill, and Rottenberg 2020.

54. Banet-Weiser, Gill, and Rottenberg 2020: 5.

55. Banet-Weiser 2012; Banet-Weiser 2018; Gill 2002; Gill 2006; Gill 2007; McRobbie 2009; McRobbie 2015; Orgad 2019; Rottenberg 2020.

56. Slaughter 2012.

57. Fielding 1999: 2.

58. Jacobs 2007.

Chapter 8: The Self-Publishing Gold Rush

1. Woodruff-Santos 2014.

2. Tucker 2011.

3. Stone 2021.

4. Thompson 2021.

5. Peter Hildick-Smith, email message to author, July 11, 2023.

6. McLoughlin 2022.

7. Talbot 2023.

8. Solomon 2009.

9. In this chapter, I use "self-publishing" and "indie publishing" interchangeably. Before the rise of digital self-publishing, "independent publisher" referred to companies not affiliated with a large corporation. To avoid confusion, I refer to such publishing houses as "small presses."

10. Curcik 2022.

11. Flood 2016.

12. Easter and Dave 2017.

13. Thompson 2012.

14. Thompson 2012: 318.

15. Waldfogel 2017: 196.

16. Book Industry Study Group 2015; Book Industry Study Group 2008.

17. Larson 2019.

18. Milliot 2023.

19. Tucker, 2011.

20. Pilkington 2012.

21. Osnos 2012; Larson and Ready 2022.

22. Crutcher 2014.

23. Kat Meyer and Kristen McLean, "The 2016 Nielsen Romance Market Snapshot," Nielsen Co. report, 2016, in the author's possession.

24. Minzesheimer and DeBarros 2013.

25. Meyer and McLean, "The 2016 Nielsen Romance Market Snapshot."

26. Milliot 2009.

27. Marble 2009.

28. Marble 2009.

29. Marble 2009.

30. Becker 2008: 97.

31. Wendell and Tan 2009: 7.

32. Rowe and Tunney 2012: 12.

33. Murray and Squires 2013.

34. Larson and Ready 2022.

35. Burt 2004.

36. Barley et al. 2020: 21.

37. Carlile 2004.

38. McPherson, Smith-Lovin, and Cook 2001.

39. Uzzi and Spiro 2005: 465.

40. Unpublished authors were actually a bit less likely to name any advice connections. Maybe they were new to RWA and didn't know as many people. Or maybe asking advice helps authors get published.

41. Padgett 2010.

42. DeLeon et al. 2015: 19.

43. Cader 2014.

44. Association of American Publishers, the Authors Guild, and Association of American Booksellers 2020.

45. Duffy 2020: 202.

46. Noble 2018.

47. Semuels 2018.

48. Flood 2019.

49. Nieborg and Poell 2018.

50. Klar 2021.

Chapter 9: #RWAShitShow

1. Cole 2019.

2. Gallup 2022.

3. Edwards and Rushin 2018.

4. *The Economist* 2023.

5. Mitchell 2019.

6. Faircloth 2020; Grady 2020; Ryan 2019; Wendell 2020.

7. Vivanco 2019b.

8. Vivanco 2019b.

9. Judish and Jacobs 2020.

10. Judish and Jacobs 2020: 19.

11. Judish and Jacobs 2020: 39.

12. Judish and Jacobs 2020: 5.

13. Beckett 2020.

14. Judish and Jacobs 2020: 5, 48.

15. Gurchiek 2021: 9.

16. Mitchell 2019.

17. Beckett 2019.

18. Jackson, Bailey, and Welles 2020.

19. Bonilla-Silva 2022.

20. Jackson, Bailey, and Welles 2020: 19.

21. Collins and Bilge 2020.

22. Stover, "The History of PAN," 3.

23. Cader 2017.

24. Kreiss, Finn, and Turner 2011: 251.

25. Putnam 2001.

26. Sarah Wendell, quoted in Flood 2019.

27. Hartwell 2021.

28. @fangirlJeanne 2021; Smith 2021.

29. Italie 2021.

30. Jackson, Bailey, and Welles 2020: 205.

31. Romance Writers of America, "RWA General Meeting Minutes," 2002, Browne Popular Culture Library.

32. Rueb and Taylor 2019.

33. Garza 2021: 20.

Conclusion

1. Garza 2021: 20.

2. The Authors Guild 2021.

3. Barnes, Koblin, and Sperling 2023; Stevens 2023.

4. Giblin and Doctorow 2022.

5. Mays 2020.

6. Regis 2007: 8.

Appendix 2: Methodology

1. Howard 2002; Neff 2012; Robinson and Anderson 2020.

2. Geertz 1973: 16.

3. Latour 1993; Callon 1986.

4. Neff 2012.

5. Anderson 2013.

6. Robinson 2018.

7. Tremblay 1957.

8. Biernacki and Waldof 1981.

9. Birt et al. 2016; Lincoln and Guba 1985.

10. US Census Bureau 2023.

11. US Census Bureau 2015.

Abbott, Andrew. 1988. *The System of Professions: An Essay on the Division of Expert Labor*. Chicago: University of Chicago Press.

Acker, J. 2006. "Inequality Regimes: Gender, Class, and Race in Organizations." *Gender & Society* 20, no. 4: 441–64. http://gas.sagepub.com/cgi/doi/10.1177/0891243206289499.

Adichie, Chimamanda Ngozi. 2009. "The Danger of a Single Story." TED video, July 2009.

Adkins, Lisa. 2001. "Cultural Feminization: 'Money, Sex and Power' for Women." *Signs* 26, no. 3: 669–95.

Adkins, Lisa, and Eeva Jokinen. 2008. "Introduction: Gender, Living and Labour in the Fourth Shift." *NORA—Nordic Journal of Feminist and Gender Research* 16, no. 3: 138–49.

Alexander, Julia. 2019. "YouTubers' First Organizing Attempt, the Internet Creators Guild, Is Shutting Down." *The Verge*. Accessed June 28, 2023. https://www.theverge.com/2019/7/11/20688929/internet-creators-guild-shutting-down-hank-green-youtube-copyright-claims-monetization.

Alexius, Susanna, and Frida Pemer. 2013. "Struggling to Challenge an Informal Field Order: Professional Associations as Standard-Setters." In *Exploring the Professional Identity of Management Consultants*, edited by Buono, Anthony, Léon de Caluwé and Annemieke Stoppelenburg. Charlotte, NC: Information Age Publishing.

Anderson, C. W. 2013. *Rebuilding the News: Metropolitan Journalism in the Digital Age*. Philadelphia: Temple University Press.

Association of American Publishers, The Authors Guild, and Association of American Booksellers. 2020. "Joint Publishing Industry Letter to Chairman Cicilline."

Author Earnings. 2016. "Romancing the Data." Presented at the Romance Writers of America conference, July 15. http://authorearnings.com/2016-rwa-pan-presentation/.

The Authors Guild. 2021. "Authors Guild Annual Report 2021." Accessed September 8, 2022. https://authorsguild.org/wp-content/uploads/2022/03/Authors-Guild-Annual-Report-2021.pdf.

Avon Books. 2019. "Avon Books Announces First Recipient of the Beverly Jenkins Diverse Voices Sponsorship." HarperCollins. Accessed September 8, 2022. https://www.harpercollins.com/blogs/press-releases/avon-books-announces-first-recipient-of-the-beverly-jenkins-diverse-voices-sponsorship.

Axelrod, Steve. 2011. "Looking Back." *Romance Writers Report*, October.

Banet-Weiser, Sarah. 2012. *Authentic TM: Politics and Ambivalence in a Brand Culture*. New York: New York University Press.

Banet-Weiser, Sarah. 2018. *Empowered: Popular Feminism and Popular Misogyny*. Durham, NC: Duke University Press.

Banet-Weiser, Sarah, Rosalind Gill, and Catherine Rottenberg. 2020. "Postfeminism, Popular Feminism and Neoliberal Feminism? Sarah Banet-Weiser, Rosalind Gill and Catherine Rottenberg in Conversation." *Feminist Theory* 21, no. 1: 3–24. http://journals.sagepub.com/doi /10.1177/1464700119842555.

Banks, Mark. 2007. *The Politics of Cultural Work*. Basingstoke, UK: Palgrave Macmillan.

Barley, William C., Ly Dinh, Hallie Workman, and Chengyu Fang. 2020. "Exploring the Relationship Between Interdisciplinary Ties and Linguistic Familiarity Using Multilevel Network Analysis." *Communication Research* 49, no. 133–66. http://journals.sagepub.com/doi /10.1177/0093650220926001.

Barnes, Brooks, John Koblin, and Nicole Sterling. 2023. "Hollywood Actors Strike: TV and Movie Actors Vote for Biggest Walkout in Four Decades." *New York Times*, August 23.

Baumbach, Laura. 2007. "RT/Hyatt Author Targeted." *Sensual Writer* (blog). http://sensualwriter .blogspot.com/2007/05/rthyatt-author-targeted.htmlRT.

Baym, Nancy K. 2000. *Tune in, Log on: Soaps, Fandom, and Online Community*. Thousand Oaks, CA: Sage Publications.

———. 2018. *Playing to the Crowd: Musicians, Audiences, and the Intimate Work of Connection*. New York: New York University Press.

Beck, Julie. 2019. "The Fan-Fiction Friendship That Fueled a Romance-Novel Empire." *The Atlantic*. Accessed July 5, 2023. https://www.theatlantic.com/family/archive/2019/02/friendship-files -twilight-fan-fiction-new-york-times-bestseller-list/583090/.

Beck, U. 2000. *The Brave New World of Work*. Malden, MA: Polity.

Becker, Howard. 2008. *Art Worlds*. Berkeley: University of California Press.

Beckett, Lois. 2019. "Fifty Shades of White: The Long Fight against Racism in Romance Novels." *The Guardian*, April 4.

———. 2020. "White Romance Writer in Racism Row Says She Was Used." *The Guardian*, January 4.

Bedford, Debbi. 1992. "Image: Here's How We Carry Our Mission Forward." *PANdora's Box*, December.

Bell, Donnell, Neringa Bryant, and Nancy Haddock. 2010. "RWA: The 'Overnight' Success. Celebrating 30 Years of Romance Writers of American." *Romance Writers Report*, January.

Bell, Ella Louise. 1990. "The Bicultural Life Experience of Career-Oriented Black Women." In "The Career and Life Experiences of Black Professionals." Special issue, *Journal of Organizational Behavior* 11, no. 6 (November): 459–77. https://onlinelibrary.wiley.com/doi /abs/10.1002/job.4030110607.

Biernacki, Patrick, and Dan Waldof. 1981. "Snowball Sampling: Problems and Techniques of Chain Referral Sampling." *Sociological Methods and Research* 10, no. 141: 141–63.

Birt, Linda, Suzanne Scott, Debbie Cavers, Christine Campbell, and Fiona Walter. 2016. "Member Checking: A Tool to Enhance Trustworthiness or Merely a Nod to Validation?" *Qualitative Health Research* 26, no. 13: 1802–11.

Bishop, Sophie, and Brooke Erin Duffy. 2022. "The Feminization of Social Media Labor." In *The Oxford Handbook of Digital Media Sociology*, edited by Deana A. Rohlinger and Sarah Sobieraj. New York: Oxford University Press.

Bobo, Jacqueline. 1988. "Black Women's Reponses to *The Color Purple.*" *JumpCut* 33: 43–51.

Boltanski, Luc, Eve Chiapello, and Gregory Elliott. 2018. *The New Spirit of Capitalism.* London: Verso.

Bonilla-Silva, Eduardo. 2022. *Racism without Racists: Color-Blind Racism and the Persistence of Racial Inequality in America.* 6th ed. Lanham, MD: Rowman & Littlefield.

Book Industry Study Group. 2008. "BISAC Subject Heading List, 2008 Edition." https://web .archive.org/web/20090821075205/http://www.bisg.org/activities-programs/activity .php?n=d&id=44&cid=20#FICTIO.

———. 2015. "Complete BISAC Subject Headings List, 2015 Edition." Book Industry Study Group. http://bisg.org/page/BISAC2015Edition.

Bowers, Anne, Joshua Wu, Stuart Lustig, and Douglas Nemecek. 2022. "Loneliness Influences Avoidable Absenteeism and Turnover Intention Reported by Adult Workers in the United States." *Journal of Organizational Effectiveness: People and Performance* 9, no. 2: 312–35.

Bradley, Deborah. 1994. "Matchmaking: Black Writers Find an Audience for Black Romance Novels." *Dallas Morning News,* October 11.

———. 1995. "Black Writers Turn a New Leaf: Romance Novels." *South Florida Sun-Sentinal,* September 5.

Braverman, Harry. 1998. *Labor and Monopoly Capital: The Degradation of Work in the Twentieth Century.* 25th anniversary ed. New York: Monthly Review Press.

Bray, Rosemary. 1982. "Love for Sale." *Black Enterprise,* December.

Brenner, Johanna, and Barbara Laslett. 1991. "Gender, Social Reproduction and Women's Self-Organization: Considering the U.S. Welfare State." *Gender & Society* 5, no. 3: 311–33.

Brockmann, Suzanne. 2018. "That RWA LTA Speech." Tiny Letter. https://tinyletter.com /SuzanneBrockmann/letters/that-rwa-lta-speech-news-from-suz.

Brown, Tina. 2009. "The Gig Economy." *The Daily Beast.* Accessed July 10, 2022. https://www .thedailybeast.com/the-gig-economy.

Bucher, Taina. 2016. "Neither Black nor Box: Ways of Knowing Algorithms." In *Innovative Methods in Media and Communication Research,* edited by Sebastian Kubitschko and Anne Kaun, 81–98. Cham: Springer International.

Burke, Ronald J., and Mary C. Mattis, eds. 2005. *Supporting Women's Career Advancement: Challenges and Opportunities.* Northampton, MA: Elgar.

Burt, Ronald. 2004. "Structural Holes and Good Ideas." *American Journal of Sociology* 110, no. 2: 349–99.

Burton, Mary. 2000. "RWA 30th Anniversary: A Look Back." *Romance Writers Report,* March.

Bush, Vannever. 1945. "As We May Think." *The Atlantic,* July. Accessed February 24, 2012. http:// www.theatlantic.com/magazine/archive/1945/07/as-we-may-think/3881/?single_page =true.

Cader, Michael. 2014. "The Discussion Over 'Author Earnings' (Part 1)." *Publishers Lunch.* Accessed July 16, 2023. https://lunch.publishersmarketplace.com/2014/02/discussion-author -earnings-part-1/.

———. 2017. "Reidy Looks forward to an Open European Market after Brexit." *Publishers Lunch.* Accessed October 29, 2022. https://lunch.publishersmarketplace.com/2017/10 /reidy-looks-forward-open-european-market-brexit/.

Cadwalladr, Carole. 2011. "Nora Roberts: The Woman Who Rewrote the Rules of Romantic Fiction." *The Guardian*, November 19. https://www.theguardian.com/books/2011/nov/20/nora-roberts-interview-romance-fiction.

Callon, Michel. 1986. "Some Elements of a Sociology of Translation: Domestication of the Scallops and the Fishermen of St. Brieuc Bay." *Power, Action, and Belief: A New Sociology of Knowledge* 32: 196–223.

Canby, Vincent. 1987. "Film: 'Where the Heart Roams,' About Romance Novelists." *New York Times*, August 19. Accessed December 7, 2021. https://www.nytimes.com/1987/08/19/movies/film-where-the-heart-roams-about-romance-novelists.html.

Capobianco, Michael, Erin M. Hartshorn, and Sean Wallace, comps. n.d. "The SFWA Bulletin Index, 1965–2018." *Science Fiction Fantasy Writers of America*. https://sfwa.org/bulletin-index/t5.htm#A72.

Carlile, Paul R. 2004. "Transferring, Translating, and Transforming: An Integrative Framework for Managing Knowledge Across Boundaries." *Organization Science* 15, no. 5: 555–68. http://pubsonline.informs.org/doi/abs/10.1287/orsc.1040.0094.

Carlson, Shirley J. 1992. "Black Ideals of Womanhood in the Late Victorian Era." *The Journal of Negro History* 77, no. 2: 61–73.

Childress, Clayton. 2015. "Regionalism and the Publishing Class: Conflicted Isomorphism and Negotiated Identity in a Nested Field of American Publishing." *Cultural Sociology* 9, no. 3: 364–81.

———. 2019. *Under the Cover: The Creation, Production, and Reception of a Novel*. Princeton, NJ: Princeton University Press.

Choyke, Kelly L. 2019. *The Power of Popular Romance Culture: Community, Fandom, and Sexual Politics*. PhD diss., Ohio University.

Click, Melissa A., Jennifer Stevens Aubrey, and Elizabeth Behm-Morawitz. 2010. *Bitten by Twilight: Youth Culture, Media, & the Vampire Franchise*. New York: Peter Lang.

Click, Melissa A., and Suzanne Scott. 2017. *The Routledge Companion to Media Fandom*. New York: Routledge.

Cohen, Jonathan. 2014. "Mediated Relationships and Social Life: Current Research on Fandom, Parasocial Relationships, and Identification." In *Media and Social Life*, edited by M. B. Oliver and A. A. Raney, 142–56. New York: Routledge.

Cohen, Nicole S. 2016. *Writers' Rights: Freelance Journalism in a Digital Age*. Montreal: McGill-Queen's University Press.

Cohen, Nicole S., and Greig De Peuter. 2020. *New Media Unions: Organizing Digital Journalists*. New York: Routledge.

Cohen, Steven A., Natalie J. Sabik, Sarah K. Cook, Ariana B. Azzoli, and Carolyn A. Mendez-Luck. 2019. "Differences within Differences: Gender Inequalities in Caregiving Intensity Vary by Race and Ethnicity in Informal Caregivers." *Journal of Cross-Cultural Gerontology* 34, no. 3: 245–63.

Cole, Alyssa (@AlyssaColeLit). 2019. "One of the reasons I believed in RWA . . ." Twitter, December 23, 8:10 p.m. https://twitter.com/AlyssaColeLit/status/1209280219175100422.

Collins, Lauren. 2009. "Real Romance: How Nora Roberts Became America's Most Popular Novelist." *The New Yorker*, June 15. https://www.newyorker.com/magazine/2009/06/22/real-romance-2.

Collins, Patricia Hill. 1990. *Black Feminist Thought: Knowledge, Consciousness, and the Politics of Empowerment*. New York: Routledge.

Collins, Patricia Hill, and Sirma Bilge. 2020. *Intersectionality*. 2nd ed. Cambridge, UK: Polity.

Coser, Lewis A., Charles Kadushin, and Walter W. Powell. 1982. *Books: The Culture and Commerce of Publishing*. New York: Basic Books.

Coultrap-McQuin, Susan Margaret. 1990. *Doing Literary Business: American Women Writers in the Nineteenth Century*. Chapel Hill: University of North Carolina Press.

Crenshaw, Kimberlé. 1990. "Mapping the Margins: Intersectionality, Identity Politics, and Violence against Women of Color." *Stanford Law Review* 43, no. 6 (July): 1241–99.

Crusie, Jennifer. 2000. "I Know It When I Read It: Defining the Romance Genre." *Jenny Cruise* (blog). Accessed September 30, 2023. https://jennycrusie.com/non-fiction/i-know-what-it-is-when-i-read-it-defining-the-romance-genre/.

Crutcher, Paige. 2014. "KDP Star, Barbara Freethy, Creates Print Imprint." *Publishers Weekly*, October 15. Accessed August 31, 2015. http://www.publishersweekly.com/pw/by-topic/industry-news/publisher-news/article/64405-kdp-star-freethy-launches-print-imprint.html.

Csicsery, George Paul, dir. 1987. *Where the Heart Roams*. Oakland, CA: Zala Films. DVD.

Cunningham, Stuart, ed. 2021. *Creator Culture: An Introduction to Global Social Media Entertainment*. New York: New York University Press.

Curcik, Dimitrije. 2022. "Romance Novel Sales Statistics." Words Rated. Accessed July 3, 2023. https://wordsrated.com/romance-novel-sales-statistics/.

Danford, Natalie. 2005. "Embraced by Romance." *Publishers Weekly*, November 18. https://www.publishersweekly.com/pw/print/20051121/21816-embraced-by-romance.html.

Davies, Celia. 1996. "The Sociology of Professions and the Profession of Gender." *Sociology* 30, no. 4: 661–78.

Davis, Kenneth C. 1984. *Two-Bit Culture: The Paperbacking of America*. Boston: Houghton Mifflin.

Deahl, Rachel. 2022. "E. L. James: PW's Publishing Person of the Year." *Publishers Weekly*. Accessed July 21, 2022. https://www.publishersweekly.com/pw/by-topic/industry-news/people/article/54956-e-l-james-pw-s-publishing-person-of-the-year.html.

DeLeon, Jana, Tina Folsom, Colleen Gleason, Jane Graves, Debra Holland, Dorien Kelly, Theresa Ragan, Denise Grover Swank, and Jacinda Wilder. 2015. *The Naked Truth about Self-Publishing*. Self-published, The Indie Voice.

de Peuter, Greig. 2011. "Creative Economy and Labor Precarity: A Contested Convergence." *Journal of Communication Inquiry* 35, no. 4: 417–25. https://doi.org/10.1177/0196859911416362.

de Peuter, Greig, Nicole S. Cohen, and Francesca Saraco. 2017. "The Ambivalence of Coworking: On the Politics of an Emerging Work Practice." *European Journal of Cultural Studies* 20, no. 6: 687–706. http://journals.sagepub.com/doi/10.1177/1367549417732997.

Deseret News. 1996. "Publishers Strike Mother Lode with Black Romance Fiction." *St. Petersburg Times*, November 15. https://www.deseret.com/1996/11/15/19277945/online-document-publishers-strike-mother-lode-with-black-romance-fiction.

Deuze, Mark. 2007. *Media Work*. Cambridge, UK: Polity.

Di Leonardo, Micaela. 1987. "The Female World of Cards and Holidays: Women, Families, and the Work of Kinship." *Signs: Journal of Women in Culture and Society* 12, no. 3: 440–53.

Dua, André, Kwellin Elindgrud, Bryan Hancock, Ryan Luby, Anu Madgavkar, and Sarah Pemberton. 2022. "Freelance Work, Side Hustles, and the Gig Economy." McKinsey & Company. Accessed June 9, 2023. https://www.mckinsey.com/featured-insights/sustainable-inclusive-growth/future-of-america/freelance-side-hustles-and-gigs-many-more-americans-have-become-independent-workers.

Duffy, Brooke Erin. 2017. *(Not) Getting Paid to Do What You Love: Gender, Social Media, and Aspirational Work*. New Haven, CT: Yale University Press.

———. 2020. "Algorithmic Precarity in Cultural Work." *Communication and the Public* 5, no. 3–4: 103–7. http://journals.sagepub.com/doi/10.1177/2057047320959855.

Duffy, Brooke Erin, and Urszula Pruchniewska. 2017. "Gender and Self-Enterprise in the Social Media Age: A Digital Double Bind." *Information, Communication & Society* 20, no. 6: 843–59. https://www.tandfonline.com/doi/full/10.1080/1369118X.2017.1291703.

du Gay, Paul. 1996. *Consumption and Identity at Work*. London: Sage Publications.

Duran, Betty. 1992. "Rabble Rouser: Grow Up!" *PANdora's Box*, December.

Dzieza, Josh. 2022. "How Kindle Novelists Are Using ChatGPT." *The Verge*. Accessed July 9, 2023. https://www.theverge.com/23520625/chatgpt-openai-amazon-kindle-novel.

Easter, Makeda, and Paresh Dave. 2017. "Remember When Amazon Only Sold Books?" *Los Angeles Times*. Accessed July 11, 2023. https://www.latimes.com/business/la-fi-amazon-history-20170618-htmlstory.html.

The Economist. 2023. "Political Protests Have Become More Widespread and More Frequent." March 10. https://www.economist.com/graphic-detail/2020/03/10/political-protests-have-become-more-widespread-and-more-frequent.

Edmunds-Stills, Zakiyah. 2020. "Black Romance Matters." *Unsuitable: Conversations about Women, History & Popular Fiction* (blog). https://sites.duke.edu/unsuitable/black-romance-matters/.

Edwards, Griffin S., and Stephen Rushin. 2019. "The Effect of President Trump's Election on Hate Crimes." Social Science Research Network. Accessed October 1, 2023. https://papers.ssrn.com/sol3/papers.cfm?abstract_id=3102652.

Elberse, Anita. 2013. *Blockbusters: Hit-Making, Risk-Taking, and the Big Business of Entertainment*. New York: Henry Holt and Company.

Ellis, Danika. 2021. "The Ripped Bodice's 2020 Racial Diversity in Romance Publishing Report." *Book Riot*. Accessed June 17, 2023. https://bookriot.com/racial-diversity-in-romance-report-2020/.

Everbach, Tracy. 2006. "The Culture of a Women-Led Newspaper: An Ethnographic Study of the Sarasota Herald-Tribune." *Journalism & Mass Communication Quarterly* 83, no. 3: 477–93. http://journals.sagepub.com/doi/10.1177/107769900608300301.

Faircloth, Kelly. 2020. "Inside the Spectacular Implosion at the Romance Writers of America." *Jezebel*. https://jezebel.com/inside-the-spectacular-implosion-at-the-romance-writers-1841002358.

@FangirlJeanne. 2021. "So, RWA has confirmed that 'inspirational romance' is white supremacist fantasies." Twitter, August 2, 2021, 11:02 p.m. https://twitter.com/fangirlJeanne/status/1422422636370432001.

Fielding, Helen. 1999. *Bridget Jones's Diary*. New York: Penguin.

Fish, Stanley Eugene. 1980. *Is There a Text in This Class? The Authority of Interpretive Communities*. Cambridge, MA: Harvard University Press. Accessed March 15, 2012. http://catalog.hathitrust.org/api/volumes/oclc/6555139.html.

Flade, Felicitas, Yechiel Klar, and Roland Imhoff. 2019. "Unite against: A Common Threat Invokes Spontaneous Decategorization between Social Categories." *Journal of Experimental Social Psychology* 85. https://doi.org/10.1016/j.jesp.2019.103890.

Flood, Alison. 2015. "When a Jew Loves a Nazi: Holocaust Romance's Award Listings Cause Outrage." *The Guardian*, August 10.

———. 2016. "Digital Reading Led by Older Women, Study Says." *The Guardian*, April 16.

———. 2019. "Plagiarism, 'Book-Stuffing,' Clickfarms . . . the Rotten Side of Self-Publishing." *The Guardian*, March 28. https://www.theguardian.com/books/2019/mar/28/plagiarism-book-stuffing-clickfarms-the-rotten-side-of-self-publishing.

———. 2020. "Nora Roberts: 'I Could Fille All the Bookstores in the Land.'" *The Guardian*, January 30.

Foucault, Michel. 1979. *Discipline and Punish: The Birth of the Prison*. New York: Vintage Books.

Fox, Margalit. 2009. "Kate Duffy, Editor Who Was a Force in Romance, Dies at 56." *New York Times*, October 5.

Fox, Susannah, and Lee Rainie. 2014. "Part 1: How the Internet Has Woven Itself into American Life." Pew Research Center. Accessed June 30, 2022. https://www.pewresearch.org/internet/2014/02/27/part-1-how-the-internet-has-woven-itself-into-american-life/.

Frederick, John T. 1975. "Hawthorne's 'Scribbling Women.'" *The New England Quarterly* 48, no. 2: 231–40. http://www.jstor.org/stable/364660.

Freelancers Union. 2018. "Freelancing in American 2018." New York: Freelancers Union. Accessed September 30, 2023. https://assets.freelancersunion.org/media/documents/freelancinginamericareport-2018.pdf.

Gallagher, Rita. 1998. "The Way We Were." *Romance Writers Report*, January.

Gallup. 2022. "Americans' Trust in Media Remains Near Record Low." Accessed October 1, 2023. https://news.gallup.com/poll/403166/americans-trust-media-remains-near-record-low.aspx.

Garcia-Navarro, Lulu. 2018. "The Billion-Dollar Romance Fiction Industry Has a Diversity Problem." NPR, April 8. https://www.npr.org/2018/04/08/600549049/the-billion-dollar-romance-fiction-industry-has-a-diversity-problem.

Garza, Alicia. 2021. *The Purpose of Power: How We Come Together When We Fall Apart*. New York: Random House.

Gatevackes, William. 2021. "Comic Creator Credit: Why Not Unionize?" *Film Buff Online* (blog). Accessed June 28, 2023. https://www.filmbuffonline.com/FBOLNewsreel/wordpress/2021/09/10/comic-creator-credit-why-not-unionize/.

Geertz, Clifford. 1973. *The Interpretation of Cultures: Selected Essays*. New York: Basic Books.

Giblin, Rebecca, and Cory Doctorow. 2022. *Chokepoint Capitalism: How Big Tech and Big Content Captured Creative Labor Markets and How We'll Win Them Back*. Boston: Beacon Press.

Gill, Rosalind. 2002. "Cool, Creative and Egalitarian? Exploring Gender in Project-Based New Media Work in Euro." *Information, Communication & Society* 5, no. 1: 70–89. http://www.tandfonline.com/doi/abs/10.1080/13691180110117668.

———. 2006. *Gender and the Media*. Malden, MA: Polity.

———. 2007. "Postfeminist Media Culture: Elements of a Sensibility." *European Journal of Cultural Studies* 10, no. 2: 147–66. http://journals.sagepub.com/doi/10.1177/1367549407075898.

Gilligan, Carol. 1982. *In a Different Voice*. Cambridge, MA: Harvard University Press.

Glynn, Sarah Jane. 2018. "An Unequal Division of Labor." Center for American Progress. Accessed June 19, 2023. https://www.americanprogress.org/article/unequal-division-labor/.

Golash-Boza, Tanya Maria. 2017. *Race and Racisms: A Critical Approach*. 2nd ed. New York: Oxford University Press.

Gottlieb, Robert. 2017. "A Roundup of the Season's Romance Novels." *The New York Times*, September 26. https://www.nytimes.com/2017/09/26/books/review/macomber-steel -james-romance.html.

Grady, Constance. 2020. "A History of Racism Led to an Implosion of the Romance Publishing World. Now Can It Change?" *Vox*. Accessed April 12, 2022. https://www.vox.com/the -highlight/2020/6/17/21178881/racism-books-romance-writers-of-america-scandal-novels -publishing.

Green, W. M. 2018. "Employee Resource Groups as Learning Communities." *Equality, Diversity and Inclusion: An International Journal* 37, no. 7: 634–48.

Grescoe, Paul. 1996. *The Merchants of Venus: Inside Harlequin and the Empire of Romance*. Vancouver, Canada: Raincoast Book.

Grinnan, Dabney. 1998. "Laurie's News & Views #56." *All About Romance*. Accessed July 16, 2023. https://allaboutromance.com/lauries-news-views-56/.

Guillaume, Yves R. F., Jeremy F. Dawson, Lilian Otaye-Ebede, Stephen A. Woods, and Michael A. West. 2017. "Harnessing Demographic Differences in Organizations: What Moderates the Effects of Workplace Diversity?" *Journal of Organizational Behavior* 38, no. 2: 276–303.

Gurchiek, Kathy. 2021. *Report: Most Companies Are "Going Through the Motions" of DE&I*. Society for HR Management, February 23. https://www.shrm.org/resourcesandtools/hr-topics /behavioral-competencies/global-and-cultural-effectiveness/pages/report-most -companies-are-going-through-the-motions-of-dei.aspx.

Hacker, Jacob S. 2008. *The Great Risk Shift: The New Economic Insecurity and the Decline of the American Dream*. Oxford: Oxford University Press.

Hall, Libby. 1994. "Growing Pains." *PANdora's Box*, May.

Hall, Stuart. 1995. "The Whites of Their Eyes: Racist Ideologes and the Media." In *Gender, Race, and Class in Media: A Text-Reader*, edited by Gail Dines and Jean McMahon Humez, 18–22. Thousand Oaks, CA: Sage Publications.

Hamilton, James. 2004. *All the News That's Fit to Sell: How the Market Transforms Information into News*. Princeton, NJ: Princeton University Press.

Harrington, C. Lee, and Denise Bielby. 2018. "Soap Fans, Revisited." In *A Companion to Media Fandom and Fan Studies*, edited by Paul Booth, 77–90. Wiley Online Library. https:// onlinelibrary.wiley.com/doi/abs/10.1002/9781119237211.ch5.

Harris, Elizabeth A. 2021. "How Crying on TikTok Sells Books." *New York Times*, March 20. https://www.nytimes.com/2021/03/20/books/booktok-tiktok-video.html.

———. 2022. "How TikTok Became a Best-Seller Machine." *New York Times*, July 1. Accessed July 7, 2023. https://www.nytimes.com/2022/07/01/books/tiktok-books-booktok.html.

Hart, Angelica. 1998. "Electronic Publishing: Catch the Wave!" *All About Romance* (blog), March 4. https://allaboutromance.com/cynthia-lawrence-on-electronic-publishing/.

Hartwell, Jenny (@_JennyHartwell). 2021. "On Saturday night, I sent a letter to the RWA board as a member, a chapter president, & someone who presented an award at the Vivians. https://T .Co/D33YoI2w0y." Twitter, August 2, 2021, 11:14 p.m. https://twitter.com/_JennyHartwell/status /1422395323113033731.

Harvey, David. 2005. *A Brief History of Neoliberalism*. Oxford: Oxford University Press.

Held, Virginia. 2006. *The Ethics of Care: Personal, Political and Global*. Oxford: Oxford University Press.

Hesmondhalgh, David. 2018. *The Cultural Industries*. 4th ed. Thousand Oaks, CA: Sage Publications.

Hesmondhalgh, David, and Sarah Baker. 2011. *Creative Labour: Media Work in Three Industries*. London: Routledge.

Hesmondhalgh, David, Richard Osborne, Hyojung Sun, and Kenny Barr. 2021. "Music Creators' Earnings in the Digital Era". *SSRN Electronic Journal*. https://doi.org/10.2139/ssrn.4089749.

Hiatt, Brenda. 2004. "So How Much Money Do You Make?" *Romance Writers Report*, May.

———. 2005. "Tough Question: How Much Money Do You Make?" *Romance Writers Report*, May.

Hills, Matt. 2002. *Fan Cultures*. London: Routledge.

Hochschild, Arlie Russell. 2012. *The Managed Heart: Commercialization of Human Feeling*. Berkeley: University of California Press.

Hochschild, Arlie Russell, and Anne Machung. 1989. *The Second Shift: Working Parents and the Revolution at Home*. New York: Viking.

Hodson, Randy. 2001. *Dignity at Work*. Cambridge: Cambridge University Press.

Hogan, Ginny. 2023. "Unionizing Freelancers: What Recent Progress Means for The Self-Employed." *Forbes*. Accessed July 7, 2023. https://www.forbes.com/sites/ginnyhogan/2023/05/04/unionizing-freelancers-what-recent-progress-means-for-the-self-employed/.

Holder, Aisha M. B., Margo A. Jackson, and Joseph G. Ponterotto. 2015. "Racial Microaggression Experiences and Coping Strategies of Black Women in Corporate Leadership." *Qualitative Psychology* 2, no. 2: 164–80.

Holson, Laura. 2016. "With Romance Novels Booming, Beefcake Sells but It Doesn't Pay." *New York Times*, March 30.

Howard, Philip N. 2002. "Network Ethnography and the Hypermedia Organization: New Media, New Organizations, New Methods." *New Media & Society* 4, no. 4: 550–74. http://journals.sagepub.com/doi/10.1177/146144402321466813.

Hsu, Andrea. 2023. "Labor's Labors Lost? A Year after Stunning Victory at Amazon, Unions Are Stalled." NPR, March 31. https://www.npr.org/2023/03/28/1165294695/labor-union-starbucks-amazon-howard-schultz-workers.

Huddy, Leonie. 2013. "From Group Identity to Political Cohesion and Commitment." In *The Oxford Handbook of Political Psychology*, edited by Leonie Huddy, David O. Sears, and Jack S. Levy, 737–73. Oxford: Oxford University Press.

Hughes, Langston. 1985. "Problems of the Negro Writer." *The Langston Hughes Review* 4, no. 1: 25–27. http://www.jstor.org/stable/26432671.

Hund, Emily. 2023. *The Influencer Industry: The Quest for Authenticity on Social Media*. Princeton, NJ: Princeton University Press.

Hurston, Zora Neale. 1950. "What White Publishers Won't Print." In *Within the Circle: An Anthology of African American Literary Criticism from the Harlem Renaissance to the Present*, edited by Angela Mitchell, 117–21. 1994. Durham: Duke University Press.

Huseby, Sandy. 1985. "Editor's Note." *Romance Writers Report*, August.

Internal Revenue Service. 2023. "Exemption Requirements: Business League." https://www.irs.gov/charities-non-profits/other-non-profits/requirements-for-exemption-business-league.

Isaacs, Susan. 1992. "Chilling Out in Phoenix." *New York Times*, May 31. https://www.nytimes
.com/1992/05/31/books/chilling-out-in-phoenix.html.

Italie, Hillel. 2021. "Romance Book Award Withdrawn after Uproar over Depiction of Genocide." *USA Today*, June 8. https://www.usatoday.com/story/entertainment/books/2021
/08/06/romance-book-award-withdrawn-at-loves-command/5520083001/.

Jackson, Sarah J., Moya Bailey, and Brooke Foucault Welles. 2020. *#HashtagActivism: Networks
of Race and Gender Justice*. Cambridge, MA: MIT Press.

Jacobs, Julie. 2007. "Jennifer Weiner: Chic Lit." *Hillel*, July 6.

Jarrett, Kylie. 2014. "The Relevance of 'Women's Work': Social Reproduction and Immaterial
Labor in Digital Media." *Television & New Media* 15, no. 1: 14–29. http://journals.sagepub
.com/doi/10.1177/1527476413487607.

Jenkins, Beverly. 2016. "RWA Keynote Speech." *Romance Writers Report*, September.

Jenkins, Henry. 2008. *Convergence Culture: Where Old and New Media Collide*. New York: New
York University Press.

———. 2012. *Textual Poachers: Television Fans and Participatory Culture*. New York: Routledge.

Judish, Julie A., and Jerold A. Jacobs. 2020. *Independent Ethics Audit Report for Romance Writers
of America*. Pillsbury, Winthrop, Shaw, Pittman LLP. Accessed February 27. https://www
.rwa.org/Online/News/2020/Audit_Documents.aspx.

Kamblé, Jayashree. 2014. *Making Meaning in Popular Romance Fiction: An Epistemology*. New
York: Palgrave Macmillan.

———. 2023. "The Origins of US Mass-Market Category Romance Novels: Black Editors and
Writers in the Early 1980s." *The Journal of American Culture*. https://doi-org.colorado.idm
.oclc.org/10.1111/jacc.13488.

Kamblé, Jayashree, Eric Murphy Selinger, and Hsu-Ming Teo. 2020. *The Routledge Research
Companion to Popular Romance Fiction*. New York: Routledge.

Kelley, Mary. 1984. *Private Woman, Public Stage: Literary Domesticity in Nineteenth-Century
America*. New York: Oxford University Press.

Kerstan, Lynn. 1998a. "Rabble Rouser." *Romance Writers Report*, October.

———. 1998b. *Romance Writers Report*, October.

Kinder, Donald R., and Cindy D. Kam. 2010. *Us against Them: Ethnocentric Foundations of American Opinion*. Chicago: University of Chicago Press.

Kirschenbaum, Matthew G. 2016. *Track Changes: A Literary History of Word Processing*. Cambridge, MA: The Belknap Press of Harvard University Press.

Kitzmiller, Chelley. 2023. "Chelley Kitzmiller, Author Page." Amazon. Accessed July 15, 2023.
https://www.amazon.com/stores/Chelley%20Kitzmiller/author/B003ZODFLY
/about.

Klar, Rebecca. 2021. "Amazon Hit with Antitrust Lawsuit Alleging E-Book Price Fixing." *The
Hill*. Accessed February 2, 2022. https://thehill.com/policy/technology/534364-amazon
-hit-with-class-action-lawsuit-alleging-e-book-price-fixing.

Klein, Gil. 2019. "NPC in History: Women's National Press Club Centennial." *National Press
Club*. Accessed June 16, 2021. https://www.press.org/newsroom/npc-history-womens
-national-press-club-centennial.

Korkki, Phyllis. 2016. *The Big Thing: How to Complete Your Creative Project Even If You're a Lazy,
Self-Doubting Procrastinator like Me*. New York: Harper.

Kreiss, Daniel, Megan Finn, and Fred Turner. 2011. "The Limits of Peer Production: Some Reminders from Max Weber for the Network Society." *New Media & Society*, 13, no. 2: 243–259. https://doi.org/10.1177/1461444810370951.

Krentz, Jayne Ann. 1992. *Dangerous Men and Adventurous Women: Romance Writers on the Appeal of the Romance*. Philadelphia: University of Pennsylvania Press.

Kuehn, Kathleen, and Thomas Corrigan. 2013. "Hope Labor: The Role of Employment Prospects in Online Social Production." *The Political Economy of Communication* 1, no. 1: 9–25.

Kumar, Sangeet. 2019. "The Algorithmic Dance: YouTube's Adpocalypse and the Gatekeeping of Cultural Content on Digital Platforms." *Internet Policy Review* 8, no. 2. https://doi.org/10.14763/2019.2.1417.

Kurtin, Kate Szer, Nina F. O'Brien, Deya Roy, and Linda Dam. 2019. "Parasocial Relationships with Musicians." *The Journal of Social Media in Society* 8, no. 2: 30–50.

Larsen, Katherine, and Lynn Zubernis. 2012. *Fandom at the Crossroads: Celebration, Shame and Fan/Producer Relationships*. Newcastle-upon-Tyne, UK: Cambridge Scholars Publishing. http://ebookcentral.proquest.com/lib/ucb/detail.action?docID=1133107.

Larson, Christine. 2012. "Mining the Power (and Profit) of Conversation." *New York Times*, September 15. http://www.nytimes.com/2012/09/16/business/van-heyst-group-aims-to-turn-company-events-into-media-gold.html?pagewanted=all&_r=0.

———. 2018. "Shades of Green: What Digital Economy Gig Workers Can Learn from Romance Writers." *Salon*, January 16. https://www.salon.com/2018/01/20/shades-of-green-what-gig-economy-workers-can-learn-from-the-success-of-romance-writers_partner/.

———. 2019. "Open Networks, Open Books: Gender, Precarity and Solidarity in Digital Publishing." *Information, Communication & Society*: 1–17.

———. 2022. "Streaming Books: Confluencers, Kindle Unlimited and the Platform Imaginary." *Communication, Culture and Critique* 15, no. 4: 520–30.

Larson, Christine, and Elspeth Ready. 2022. "Networking Down: Networks, Innovation, and Relational Labor in Digital Book Publishing." *New Media & Society*. https://doi.org/10.1177/14614448221090195.

Larson, Magali Sarfatti. 2012. *The Rise of Professionalism: Monopolies of Competence and Sheltered Markets*. New Brunswick: Transaction Publishers.

Latour, Bruno. 1993. *We Have Never Been Modern*. Cambridge, MA: Harvard University Press.

Lawrence, K. S. 2017. "Sisters in Crime: Raising Women's Voices for 30 Years." *Sisters in Crime*. https://cdn.ymaws.com/www.sistersincrime.org/resource/resmgr/summit_report/RaisingWomensVoices-2017-Pub.pdf.

Lee & Low Books. 2020. "Where Is the Diversity in Publishing? The 2019 Diversity Baseline Survey Results." *Lee & Low* (blog). Accessed April 25, 2022. https://blog.leeandlow.com/2020/01/28/2019diversitybaselinesurvey/.

Leviton, Laura C., Carla Herrera, Sarah K. Pepper, Nancy Fishman, and David P. Racine. 2006. "Faith in Action: Capacity and Sustainability of Volunteer Organizations." *Evaluation and Program Planning* 29, no. 2: 201–7. https://www.sciencedirect.com/science/article/pii/S0149718906000164.

Liebers, Nicole, and Holger Schramm. 2019. "Parasocial Interactions and Relationships with Media Characters—An Inventory of 60 Years of Research." *Communication Research Trends* 38, no. 2: 4–31.

Lincoln, Yvonna S., and Egon G. Guba. 1985. *Naturalistic Inquiry*. Beverly Hills, CA: Sage Publications.

Lipsitz, George. 2006. *The Possessive Investment in Whiteness: How White People Profit from Identity Politics*. Philadelphia: Temple University Press.

Lobato, Ramon. 2019. *Netflix Nations: The Geography of Digital Distribution*. Critical Cultural Communication. New York: New York University Press.

Lois, Jennifer, and Joanna Gregson. 2015. "Sneers and Leers: Romance Writers and Gendered Sexual Stigma." *Gender & Society* 29, no. 4: 459–83.

———. 2019. "Aspirational Emotion Work: Calling, Emotional Capital, and Becoming a 'Real' Writer." *Journal of Contemporary Ethnography* 48, no. 1: 51–79.

Lowe, Travis Scott. 2018. "Perceived Job and Labor Market Insecurity in the United States: An Assessment of Workers' Attitudes from 2004–2014." *Work and Occupations* 45, no. 3: 313–45.

MacLean, Sarah. 2019. "2019 RWA RITA Awards Ceremony." RWA. YouTube video, August 15. https://www.youtube.com/watch?v=e4uqBSIuZbQ.

Macpherson, W. 1999. "The Stephen Lawrence Inquiry." Report to Parliament, February. https://assets.publishing.service.gov.uk/government/uploads/system/uploads/attachment_data/file/277111/4262.pdf.

Maltese, Racheline. 2016. "RWA Issues Apology for Infamous 'One Man, One Woman' Romance Definition Poll." *Avian30* (blog). Accessed September 13, 2022. https://avian30.com/2016/04/04/rwa-issues-apology-for-infamous-one-man-one-woman-romance-definition-poll/.

——— (@racheline_m). 2020. "Anyone outside of Romancelandia trying to do a hot take about our genre _really_ needs to understand that, broadly speaking, we have both a liberation wing (protagonists bend the world to find their joy) and a compliance wing (protagonists bend themselves to find their joy)." Twitter, October 23, 11:12 a.m. https://twitter.com/racheline_m/status/1319657948264660999.

Marble, Ann. 2009. "The Harlequin Horizons Debacle: All About Romance %." *All About Romance* (blog). Accessed July 24, 2022. https://allaboutromance.com/the-harlequin-horizons-debacle/.

Markert, John. 2016. *Publishing Romance: The History of an Industry, 1940s to the Present*. Jefferson, NC: McFarland & Company.

Max, Daniel. 1992. "McMillan's Millions." *New York Times Magazine*, August 9.

Mays, Jeffery C. 2020. "How a Brooklyn Sisterhood of Black Women Became National Power Brokers." *New York Times*, November 27. https://www.nytimes.com/2020/11/27/nyregion/black-women-politics-olori-sisterhood.html.

McCormick, Casey J. 2018. "Active Fandom: Labor and Love in the Whedonverse." In *A Companion to Media Fandom and Fan Studies*, edited by Paul Booth, 369–84. Wiley Online Library. https://onlinelibrary.wiley.com/doi/abs/10.1002/9781119237211.ch23.

McLean, Kristin. 2023. "Soaring Sales of LGBTQ Fiction Showcase Diversity in Storytelling." Circana. Accessed June 19, 2023. https://www.circana.com/press-releases/2023/soaring-sales-of-lgbtq-fiction-defy-book-bans-and-showcase-diversity-in-storytelling/.

McLoughlin, Danny. 2022. "Amazon Kindle, E-Book, and Kindle Unlimited Statistics." Words Rated. Accessed July 10, 2023. https://wordsrated.com/amazon-kindle-e-book-and-kindle-unlimited-statistics/.

McPherson, M., L, Smith-Lovin, and J. M. Cook. 2001. "Birds of a Feather: Homophily in Social Networks." *Annual Review of Sociology* 27, no. 1: 415–44.

McRobbie, Angela. 2002. "Clubs to Companies: Notes on the Decline of Political Culture in Speeded up Creative Worlds." *Cultural Studies* 16, no. 4: 516–31.

———. 2009. *The Aftermath of Feminism: Gender, Culture and Social Change.* Los Angeles: Sage Publications.

———. 2010. "Reflections on Feminism, Immaterial Labor and the Post-Fordist Regime." *New Formations* 70, no. 1: 60–76.

———. 2015. *Be Creative: Making a Living in the New Culture Industries.* Cambridge, UK: Polity.

Menger, Pierre-Michel. 2014. *The Economics of Creativity: Art and Achievement under Uncertainty.* Translated by Steven Rendall, Amy Jacobs, Arianne Dorval, Lisette Eskinazi, Emmanuelle Saada, and Joe Karaganis. Cambridge, MA: Harvard University Press.

Milella, Jan, Janice Young Brooks, and Janece Hudson. 1987. "The Way We Were: Looking Back to the Founding of RWA." *Romance Writers Report*, February.

Milliot, Jim. 2009. "Harlequin, Author Solutions Form Self-Publishing Imprint Harlequin Horizons." *Publishers Weekly.* Accessed July 24, 2022. https://www.publishersweekly.com/pw/by-topic/industry-news/publisher-news/article/26993-harlequin-author-solutions-form-self-publishing-imprint-harlequin-horizons.html.

———. 2023. "Romance Books Were Hot in 2022." *Publishers Weekly.* Accessed June 11, 2023. https://www.publishersweekly.com/pw/by-topic/industry-news/bookselling/article/91298-romance-books-were-hot-in-2022.html.

Minzesheimer, Bob, and Anthony DeBarros. 2013. "What 20 Years of Best Sellers Say About What We Read." *USA Today*, October 30. https://www.usatoday.com/story/life/books/2013/10/30/twenty-years-of-usa-today-best-selling-books-list/3188685/.

Mitchell, Travis. 2019. "Race in America 2019." Pew Research Center. Accessed April 29, 2021. https://www.pewresearch.org/social-trends/2019/04/09/race-in-america-2019/.

Modleski, Tania. 2008. *Loving with a Vengeance: Mass-produced Fantasies for Women.* 2nd ed. New York: Routledge.

Moody-Freeman, Julie. 2020. "Vivian Stephens-Part One." *Black Romance Podcast*, September 8. Podcast. https://podcasts.apple.com/us/podcast/black-romance-podcast/id1528266279.

Moreno, J. Edward, and Neal E. Boudette. 2023. "UAW Expands Strikes at Automakers." *New York Times*, September 29.

Mulcahy, Diane. 2019. "How Can We Stop Companies from Misclassifying Employees as Independent Contractors?" *Forbes.* Accessed June 23, 2023. https://www.forbes.com/sites/dianemulcahy/2019/06/25/how-can-we-stop-companies-from-misclassifying-employees-as-independent-contractors/.

Murolo, Priscilla. 1997. *The Common Ground of Womanhood: Class, Gender, and Working Girls' Clubs, 1884–1928.* Urbana: University of Illinois Press.

Murray, Padmini Ray, and Claire Squires. 2013. "The Digital Publishing Communications Circuit." *Book 2.0* 3, no. 1: 3–23.

National League of American Pen Women. 2019. "Pen Women Then and Now." Accessed June 16, 2021. https://www.nlapw.org/history/.

Nava, Michael. 2021. "Los Angeles Review of Books." *Los Angeles Review of Books.* Accessed February 24, 2022. https://lareviewofbooks.org/article/creating-a-literary-culture-a-short-selective-and-incomplete-history-of-lgbt-publishing-part-i/.

Neff, Gina. 2012. *Venture Labor: Work and the Burden of Risk in Innovative Industries.* Cambridge, MA: MIT Press.

Neff, Gina, Elizabeth Wissinger, and Sharon Zukin. 2005. "Entrepreneurial Labor among Cultural Producers: 'Cool' Jobs in 'Hot' Industries." *Social Semiotics* 15, no. 3: 307–34.

Newman, Mark E. J. 2002. "Assortative Mixing in Networks." *Physical Review Letters* 89, no. 20. https://doi.org/10.1103/PhysRevLett.89.208701.

New York Times. 1912. "Authors' League Launched: Writers Protective Agency Gets Its Certificate of Incorporation." December 17.

Nieborg, David B., and Thomas Poell. 2018. "The Platformization of Cultural Production: Theorizing the Contingent Cultural Commodity." *New Media & Society* 20, no. 11: 4275–92. http://journals.sagepub.com/doi/10.1177/1461444818769694.

Nightline. 1983. "Fandom—Patricia Frazer Lamb Interview—Romance Novels—Ted Koppel." YouTube video, August 5, 2017. https://www.youtube.com/watch?v=I7ACIHpJlck.

Noble, Safiya Umoja. 2018. *Algorithms of Oppression: How Search Engines Reinforce Racism.* New York: New York University Press.

Novelists, Inc. n.d. "Member Demographics." https://ninc.com/about-ninc/member-demographics/.

NPD Books. 2017. "The Romance Book Buyer 2017: A Study by NPD Book for Romance Writers of America." Report provided at the Romance Writing Summit, 2017.

O'Meara, Victoria. 2019. "Weapons of the Chic: *Instagram* Influencer Engagement Pods as Practices of Resistance to *Instagram* Platform Labor." *Social Media + Society* 5, no. 4. https://doi.org/10.1177/2056305119879671.

O'Neil, Sharon Lund, and Cheryl L. Willis. 2005. "Challenges for Professional Organizations: Lessons from the Past." *Delta Pi Epsilon Journal* 47, no. 3: 143–53. https://colorado.idm.oclc.org/login?url=https://search.ebscohost.com/login.aspx?direct=true&AuthType=ip,sso&db=ofm&AN=507833591&site=ehost-live&scope=site.

Orgad, Shani. 2019. *Heading Home: Motherhood, Work, and the Failed Promise of Equality.* New York: Columbia University Press.

Osborne, Maggie. 1985. "President's Column." *Romance Writers Report*, February.

Osnos, Peter. 2012. "How 'Fifty Shades of Grey' Dominated Publishing." *The Atlantic*, August 8. Accessed December 31, 2021. https://www.theatlantic.com/entertainment/archive/2012/08/how-fifty-shades-of-grey-dominated-publishing/261653/.

Padgett, John F. 2010. "Open Elite? Social Mobility, Marriage, and Family in Florence, 1282–1494." *Renaissance Quarterly* 63, no. 2: 357–411.

Padgett, John, and Walter W. Powell, eds. 2012. *The Emergence of Organizations and Markets.* Princeton, NJ: Princeton University Press.

PANdora's Box. 1990. "Our Professional Image." June.

———. 1993. "Letter to the Editor: Are We Cutting Our Own Throats?" March.

Papdakis, Maria. 2000. "Complex Picture of Computer Use in the Home Emerges." National Science Foundation. Accessed July 9, 2023. https://www.nsf.gov/statistics/issuebrf/sib00314.htm.

Paretsky, Sara. n.d. "FAQs." *Sara Paretsky* (blog). https://saraparetsky.com/faqs/.

Pearce, Lynne, and Jackie Stacey, eds. 1995. *Romance Revisited.* New York: New York University Press.

Pedroni, Marco. 2023. "Two Decades of Fashion Blogging and Influencing: A Critical Overview." *Fashion Theory* 27, no. 2: 237–68.

Petre, Caitlin, Brooke Erin Duffy, and Emily Hund. 2019. "'Gaming the System': Platform Paternalism and the Politics of Algorithmic Visibility." *Social Media + Society* 5, no. 4. https://doi.org/10.1177/2056305119879995.

Pilkington, Ed. 2012. "Amanda Hocking: The Writer Who Made Millions by Self-Publishing." *The Guardian*. https://www.theguardian.com/books/2012/jan/12/amanda-hocking-self-publishing.

Poell, Thomas, David B. Nieborg, and Brooke Erin Duffy. 2021. *Platforms and Cultural Production*. Medford, MA: Polity.

Powell, Walter W. 1990. "Neither Market nor Hierarchy: Network Forms of Organization." *Research in Organizational Behavior* 12: 295–336.

Powell, Walter W., and Jason Owen-Smith. 2012. "An Open Elite: Arbiters, Catalysts, or Gatekeepers in the Dynamics of Industry Evolution." *The Emergence of Organizations and Markets*, by John F. Padgett and Walter W. Powell, 466–95. Princeton, NJ: Princeton University Press.

Project Gutenberg. 2022. "About Project Gutenberg." Accessed September 8, 2022. https://www.gutenberg.org/about.

Pryde, Jessica P., ed. 2022. *Black Love Matters: Real Talk on Romance, Being Seen, and Happily Ever Afters*. New York: Berkley.

Putnam, Robert D. 2001. *Bowling Alone: The Collapse and Revival of American Community*. New York: Simon & Schuster.

Quinn, Judy. 1998. "Nora Roberts: A Celebration of Emotions." *Publishers Weekly*. Accessed May 25, 2021. https://www.publishersweekly.com/pw/by-topic/authors/interviews/article/28010-pw-nora-roberts-a-celebration-of-emotions.html.

Radway, Janice A. 1991. *Reading the Romance: Women, Patriarchy, and Popular Literature*. Chapel Hill: University of North Carolina Press.

Regis, Pamela. 2007. *A Natural History of the Romance Novel*. Philadelphia: University of Pennsylvania Press.

Reid, Calvin. 2006. "Genesis Sues Authors for Millions." *Publishers Weekly*, November 3. https://www.publishersweekly.com/pw/print/20061106/9804-genesis-publisher-sues-writers-for-millions.html.

Rheingold, Howard. 2000. *The Virtual Community: Homesteading on the Electronic Frontier*. Cambridge, MA: MIT Press.

RIAA. 2022. "US Recorded Music Revenues by Format." Accessed October 1, 2023. https://www.riaa.com/u-s-sales-database/.

Roach, Catherine M. 2018. *Happily Ever After: The Romance Story in Popular Culture*. Bloomington: Indiana University Press.

Roberts, Nora. 2007. "My First Sale by Nora Roberts." *Dear Author* (blog). Accessed July 16, 2023. https://web.archive.org/web/20211208095409/https://dearauthor.com/features/interviews/my-first-sale-by-nora-roberts/.

———. 2019. "My POV on RWA." *Fall Into the Story* (blog). https://fallintothestory.com/my-pov-on-rwa/#:~:text=Again%2C%20I%20regret%20all%20the,was%20all%20those%20years%20ago.

Robinson, Sue. 2018. *Networked News, Racial Divides: How Power and Privilege Shape Public Discourse in Progressive Communities*. Cambridge: Cambridge University Press.

———. 2023. *How Journalists Engage: A Theory of Trust Building, Identities, & Care*. New York: Oxford University Press.

Robinson, Sue, and C. W. Anderson. 2020. "Network Ethnography in Journalism Studies: A Mixed-Method Approach to Studying Media Ecologies." *Journalism Studies* 21, no. 7: 984–1001. https://www.tandfonline.com/doi/full/10.1080/1461670X.2020.1720519.

Rodale, Maya. 2015. *Dangerous Books for Girls: The Bad Reputation of Romance Novels Explained*. Self-published, CreateSpace Independent Publishing Platform.

Rodgers, M. J. 1996. "Train Wreck 'Derails' June Sales." *Romance Writers Report*, December.

Romance Writers of America. 2020a. "Discussion on History of Black Category Rom." Paper presented at the RWA National Convention, August 26. https://www.rwa.org/ItemDetail?iProductCode=VIDEO20CDBCR&Category=VIDEOS&WebsiteKey=c531524b-2ea0-41e7-a099-7e5a27062137.

———. 2020b. "RWA2020 Video: Discussion on History of Black Category Rom." Video. https://www.rwa.org/ItemDetail?iProductCode=VIDEO20CDBCR&Category=VIDEOS&WebsiteKey=c531524b-2ea0-41e7-a099-7e5a27062137.

———. 2023a. "About the Romance Genre." Accessed July 16, 2023. https://www.rwa.org/Online/Romance_Genre/About_Romance_Genre.aspx.

———. 2023b. "Antitrust Statement." Accessed July 12, 2023. https://www.rwa.org/Online/About/Governance_Folder/Antitrust_Statement.aspx.

Romance Writers Report. 1984. "Sharing Information." December.

———. 1985. "Romance Writers of America—Writers' Survey." January-February.

———. 1988. "Membership Update." March.

———. 2010. "Romance Writers of America Celebrates 30 Years." April.

Rosen, Judith. 2004. "Arabesque Sets Events to Mark 10th Anniversary." *Publishers Weekly*, May 21.

Rosen, Sherwin. 1981. "The Economics of Superstars." *The American Economic Review* 71, no. 5: 845–58.

Rosenwald, Michael. 2018. "Mark Twain's Typewriter—'full of Defects, Devilish Ones'—Nearly Drove Him Bonkers." *Washington Post*, November 16. Accessed July 2, 2022. https://www.washingtonpost.com/history/2018/11/16/mark-twains-typewriter-full-defects-devilish-ones-nearly-drove-him-bonkers/.

Ross, Andrew. 2004. *No-Collar: The Humane Workplace and Its Hidden Costs*. Philadelphia: Temple University Press.

Rothschild, Jennifer, and Meredith Schwartz. 2018. "Research: Romance Writers Survey: Lack of Inclusion." *Library Journal*, September 1.

Rottenberg, Catherine. 2020. *The Rise of Neoliberal Feminism*. New York: Oxford University Press.

Roux, Mathilde. 2021. "5 Facts About Black Women in the Labor Force." *Department of Labor* (Blog). Accessed July 7, 2023. http://blog.dol.gov/2021/08/03/5-facts-about-black-women-in-the-labor-force.

Rowe, Julie, and Donna Tunney. 2012. "The New Frontier: Self-Published Author Collectives." *Romance Writers Report*, November.

Rueb, Emily S., and Derrick Bryson Taylor. 2019. "Obama on Call-Out Culture: 'That's Not Activism.'" *New York Times*, October 31. https://www.nytimes.com/2019/10/31/us/politics /obama-woke-cancel-culture.html.

Ryan, Claire. 2019. "The Implosion of the RWA." *Claire Ryan* (blog). Accessed July 13, 2023. https://claireryanauthor.com/blog/2019/12/27/the-implosion-of-the-rwa/.

Salcedo, Nicki. 2018. "Dear Suzanne Brockmann." *Medium*. Accessed September 13, 2022. https://medium.com/@nicki.salcedo/dear-suzanne-brockmann-5d67d5a1a41f.

Samuels, Barbara. 1993. "What Does a Romance Writer Look Like?" *PANdora's Box*, April.

Semuels, Alina. 2018. "The Authors Who Love Amazon." *The Atlantic*, June 20. https://www .theatlantic.com/technology/archive/2018/07/amazon-kindle-unlimited-self-publishing /565664/.

Seressia says PREORDER GAME ON [@seressia]. 2020. "In other dumpster fire news interim ED new email: 'RWA has failed to protect its members of color and its members from the LGBTQ+ and disabled communities, and failed to offer a safe and inclusive place for all our members, because of its systemic issues with racism and bias.'" Twitter, February 5, 1:53 p.m. https://twitter.com/seressia/status/1225130285479743489.

Shock, Marianne. 1985. "The 1985 RWR Writers' Survey." *Romance Writers Report*, July–August.

Sisters in Crime. 2017. "A History of Sisters in Crime." https://www.sistersincrime.org/page /history.

Skarupski, Kimberly A., and Kharma C. Foucher. 2018. "Writing Accountability Groups (WAGs): A Tool to Help Junior Faculty Members Build Sustainable Writing Habits." *The Journal of Faculty Development* 32, no. 3: 47–54.

Slaughter, Anne-Marie. 2012. "Why Women Still Can't Have It All." *The Atlantic*. Accessed July 5, 2022. https://www.theatlantic.com/magazine/archive/2012/07/why-women-still-cant -have-it-all/309020/.

Smith, Chris Gordon, and Linda Duxbury. 2019. "Attitudes towards Unions through a Genera- tional Cohort Lens." *The Journal of Social Psychology* 159, no. 2: 190–209.

Smith, Deb. 1997. "Rabble Rouser." *Romance Writers Report*, June.

Smith, Dorothy. 1974. "Women's Perspective as a Radical Critique of Sociology." *Sociological Inquiry* 44, no. 1: 7–13.

Smith, V. 2010. "Review Article: Enhancing Employability: Human, Cultural, and Social Capital in an Era of Turbulent Unpredictability." *Human Relations* 63, no. 2: 279–300. http://hum .sagepub.com/cgi/doi/10.1177/0018726709353639.

Smith, Wendy (@wendys_smith). 2021. "This book winning an award shows nothing's really changed at RWA. The 'hero' takes part in the Wounded Knee massacre at the start of the book." Twitter, August 1, 12:24 a.m. https://twitter.com/wendys_smith/status/142168826024639 2835.

Snitow, Ann Barr. 2003. "Mass Market Romance: Pornography for Women Is Different." In *Gender, Race and Class in Media*, edited by Gail Dines. Thousand Oaks, CA: Sage Publications.

Snyder, Suleikha. 2023. "RWA15 in NYC: A Tale of Two Conferences." *Suleikha Synder* (blog). Accessed July 9, 2023. http://www.suleikhasnyder.com/2015/07/rwa15-in-nyc-tale-of-two -conferences.html.

Solomon, Deborah. 2009. "Book Learning." *New York Times*, December 2. https://www.nytimes.com/2009/12/06/magazine/06fob-q4-t.html.

Soloski, Alexis. 2020. "For Television and Romance Novels, Love at Last?" *New York Times*, December 28. https://www.nytimes.com/2020/12/28/arts/television/bridgerton-outlander-romance-novels.html.

Stevens, Matt. 2023. "What to Know about the Actors' Strike." *New York Times*. July 14.

Stewart, Barbara. 1996. "A Magazine for Romance Novels and the Women Who Love Them." *New York Times*, December 10. https://www.nytimes.com/1996/12/10/nyregion/a-magazine-for-romance-novels-and-the-women-who-love-them.html.

Stone, Brad. 2021. *Amazon Unbound: Jeff Bezos and the Invention of a Global Empire*. New York: Simon & Schuster.

Stone, Lawrence, and Jeanne C. Fawtier Stone. 1986. *An Open Elite?: England, 1540–1880*. New York: Oxford University Press.

Swartz, Mimi. 2020. "Vivian Stephens Helped Turn Romance Writing into a Billion Dollar Industry. Then She Got Pushed Out." *Texas Monthly Magazine*, September. https://www.texasmonthly.com/arts-entertainment/vivian-stephens-helped-turn-romance-writing-into-billion-dollar-industry/.

Talbot, Dean. 2023. "Amazon Publishing Imprints Statistics." Words Rated. Accessed July 11, 2023. https://wordsrated.com/amazon-publishing-imprints-statistics/.

Testa, Jessica. 2021. "New York City Sues L'Officiel Magazine for Not Paying Freelancers." *New York Times*, December 2. https://www.nytimes.com/2021/12/02/style/lofficiel-magazine-lawsuit.html.

Thompson, John B. 2012. *Merchants of Culture: The Publishing Business in the Twenty-First Century*. 2nd ed. New York: Plume.

———. 2021. *Book Wars: The Digital Revolution in Publishing*. Medford, MA: Polity.

Toossi, Mitra, and Teresa L. Morisi. 2017. "Women in the Workforce Before, During, and after the Great Recession." US Bureau of Labor Statistics. https://www.bls.gov/spotlight/2017/women-in-the-workforce-before-during-and-after-the-great-recession/home.htm.

Tremblay, Marc-Adelard. 1957. "The Key Informant Technique: A Nonethnographic Application." *American Anthropologist* 59, no. 4: 688–701.

Tronto, Joan C. 1993. *Moral Boundaries: A Political Argument for an Ethic of Care*. New York: Routledge.

———. 2013. *Caring Democracy: Markets, Equality, and Justice*. New York: New York University Press.

Tucker, Neely. 2011. "Novel Rejected? There's an e-Book Gold Rush!" *Washington Post*, May 7. Accessed June 20, 2022. https://www.washingtonpost.com/lifestyle/style/novel-rejected-theres-an-e-book-gold-rush/2011/04/09/AFZdqb9F_story.html.

Turner, Fred. 2006. *From Counterculture to Cyberculture: Stewart Brand, the Whole Earth Network, and the Rise of Digital Utopianism*. Chicago: University of Chicago Press.

US Bureau of Labor Statistics. 2017. "A Look at Women's Education and Earnings since the 1970s." Accessed July 7, 2022. https://www.bls.gov/opub/ted/2017/a-look-at-womens-education-and-earnings-since-the-1970s.htm.

US Census Bureau. 2015. "American Community Survey." https://data.census.gov/table?q=2015+US+population+white.

———. 2023. "Educational Attainment in the United States: 2015." Accessed July 15, 2023. https://www.census.gov/library/publications/2016/demo/p20-578.html.

Uzzi, Brian. 1996. "The Sources and Consequences of Embeddedness for the Economic Performance of Organizations: The Network Effect." *American Sociological Review* 61, no. 4: 674–98.

Uzzi, Brian, and Jarrett Spiro. 2005. "Collaboration and Creativity: The Small World Problem." *American Journal of Sociology* 11, no. 2: 447–504.

van Dijk, Teun A. 1997. *Discourse as Structure and Process.* London: Sage Publications.

Vida. 2012. "Vida Count." Accessed March 15, 2012. http://www.vidaweb.org/the-count.

Vivanco, Laura. 2019a. "Race and the Ritas." *Teach Me Tonight* (blog). http://teachmetonight.blogspot.com/.

———. 2019b. "Teach Me Tonight: Racism and the Corporate Romance Buyer: A 'Little Fiasco' Involving Sue Grimshaw." *Teach Me Tonight* (blog). Accessed July 13, 2023. https://teachmetonight.blogspot.com/2019/08/racism-and-corporate-romance-buyer.html.

Waite, Olivia. 2018. "Golden Heartbroken." *The Seattle Review of Books.* Accessed April 19, 2022. http://www.seattlereviewofbooks.com/notes/2018/09/20/golden-heartbroken/.

——— (@O_Waite). 2021. "Thinking about fiction and ethics and so it's a rambly thread! One of the things I find interesting about romance is the moral dimension. We've come to call the leads heroes and heroines because there absolutely is a sense that they have a moral role." Twitter, December 26, 7:07 p.m. https://twitter.com/O_Waite/status/1475257054537216004.

Waldfogel, Joel. 2017. "How Digitization Has Created a Golden Age of Music, Movies, Books, and Television." *Journal of Economic Perspectives* 31, no. 3: 195–214.

Waldfogel, Joel, and Imke Reimers. 2015. "Storming the Gatekeepers: Digital Disintermediation in the Market for Books." *Information Economics and Policy* 31: 47–58.

Walker, Vanessa Siddle, and John R. Snarey, eds. 2004. *Race-Ing Moral Formation: African American Perspectives on Care and Justice.* New York: Teachers College Press.

Walters, Ray. 1981. "Paperback Talk." *New York Times,* June 21.

———. 1982. "Paperback Talk." *New York Times,* May 9.

Watkins, Mel. 1981. "Hard Times for Black Writers." *New York Times,* February 22. Accessed March 3, 2022. https://www.nytimes.com/1981/02/22/books/hard-times-for-black-writers.html.

Weiner, Jennifer. 2007. "Jennifer Weiner on Taking Women Writers Seriously." *Elle,* July. https://www.elle.com/culture/books/reviews/a14119/women-in-black-and-white/.

Wellman, Barry, and Scot Wortley. 1990. "Different Strokes from Different Folks: Community Ties and Social Support." *American Journal of Sociology* 96, no. 3: 558–88.

Wendell, Sarah. 2009. "In Memory of Kate Duffy." *Smart Bitches, Trashy Books* (blog).

———. 2020. "RWA 2020: No Happy Ending in Sight, Just Hollow Women: Smart Bitches, Trashy Books." *Smart Bitches, Trashy Books* (blog). Accessed July 13, 2023. https://smartbitchestrashybooks.com/2020/02/rwa-2020-no-happy-ending-in-sight-just-hollow-women/.

Wendell, Sarah, and Candy Tan. 2009. *Beyond Heaving Bosoms: The Smart Bitches' Guide to Romance Novels.* New York: Simon & Schuster.

Wheeler, André. 2020. "Novelist Terry McMillan on Love, Death and 'Dirty Secrets.'" *The Guardian,* March 31. Accessed April 26, 2022. https://www.theguardian.com/books/2020/mar/31/novelist-terry-mcmillan-interview-its-not-all-downhill-from-here.

White, Ann Yvonne. 2008. *Genesis Press: Cultural Representation and the Production of African American Romance Novels*. PhD diss., University of Iowa. https://www.proquest.com /pqdtglobal/pagepdf/304609546/Record/7F61F36337FF4F54PQ/1?accountid=14503.

Whitehead, S. 2003. "Identifying the Professional 'Man'Ager: Masculinity, Professionalism and the Search for Legitimacy." *Gender and the Public Sector*, edited by Jim Barry, Mike Dent, and Maggie O'Neill, 75–86. New York: Routledge.

Wiessner, Daniel. 2023. "Union-Friendly Changes in the Works at U.S. Labor Board." *Reuters*, January 3. Accessed July 1, 2023. https://www.reuters.com/legal/litigation/union-friendly -changes-works-us-labor-board-2023-01-03/.

Wight, Vanessa R., Suzanne M. Bianchi, and Bijou R. Hunt. 2013. "Explaining Racial/Ethnic Variation in Partnered Women's and Men's Housework: Does One Size Fit All?" *Journal of Family Issues* 34, no. 3: 394–427.

Williams, Rachel, and Michele Andrisin Wittig. 1997. "'I'm Not a Feminist, But . . .': Factors Contributing to the Discrepancy between Pro-Feminist Orientation and Feminist Social Identity." *Sex Roles* 37, no. 11: 885–904.

Winter, Thomas. 2004. "Professionalism." In *American Masculinities: A Historical Encyclopedia*, edited by Bret Carroll. Thousand Oaks, CA: Sage Publications. https://doi.org/10.4135 /9781412956369.

Woodruff-Santos, Mandi. 2014. "These Romance Writers Ditched Their Publishers for Ebooks—and Made Millions." *Yahoo Finance*. Accessed July 12, 2022. http://finance.yahoo .com/news/independent-romance-writers-get-the-last-laugh-%E2%80%94-all-the-way-to -the-bank-213437913.html.

Young, John K. 2010. *Black Writers, White Publishers: Marketplace Politics in Twentieth-Century African American Literature*. Jackson: University Press of Mississippi.

Yuan, Shupei, and Chen Lou. 2020. "How Social Media Influencers Foster Relationships with Followers: The Roles of Source Credibility and Fairness in Parasocial Relationship and Product Interest." *Journal of Interactive Advertising* 20, no. 2: 133–47.

INDEX

Note: Illustrations are indicated by **bold** page numbers.

A NOTE ON THE TYPE

This book has been composed in Arno, an Old-style serif typeface in the
classic Venetian tradition, designed by Robert Slimbach at Adobe.